After the Boom

**People, Passions, and Power: Social Movements,
Interest Organizations, and the Political Process**
John C. Green, Series Editor

This new series explores the people, activities, and institutions that animate the political process. The series emphasizes recent changes in that process—new actors, new movements, new strategies, new successes (or failures) to enter the political mainstream or influence everyday politics—and places these changes in context with the past and the future. Books in the series combine high quality scholarship with accessibility so that they may be used as core or supplementary texts in upper division political science, sociology, and communication studies courses. The series is consciously interdisciplinary and encourages cross-discipline collaboration and research.

The State of the Parties, Second Edition: The Changing Role of Contemporary American Parties (1996) edited by John C. Green and Daniel M. Shea

After the Boom: The Politics of Generation X (1997) edited by Stephen C. Craig and Stephen Earl Bennett

Social Movements and American Political Institutions (forthcoming) edited by Anne Costain and Andrew S. McFarland

Multi-Party Politics and American Democracy, edited by Paul S. Herrnson and John C. Green

The Social Movement Society: Comparative Perspectives, edited by David Meyer and Sidney Tarraw

After the Boom

The Politics of Generation X

Edited by
STEPHEN C. CRAIG
and
STEPHEN EARL BENNETT

ROWMAN & LITTLEFIELD PUBLISHERS, INC.
Lanham • Boulder • New York • London

ROWMAN & LITTLEFIELD PUBLISHERS, INC.

Published in the United States of America
by Rowman & Littlefield Publishers, Inc.
4720 Boston Way, Lanham, Maryland 20706

3 Henrietta Street
London WC2E 8LU, England

British Cataloging in Publication Information Available

Library of Congress Cataloging-in-Publication Data

After the boom : the politics of Generation X / edited by Stephen C. Craig, Stephen Earl
     Bennett.
       p. cm.— (People, passions, and power)
     Includes bibliographical references and index.
       ISBN 0–8476–8359–1 (cloth : alk. paper).—ISBN 0–8476–8360–5 (pbk.: alk. paper)
       1. Generation X—United States—Attitudes.   2. Generation X—United States—
Political activity.   I. Craig, Stephen C.   II. Bennett, Stephen Earl.   III. Series.
HQ799.7.A35   1997
305.23′15—dc21   96–51719
                                                                                          CIP

ISBN 0-8476-8359-1 (cloth : alk. paper)
ISBN 0-8476-8360-5 (pbk. : alk. paper)

Printed in the United States of America

⊚ ™ The paper used in this publication meets the minimum requirements of American
National Standard for Information Sciences—Permanence of Paper for Printed Library
Materials, ANSI Z39.48–1984.

Contents

95310

List of Tables and Figures

1

Generations and Change: Some Initial Observations

Stephen Earl Bennett and Stephen C. Craig
with Eric W. Rademacher

The Baby Boomers [mucked] up the entire planet!
Hope they had fun.
Oh, by the way,
Thanks for the:
Debt
AIDS
Ozone Hole
and lack of jobs out there.

—*Generation X*
Seen on the wall of a men's bathroom stall
at the University of Cincinnati

Thirty years ago, the battle cry "Don't trust anyone over thirty!" became one of the symbols of a generation gap that was said to pit the values and interests of post-World War II baby boomers against those of their parents and grandparents. Born between the late 1940s and early 1960s, the first wave of boomers was just starting to come of age during that turbulent period, and its less-than-subtle arrival—in numbers that would eventually reach 80 million or more—seemed at times to mark the beginnings of a transformation that would fundamentally reshape the character of U.S. society and politics (Reich 1970).

A large portion of the postwar birth cohort (those under age twenty-five) was cited as *Time* magazine's Man of the Year in 1967. As publisher Bernhard Auer described them, boomers were "anything but silent. . . . [They] exhibit many features, make many statements, suggest many pictures, often conflicting—they are well educated, affluent, rebellious, responsible, pragmatic, idealistic, brave, 'alienated,' and hopeful" (Auer 1967, 11). The boomers' numbers, as well as their extremely visible forays into social and political activism, help to explain the popular media's love affair with them in the 1960s and early 1970s—an affair that, in certain respects, continues even today.

The attraction is not difficult to understand. Initially, boomers (at least some of them) made for "good copy" with their unconventional lifestyles and apparent willingness to challenge society's major institutions. Now, in the 1990s, boomers are still deemed newsworthy as they go about replacing the "silent generation" that preceded them in the spheres of government, business, and nearly every other aspect of American life. The symbolism of First Boomer Bill Clinton's successful quest for the presidency in 1992—which many felt was a generational turning point—did not escape the media's attention.

The baby-boom cohort's ultimate impact is still being debated (Delli Carpini 1986; Jones 1980; Wheeler 1984; Light 1988). Yet one thing no one expected back in the late 1960s and early 1970s was that a generation later, as the graffito quoted earlier suggests, boomers would find themselves in the uncomfortable position once occupied by their own elders: under assault by a newly arrived group of young people possessing what appears to be a finely honed sense of grievance directed squarely at what they perceive as the excesses and failures of those who preceded them. But this time there is a difference. More than twenty years after being chosen as its Man of the Year, American youth once again graced the cover of *Time*—as "twenty-somethings," a group whose collective portrait was far less flattering than that of their counterparts in 1967. Twentysomethings in the 1990s were described as indecisive, lacking in ambition, and as having "few heroes, no anthems, no style to call their own. They crave entertainment but their attention span is as short as one zap of a TV dial. . . . They postpone marriage because they dread divorce. . . . They possess only a hazy sense of their own identity but a monumental preoccupation with all the problems the preceding generation will leave for them to fix" (Gross and Scott 1990, 57). Early media coverage was dominated by similarly critical accounts of this new cohort.

Still, there is no escaping the fact that Generation X in the United States currently comprises roughly 50 million young adults, a number that exceeds the total population of many nations, including South Korea, Spain, and Canada (Dunn 1993, 154). Like boomers before them, Xers have captured the attention of marketing and communications specialists who are continually looking for ways of attracting the gen-X audience and its dollars. When the popular TV show *Friends* became a hit during the 1994–95 network programming season, it seemed as if every new sitcom introduced the following fall was some sort of clone (a trend duly noted by most television critics).

Speaking of baby boomers, advertising executive Barbara Feigan told the *New York Times* a few years ago, "No marketer on earth could have ignored those 75 million or whatever baby boomers. Obviously that was one of the hugest marketing opportunities of the century. It was imperative to comprehend not only the shared chronological age but the mind-set, the common attitudes, sociology and psychology—what values that unique group brought to the marketplace" (Isreal 1993, 1). Now it is gen-Xers' turn, as they face an onslaught of products designed to appeal to their presumably distinctive "mind-set" and "common attitudes" and to tastes that are thought to be different from those of older citizens. The problem, of course, is that no one has yet managed to figure out what the "mind-set" and "common attitudes" of Generation X actually are. Stereotypes abound, but the collective identity of gen-Xers—sociologically, culturally, politically—remains elusive.

The chapters that follow represent an effort to add substance to our heretofore limited knowledge of Xers' specifically political characteristics. Covering a wide array of topics, these chapters provide an informative and occasionally unexpected (partial) profile of a birth cohort that will one day inherit the responsibility for shaping America's future. Authors were asked to draw upon prior research whenever possible (while not overlooking the impressionistic and largely anecdotal media portrayals of Generation X) and to utilize the best data they could find in pursuing their investigations.

Nevertheless, scholars must exercise caution when trying to identify the dynamics of generational change in this or any era. Young people sometimes think and act differently from their elders simply because they are young and not because they have spent their "formative years" being influenced by the tides of history. In other instances, the attitudes and behavior of young and old alike will shift in a similar direction (and perhaps to a similar degree) because both have been exposed to and affected by the same historical forces and events. Finally, generational scholars must be careful not to describe all members of a given birth cohort in terms of traits and tendencies that may apply to only a relatively small percentage of them. With these and other potential pitfalls in mind, we believe that a brief review of some of the important ideas associated with the study of political generations is in order.

Political Generations and Related Concepts

The chapters in this book contain numerous references to such concepts as political generations, aging (or maturation) and the life cycle, birth cohorts, historical periods, and so on. Some general background information about these terms and the theoretical frameworks from which they are drawn might help readers to put them into proper perspective and see how they add to (or detract from) our understanding of the issues surrounding generational change in American politics.

First, a warning: There often are ambiguities and/or multiple meanings associated with the terms we will be discussing. Take *generation*, for example. When demographers—the people who study population trends—talk about a generation, they typically refer to a period of roughly twenty-five years, which is the time required for a newborn child to grow up, mature, and begin to produce offspring. Social scientists generally define the length of a generation in terms of the critical events that mark its beginning and end. Because the periodicity of such events is not altogether predictable, some generations may be longer or shorter than others. Complicating matters further is the lack of scholarly consensus concerning which critical events have been powerful enough to shape the collective identity of an entire group of young people—the Civil War and Reconstruction? the Industrial Revolution? the Great Depression? Vietnam and the civil rights movement of the 1960s?—and when, exactly, one generation ends and a new one commences. For example, should we mark the start of Generation X (and the end of the baby-boom era) as the mid-1970s, the late 1970s, or the early 1980s? Should boomers be treated as a single bloc or divided into two separate groups (see below, as well as Chapters 2 and 8)? How old must a person be (fifteen, seventeen, twenty-one, or some other age) when critical events occur in order that his or her political identity is likely to be shaped by them? As will become apparent, no two of our authors have answered these questions (especially the last one) in precisely the same way.

This lack of agreement notwithstanding, researchers who study political generations have little choice but to take into account not only biology but also history. That is, "the logic behind generational development lies in the assumption that there is an *interaction* between age and experience" (Delli Carpini 1989, 18; emphasis added). In the 1920s, Karl Mannheim (1952), a German sociologist, published a famous essay entitled "The Problem of Generations," which remains a touchstone for students of generational issues. In it, Mannheim was critical of the inexact manner in which writers had used the term *generation* to explain historical change ever since the seventeenth century (also see Bengtson et al. 1974). For clarity, he introduced the concept of a *generation unit* to describe a group of people born during the same period who at a relatively young age experienced some major event—for example, war, political upheaval, or economic catastrophe—that left them with a sense of having shared a common history and with feelings of kinship connecting them to others of approximately the same age.

There are two points we need to consider here, each of which generates contention among scholars. First, even though all or most members of society may experience a major event, its psychological impact will not be the same on everyone. Dates such as December 7, 1941 (when the Japanese bombed Pearl Harbor) or November 22, 1963 (when President John F. Kennedy was assassinated) mean different things to different people, depending, among other things, on how old they were when the incident occurred. Those who are too young to appreciate an event's significance will not react in the same way as older people who are fully aware of the world around them. Or, an individual well advanced in years will not feel the same as someone who is just coming of age and beginning to understand the historical importance of contemporary events.

Getting back to Mannheim and his notion of generation units, it seems doubtful that any event will have the required impact (that is, creating a sense of common identity and shared experience) on a group of citizens unless they are both (1) old enough to comprehend it and (2) young enough to be malleable, or psychologically adaptable. In general, it is believed that an event will most strongly affect those who are coming of age at the time it happens. But what does *coming of age* mean? Generational scholars have answered this question in a variety of ways (see Braungart and Braungart 1984; Delli Carpini 1989). It is widely agreed that the critical period is during adolescence and early adulthood, when young people begin to leave the concerns of childhood behind and assume adult roles. The sort of transition we are describing, however, can take place at different points in the life cycle for different societies, or even within the same society at different times.

For example, young Americans were not permitted to vote in federal elections before turning twenty-one (which was also the minimum age for males entering the military prior to World War I) until passage of the Twenty-Sixth Amendment to the Constitution in 1971, at which point the age of eligibility was lowered to eighteen (the age when young men could be drafted for twentieth-century wars). So, does coming of age in the United States mean being about eighteen years old? Did it mean being twenty-one years old in earlier times? In fact, with political socialization studies making it clear that many young people are politically attentive before they reach age eighteen (Kinder and Sears 1985), it may be appropriate to include those in middle or even early adolescence when setting the boundaries of a particular generation or generation unit.

A second consideration raised by Mannheim (1952) has to do with where one is in the social structure when he or she experiences a major event. The impact of the Great Depression in the 1930s, and of the nation's shift from agriculture to industry in the late nineteenth and early twentieth centuries, was much more devastating for those from lower- and working-class families than for the well-to-do. Similarly, the lasting impression left by Vietnam was surely greater, or at least different, for those who served in the armed forces during the war (and for their families)—a disproportionate share of whom came from society's less privileged elements. Children from middle- and especially upper-class families were considerably more likely to avoid military service altogether (perhaps through educational draft defer-ments) or, if they served, to do so as officers rather than as enlisted personnel (which reduced to some degree the likelihood of their seeing combat).[1]

Although we and our fellow contributors typically use the term *genera-tion* (or *birth cohort*; see Bennett and Bennett 1990, also Chapter 2) rather than *generation unit*, we do so more to conform with conventional usage than because of any argument with Mannheim's distinction between the two. In addition, readers should understand that this book was put together for the purpose of examining *inter*generational differences in the 1990s. If the differences we find are less dramatic than media accounts might lead us to expect (and they are), so be it. The most crucial age-related differences in political attitude and behavior today may very well be between *parts* of one generation and parts of one or more others or between different parts of a single generation. Either way, scholars who study the dynamics of genera-tional change must take care not to assume that all persons of a similar age—even those who have lived together through some sort of major social or political transformation—will have the same outlook, much less that they will share a common psychological identity as a result of their experiences.

These are not, of course, the only hazards associated with generational analysis. As we have indicated, political generations are presumed to be the product of critical events that have their greatest impact on the malleable young. Some events, though, are powerful enough to shape the political views of virtually all citizens regardless of age. Over the course of U.S. history, one imagines that the Civil War (1860s), the Great Depression (1930s), and perhaps Vietnam (1960s–70s) were so devastating in their di-rect impact on so many people that no age group was left untouched. Events of comparable scope and magnitude in other countries would probably in-clude the Russian Revolution of 1917 (and the breakup of the Soviet Union more than seventy years later), the Chinese Revolution of the 1940s, the Nazi takeover of Germany in the 1930s, and the ethnic civil war that has raged in Bosnia throughout much of the 1990s.

When the consequences of an event ripple through almost every group in society irrespective of age, when the event has "an impact on the entire population in a similar way" (Delli Carpini 1986, 21), the result is called a *period effect*. Whereas many analysts predicted that Vietnam, Watergate, and other alienating events that occurred during the late 1960s and early 1970s would cause baby boomers to be an unusually "cynical" generation, the evidence shows that levels of trust in government have dropped sharply among young and old alike over the past three decades (Craig 1996b). This is basically how a period effect works. We need to be cautious, however, because certain events will affect citizens of all ages but exert their strongest impact on the young (Converse 1976; Markus 1979). In Chapter 6, Kevin Hill reports that the apparent increase in political tolerance observed between the 1950s and the 1970s may fall into this category. As a rule of thumb, analysts should not interpret signs of change among the young as a generational effect without first determining whether the same kinds of changes have also taken place (and to about the same degree) among older people as well.

A more intricate problem stems from the need to distinguish between generational and *aging* (or *life-cycle*) effects. Barring accident or illness, an individual is born and then moves through childhood, adolescence, early adulthood, middle age, old age and, finally, death. Part of this progression is biological, part is psychological, and part is social (see Erikson 1963, 1968; Keniston 1968; Flacks 1971). Most of us—regardless of when we were born or our location in the social structure—face the same options and problems (formal schooling, pursuing a job or career, choosing a life partner, raising children, retiring) at a similar point in our lives. As people age, they change, and these changes are essentially the same for almost everyone. We know, for example, that as people move from adolescence to early adulthood to middle age, they tend to become increasingly set in their ways: resistant to new ideas, new values and lifestyles, and even new political movements or parties (Converse 1976; Butler and Stokes 1976). This is why events that have a major impact on young people may not be powerful enough to shift adults (especially the elderly) out of established patterns of behavior.

The best approach to studying aging or life-cycle effects would be for scholars to examine periodically the same group of individuals over the entire course of their lives, comparing areas of stability and change and, in each instance, determining whether the patterns observed in the target group matched what was happening in the overall population over the same period. Under the circumstances, it is not surprising that very few such studies have been undertaken by social scientists. One fascinating example is the work of Duane Alwin and his colleagues (1991), who recently completed a fifty-year study of women who graduated from Bennington College in 1939. Another, slightly less ambitious, effort is that of M. Kent Jennings and Richard Niemi (1974, 1981; also see Jennings 1987), who followed a group of high-school seniors and their parents beginning in 1965 and extending into the early 1980s.

Although such a long-term research focus is rare (and extraordinarily difficult to execute), those who study political generations must nonetheless consider the possibility that whatever age-based differences they observe in their (usually) cross-sectional data are due to life-cycle factors rather than generational change. If, for example, we look at a public opinion survey in 1996 and learn that young adults are less likely to identify with a political party than are older citizens, should we assume that this is because the former constitute a less partisan generation, that is, they have been shaped by events in such a way that they will probably remain less supportive of parties for the rest of their lives? Or is it because the political identities of young people have not yet fully developed, and thus they tend in any historical era to be less partisan than their elders? If our only data base is the 1996 survey, there is no way of answering that question. We would need to track today's young adults as they aged and see whether their partisan attachments grew stronger (in which case the 1996 results probably could be attributed to life-cycle effects) or remained relatively weak (which would indicate an enduring generational effect).

The dilemma facing each of our authors is that members of Generation X are still fairly young. As a result, it is impossible to know for certain whether any differences that currently exist between Xers and older cohorts will endure. The problem is most acute with respect to areas where, according to prior research, young people normally tend to differ from their elders (for example, partisanship; see Chapters 3 and 4), but it applies to some extent across the board. In the absence of longitudinal data,[2] sometimes the best we can do is to compare the attitudes and behavior patterns of today's youth with those of older cohorts when the latter were themselves young. And given that many of the questions asked in contemporary surveys were not asked in years past, even this limited test may be unavailable.

In fact, it is difficult under the best of circumstances to separate out the effects of generation (or birth cohort), period, and life cycle in any single analysis. The main reason for this is that the three phenomena are interrelated, and hence it is almost impossible to isolate all three at the same time (Glenn 1977). Being of a malleable age when exposed to specific historical events (generation) depends on when one was born, but when one was born also determines one's chronological age (life cycle) and one's exposure to events that have a greater or lesser impact on all groups in society (period, or period plus generation), and so on. These truisms mean that a researcher can never be entirely sure about the source of observed differences in outlook or behavior between old and young. We therefore offer, with a fair measure of humility, the following observations about Generation X and its predecessors. Although *After the Boom* is not the first effort to look at generational change in the 1990s, it is certainly one of the first to do so systematically. We recognize, however, that definitive answers to the questions raised here must await the passage of time and a good deal more research.[3]

Popular Conceptions of Boomers and Xers

A troublesome tendency in both the 1960s and 1990s has been for media accounts to depict the youngest cohort as if it were a cohesive whole, that is, to ignore or downplay, first with boomers and later with Xers, some notable intracohort differences concerning members' attitudes and behavior patterns. *Time*'s 1967 Man of the Year cover story described young Americans as having enjoyed "unprecedented affluence" and possessing "a sense of economic security unmatched in history" (Jones and Demarest 1967, 18); this facilitated what was said to be their greater commitment to "the fundamental Western ethos—decency, tolerance, brotherhood—than almost any generation since the age of chivalry. If they have an ideology, it is idealism; if they have one ideal, it is pragmatism" (20). Yet along with such admirable qualities (plus higher levels of educational attainment) came increasingly vocal challenges to the "establishment" and, in turn, the inevitable discussion of a generation gap. For sociologist David Riesman, the generation gap in the mid- to late 1960s was "wider than I've ever seen it in my lifetime" (Jones and Demarest 1967, 23).

In late 1969, a discourse in *U.S. News & World Report* entitled "One Generation Speaks to Another" illuminated some of the feelings of those on both sides of the gap. Marc Machiz, a high school student and self-professed "radical," offered the following perspective: "From my vantage point, we are confronted with a worn-out set of values. For once, our underlying values are in direct conflict with the sort of institutional change required by political and socioeconomic circumstance, and the youth of today find themselves confronted with a majority firm in the conviction that the old values remain valid" (*U.S. News & World Report* 1969, 28). Machiz's letter was in response to a speech made by James L. Robertson and reprinted in his book *What Generation Gap?* (1970). Robertson expressed a somewhat different view from his side of the gap: "Today, we appear to have too many people, mostly young ones, who think of themselves as problem solvers and activists but who want to *undo* something. They want to undo and destroy what it has taken . . . centuries to build. They have an almost ferocious conviction of their own righteousness and wisdom. They see themselves as the only real devotees in the world of the true, the good, and the beautiful" (Robertson 1970, 20).

Sociologist Andrew Greeley was one who questioned the reality of a generation gap in the late 1960s. In his analysis, Greeley observed greater differences of political outlook between college-educated and lesser-schooled baby boomers than between boomers as a whole and older Americans (quoted in Rosenberg et al. 1970, 68–73); over a period of time, numerous empirical studies confirmed that basic finding.[4] As popular novelist and former sixties activist Scott Turow recently remarked, "To recite the names of the various political hotbeds [Berkeley, Cambridge, etc.] . . . is to recognize that the cutting edge was traveled most often by the children of privilege. Generally speaking, blue-collar kids weren't the ones out there chanting; they still wanted their piece of the American dream. (And they—and the poor—were, by and large, the kids doing the dying in Vietnam.)

Richard Nixon was right: there was a silent majority out there. And it agreed with him, not us" (Turow 1996, 47). Thus, when all was said and done, a generation gap that seemed authentic to many—especially in the media—turned out to be less important than the education gap that existed within the boomer cohort itself.

Almost thirty years later, boomers are now seen as the target of great antipathy from gen-Xers (Mitchell 1993)—and vice versa (Giles 1994). Just as in the 1960s and early 1970s, the media have happily provided a forum for the angst of young and not-so-young alike, thereby helping to provoke a new storm over the growing conflict between generations. The direction from which this storm originated depends largely on whom you talk to. Neil Howe and William Strauss (1992, 79), for example, contend, "Over the past decade Boomers have begun acting on the assumption that Thirteeners [their term for Generation X] are 'lost'—reachable by pleasure-pain conditioning perhaps, but closed to reason or sentiment." In fact, "This generation—more accurately this generation's *reputation*—has become a Boomer metaphor for America's loss of purpose, disappointment with institutions, despair over the culture, and fear for the future" (Howe and Strauss 1992, 79; emphasis in original). According to Karen S. Peterson (1993, D1), boomers "are having a heyday calling [Xers] apathetic, shiftless, causeless navel-gazers. And that's when boomers notice them at all."

Taking the other side, one boomer laments the attacks that he believes originated with Xers. Ever since the publication of Douglas Coupland's oft-cited novel *Generation X: Tales for an Accelerated Culture* (1991), says David Martin (1993, 10), baby boomers have been subjected to a barrage of op-ed pieces and articles blaming them

> for the sad face of the twentysomething generation. . . . If you believe the Generation X essayists, all the troubles of the world can be traced to us forty-somethings. Well, enough is enough. As a baby boomer, I'm fed up with the ceaseless carping of a handful of spoiled, self-indulgent, overgrown adoles-cents. . . . If these pusillanimous purveyors of pseudo-angst would put as much effort into getting a life as they do into writing about their horrible fate, we'd be spared the weekly diatribes that pass for reasoned argument in newspapers and magazines.

Regardless of whether gen-Xers initiated this exchange of acrimony, at least some of them have worked hard to keep it alive. One Xer recently blasted boomers for being boring, irrelevant, without substance, consumed with the pursuit of profit, and generally so useless as to encourage their children to entertain thoughts of euthanasia (Nelson 1994). Another, with considerably less hostility, nevertheless complained: "I'm not in love with everything your parents did, but at least they gave you a chance. . . . For most of us, all we've been left with are the erotic fantasies, aggressive tendencies and evanescent funds of youth. Pretty soon we won't have youth *or* money, and that's when we may get a little angry" (Smith-Rowsey 1991, 11; emphasis in original). Are these feelings typical of gen-Xers? Probably not. Still, the debate goes on.

Economic claims seem slowly to be taking over as the primary source of discontent among gen-Xers—and with good reason, since recent developments have not been overwhelmingly positive (see Penny and Schier 1996; also Chapter 8 in this volume). In the early 1990s, the U.S. Labor Department released figures suggesting that "over the next dozen years about 30 percent of new college graduates will be either under-employed or unemployed" (Van Sant 1993, A1). It is likely, then, that the anger felt by many gen-Xers stems from their sense that they have been relegated to serving as the "reckless bicycle messengers, pizza drivers, yard workers, Wal-Mart shelf-stockers, health-care trainees, and miscellaneous scavengers, hustlers, and McJobbers in the low-wage/low-benefit service economy" (Howe and Strauss 1992, 74–5). Making matters worse, there is a growing recognition and resentment among younger people that while they are paying as much as twenty times more than previous generations (adjusting for inflation) in Social Security taxes, their return may be as low as 1.5 or 2 percent (Malkin 1994).

Yet the overall economic picture for Generation X and its future is by no means the subject of consensus. Howe and Strauss (1993b, 641), taking one side of the argument, assert that Xers will not enjoy the same standard of living that their parents enjoyed; to the contrary, it will be lower. As evidence, they point to the fact that the poverty rate among under-thirty households has more than doubled since the early 1970s. Howe and Strauss further maintain that the youngest birth cohort "has a weaker middle class than any other born in this century"; that is, the distance between those who are "beating the average" and those who fall beneath it has grown wider (641).

The opposing view comes from economist Robert Samuelson (1993, 641), who contends: "The pop theory that today's young won't live (in a material sense) as well as their parents is almost certainly wrong. As long as productivity rises modestly, Americans' material prosperity will gradually increase. True, we aren't getting ahead as fast as before. But this is not the same as slipping backward. . . . Even if standards of living [have] stagnated, they're dramatically higher than a half century ago." Without a crystal ball, it is impossible to know exactly what the future holds for gen-Xers or anyone else. What we can, and in the next section will do, however, is take a closer look at the *current* economic circumstances of different cohorts and assess whether there are age-related variations in how people *perceive* their own and the nation's economic prospects in both the long and short term.

But pocketbook factors are not the only source of friction between gen-

Xers and their elders. There also are questions relating to family life, the character of which has been rather different for baby boomers and their children. William Dunn (1993, 29) quoted one Xer's complaint that, "For the past 18 to 24 years, boomers have not been overly concerned about their children's welfare." The anger here derives primarily from higher rates of divorce among boomers, a larger number of single-parent families, and a surge in the number of children in child care as opposed to home care. Divorce has been an especially critical element; by the 1970s, the United States had achieved "the dubious honor of the world's highest divorce rate, with about 40 percent of marriages likely to end in divorce" (Dunn 1993, 16). Adding to the familial tension is the recent tendency for young adults to "leave the nest" and to get married at an older age than in the past.

Dunn (1993, 90–91) provided some telling statistics on this latter point: In 1992, a record 13.2 million persons aged eighteen to twenty-four (54 percent) were living at home with their parents—up from 11 million (47 percent) in 1970. Twelve percent of adults aged twenty-five to thirty-four lived with their parents in 1992; two decades earlier only 8 percent did. On average, gen-Xers are marrying later than any generation in the twentieth century. The median age at first marriage in 1992 was 26.5 for men and 24.4 for women. As recently as 1975, when many boomers were tying the knot, the comparable figure was 23.5 for men and 21.1 for women.

Regardless of whether one approves or disapproves, these developments have left the impression in certain quarters that gen-Xers are somehow less intelligent, more apathetic, less active, and more reliant on others than previous birth cohorts when they were young. Again, herein lies one of the problems associated with generational analysis: The term *generation* can be taken to imply that a particular age group is pretty much the same throughout, for example, in terms of its basic values and life experiences. The negative characterizations of Generation X may or may not be true as a matter of general tendency. Yet there are some gen-Xers who clearly defy the "apathetic and detached" stereotype by undertaking leadership roles in community center programs, by promoting juvenile justice and safety issues, and by addressing "such ills as poor education, street violence, poverty and joblessness" (Dowdy 1993, A1). Others are gathering in groups like the San Francisco Urban Service Project, which is aimed at helping Alzheimer's patients, the homeless, and those infected with the AIDS virus (Minton 1993, D7). Still others have joined political advocacy groups like Third Millennium (see Chapter 7), an organization with hundreds of members who are dedicated to speaking out on behalf of the interests of their age group (Bash 1993).

The actions of these individuals reinforce our warning that Generation X, like baby boomers, cannot be described simply in terms of a single set of underlying orientations (including feelings of enmity or anger directed at their parents' generation) that are shared by all or even most of its members. Significant portions of the popular media made that mistake in the 1960s and are in danger of making it again today. As several chapters in this book illustrate, there is considerable diversity within the Xer cohort—and more than a few similarities between Xers collectively and boomers collectively. Yet there *are* some aspects of the life experiences—past, present, and future—of today's young adults that are different from those of citizens who came of age at an earlier time. As we have already noted, many observers (gen-Xers among them) believe that the most important of these differences revolve around issues of economic opportunity. Let us take a moment to see if we can determine whether current economic patterns support such a conclusion and, more to the point, whether Xers as a whole buy in to the notion that their prospects are as bleak as has been suggested.

Cohort Differences in Economic Outlook

Is it true that Generation X faces a lifetime of economic hardship, especially relative to its baby-boom predecessors? Psychologically, gen-Xers are sometimes said to be experiencing a profound sense of limited fortune due to reduced educational opportunities and an uncertain long-term outlook for the overall economy. Whether the images be of decaying Rust-Belts or menial "McJobs," many Xers supposedly feel threatened by an economic calamity waiting to happen. In contrast, the general prosperity of postwar America is thought to have freed a majority of baby boomers (especially early boomers; see note 6) from want and encouraged them to take their and the nation's long-term economic security for granted.

Census Bureau and polling data alike attest to the lower educational achievements among gen-Xers (*New York Times* 1984; U.S. Department of Commerce 1993). For example, according to the 1992 American National Election Study (ANES) survey,[5] 21 percent of "early" boomers[6] reported receiving advanced college degrees, compared with just 10 percent of "late" boomers and a mere 4 percent of gen-Xers. Although it is likely that a larger proportion of today's young adults will eventually go on to pursue postbaccalaureate studies, three factors work against any expectation that Xers will reach the same level of advanced training as early boomers. First, many males among the early boomers remained in school past receiving their bachelor's degrees in order to remain clear of the Vietnam-era draft (*New York Times* 1984)—not a consideration for male Xers. Second, whereas the parents of both early and late boomers frequently had sufficient resources to underwrite extended stays in college, fewer Xers are in as enviable a position. Third, public support for higher education has dropped sharply over the past ten to fifteen years, making it more difficult for young people today to obtain advanced university training.

A related problem has to do with Generation X's allegedly straitened economic plight. A large number of Xers, we are told, find themselves locked into low-paying, dead-end jobs, and as a result they have developed a finely honed sense of economic grievance aimed at older citizens in general and baby boomers in particular. However, preliminary tests of this argument using survey data would seem to suggest otherwise (see Ladd 1993). And even if we were to learn that Xers do tend to be more disgruntled about their personal financial situations, any comparison of people under thirty (when many are still in college or just beginning careers) with people over thirty (most of whom have finished school and are established in jobs and careers) can be seriously misleading because of the presence of life-cycle rather than generational differences. If, as a Gallup poll from the early 1990s showed, Xers are less likely than their elders to enjoy the time they spend at work, this may stem "not [from] generational experience, but [from] such things as young people typically having less interesting jobs . . . and, as well, having more things they want to do off the job" (Ladd 1993, 16).

Fortunately, the ANES election-year surveys allow us to compare the financial conditions and expectations of gen-Xers today with those of boomers in the 1970s and 1980s, when the latter were roughly the same age as Xers are now. We start with reports of total family income, which has been broken into quintiles in order to control for the effects of inflation between 1972 and 1992. What the data clearly reveal is a tendency for Xers to fall into lower income brackets in the 1990s than did either of the two baby-boom cohorts in earlier years (see Bennett and Rademacher 1994). Specifically, the 1992 ANES shows between a quarter and a third of Xers with family incomes in the lowest quintile, about one-sixth in the middle quintile, and from one-twelfth to one-sixth in the highest quintile. By comparison, only about one-eleventh of the early boomers said their family incomes in 1972 fell in the lowest quintile, while a quarter were in the middle quintile, and from one-sixth to one-fifth had family incomes in the highest income quintile. Finally, if the ANES data are accurate, late boomers' family incomes in 1980 fell somewhere in between those of early boomers in 1972 and Xers in 1992.[7]

Interestingly, though, it appears that gen-Xers' perceptions of their economic circumstances are not as negative as one might expect (see Bennett and Rademacher 1994). When asked how their family finances had fared during the last year, Xers' answers in 1992 were not materially different from those given by early and late boomers in the 1970s and 1980s. And when asked to anticipate how their family finances would fare in the coming twelve months, Xers were no more pessimistic than the older cohorts had been at a comparable age. Most impressively, the 1992 ANES included a question asking respondents whether they believed that "twenty years from now, the standard of living for the people who are just children now will be better, about the same, or worse than it is today." We cannot track this question back in time, nor does it directly address the matter of Xers' own longer-term prospects. Nevertheless, there is nothing to indicate that young adults are more prone than anyone else to expect that economic hard times lie ahead.[8]

All in all, survey evidence bearing on the finances of Generation X points to some troublesome objective trends accompanied by guarded perceptions of the future—but perceptions that are more similar to than different from those of older cohorts. The trend data (relating to education and income) do, however, raise an intriguing question: Do variations in economic experiences across birth cohorts have any effect on people's basic expectations along the lines suggested by political scientist Ronald Inglehart (1971, 1977, 1990)?

Inglehart's thesis concerning generational and value change in Western societies began with the notion that, when pursuing various goals, individuals tend to give higher priority ("maximum attention") to those "things they sense to be the most important unsatisfied needs at a given time," for example, a thirsty man lost in the desert devoting almost all of his energy to finding water, or someone who is hungry becoming obsessed with the gathering of food (Inglehart 1971, 991). Once such needs are satisfied, other goals presumably can be attended to—except that Inglehart raises the additional possibility that people who have been socialized during periods of economic scarcity (for example, the Great Depression) may continue to emphasize material needs, relatively speaking, throughout their entire lifetimes.

Building on Abraham Maslow's (1954) theory of the hierarchy of human needs, Inglehart hypothesized that if during their childhood and adolescence (the formative years), people's basic human needs for sustenance and security were not met, they would as adults usually pursue goals aimed at achieving these "bourgeois" or "materialist" values over other ends. Alternatively, if they were fortunate to be reared during a period of widespread peace and prosperity, people would tend to put less emphasis on pursuing security and sustenance needs and instead stress "postbourgeois" or "postmaterialist" goals such as self-actualization and belongingness. While not without his critics (e.g., Duch and Taylor 1993, 1994), Inglehart (1990; also see Inglehart and Abramson 1994; Abramson and Inglehart 1994) insists that data from Europe and elsewhere are generally consistent with his line of reasoning.

As for the United States,[9] Inglehart's argument seems to have definite implications for our analysis of generational change: If it is true that Xers have faced and will continue to face less favorable economic circumstances than did boomers (especially early boomers) in their youth, then we would expect that the former would be much more likely than the latter to express materialist value priorities. As it happens, ANES surveys since 1972 have included two items developed by Inglehart to test hypotheses about the impact of economic and political conditions on different cohorts' underlying value priorities. Specifically, respondents are asked to identify which of four national goals they consider to be (1) most desirable and (2) second most desirable. In Inglehart's formulation, two of the stated goals (maintaining order in the nation; fighting rising prices) tap materialist values while the other two (giving the people more say in important political decisions; protecting freedom of speech) reflect a postmaterialist slant. Despite our reservations about what these items actually measure, we believe they can at least help us to determine whether gen-Xers are as fixated on the issue of economic security as they are sometimes said to be—and whether boomers are indeed more likely than their generational successors to take that security for granted.

We tested for this by comparing the proportion of different birth cohorts (see note 6) who listed each of the four national goals as their number-one priority for the years 1972–1992. Results (not shown) lead us to the following conclusions: First, as Inglehart predicted, there is a relationship between preferences and short-term fluctuations in the macroeconomy; that is, the percentage of respondents choosing "fighting rising prices" as their top priority increased (among all cohorts except Xers, who are not represented in the ANES surveys until 1984) in 1976 (when Jimmy Carter defeated Gerald Ford for president, partly due to worries about inflation) and 1980 (when unemployment and inflation were both high, leading to the election of Ronald Reagan), then dropped thereafter (including 1992, when unemployment was high but inflation low).

Second, there is relatively little variation in the structuring of national priorities across our five cohorts. Third, and for present purposes most important, we do not find much here to distinguish between the priorities of gen-Xers and the two boomer cohorts. Young people today may believe that they are experiencing financial hard times, but, if so, this does not significantly influence how they rank these national goals. Admittedly, our findings might be different if the options provided by Inglehart's measure included "promoting economic growth" rather than "fighting rising prices," but given the overall similarities across cohorts which exist on other types of economic evaluations, we would have to be persuaded. Perhaps, as Steven Schier concludes in Chapter 7, young Americans should be more concerned about their future than they apparently are, and perhaps one day soon they will be. Our data suggest that day has not yet arrived.

Conclusion

At the end of Chapter 2, Bennett and Rademacher cite Everett Carll Ladd's (1993, 14) observation that too much of the generational literature "abounds with hyperbole and unsubstantiated leaps from available data." This book is intended as a partial corrective to that problem. As noted, many of our contributors report findings that show more similarity than difference between gen-Xers and baby boomers or, in some instances, between Xers and older age groups in American society. At the same time, however, Xers do exhibit certain distinctive traits. We may have to await the passage of time to know whether those traits are a product of generational experience (thus, in all probability, enduring) or of age per se (thus transitory). Yet at least we have provided a starting point from which to track the political attitudes and behavior of young people in the years to come. Generational differences do not necessarily need to be dramatic or to generate bitter conflict in order to be important. Fairly modest changes due to generational turnover can lead, if sometimes gradually, to major social and political transformations. It should therefore be useful to identify where the potential for such change is present—and where the popular media and other social critics may have overestimated the likelihood of its occurring in either the long or short term.

Of the seven essays that follow, five are based on analyses of survey data from the United States. In Chapter 2, Stephen Earl Bennett and Eric Rademacher consider whether gen-Xers are as inactive, inattentive, and generally disengaged from the world of government and public affairs as they often appear to be—and are accused of being. This is followed in Chapter 3 by a look at the partisan makeup of Generation X (Jack Dennis and Diana Owen), and in Chapter 4 by a discussion of the policy views and ideological belief structures of various cohorts (Stephen Craig and Angela Halfacre); in both cases, the patterns of generational change are subtle and yet significant in ways that could portend continuing troubles for our existing party system. Chapter 5 (Diana Owen) is an examination of generational differences in feelings of political trust and support, while Chapter 6 (Kevin Hill) tackles the question of whether Xers display the sort of cultural liberalism and support for democratic values that have frequently been attributed to young people in general—and to baby boomers, when they were young, in particular.

Steven Schier moves away from our overall focus on attitudes and behavior in Chapter 7, painting a rather bleak portrait of Generation X's economic future should political leaders fail to confront the problem of large, persistent budget deficits; Schier is among those who feel that Xers are not as distressed by their circumstances as they need and deserve to be. Finally, in Chapter 8, Michael Martinez provides a comparative perspective with his analysis of Generation X in Canada; although the critical issues there are not the same as in the United States, our neighbors to the north currently face some hard choices and generational tensions of their own.

In closing, we want to alert readers to the fact that our contributors do not all interpret the "generational rhythm" (Elazar 1976) of U.S.—or

Canadian—political history in exactly the same way. It was noted earlier that the results one gets from studying birth cohorts depend substantially on the manner in which those cohorts are defined. The various age breaks employed in this book are outlined in Table 1.1. Notice that some authors designate four cohorts (Chapters 3, 6, and 8) and others use five (Chapters 1, 2, and 5) or even as many as six (Chapter 4). Each has interpreted the flow of historical events and their impact on young people in a slightly different fashion, and that is as it should be. We made the decision *not* to impose uniform age breaks throughout the book because, in our view, no one has yet determined what the "correct" breaks actually are.

The truth is that generational scholarship is still at the exploratory stage, and it would be presumptuous for us to think that we have all the answers. Nevertheless, readers need to recognize that the empirical findings presented here are not strictly comparable. They are informative, they are suggestive, they are occasionally provocative, and we hope they will help to clear up some questions and misperceptions while identifying others that require ad-

---

Table 1.1
Cohort Age Breaks by Chapter*

Chapter 2 (Bennett and Rademacher)
  Pre-cold warriors: up to 1929
  Cold warriors: 1930-1945
  Early boomers: 1946-1954
  Late boomers: 1955-1964
  Gen-Xers: 1965-

Chapter 5 (Owen)
  Oldest Generation: 1901-1929
  Silent Generation: 1930-1945
  Early boomers: 1946-1954
  Late boomers: 1955-1964
  Gen-Xers: 1965-

Chapter 3 (Dennis and Owen)
  G.I. Generation: up to 1924
  Silent Generation: 1925-1942
  Baby boomers: 1943-1960
  Gen-Xers: 1961-

Chapter 6 (Hill)
  G.I. Generation: up to 1924
  Silent Generation: 1925-1942
  Baby boomers: 1943-1963
  Gen-Xers: 1964-

Chapter 4 (Craig and Halfacre)
  Pre-Depression cohort: up to 1911
  Great Depression cohort: 1912-1922
  World War II/cold war cohort: 1923-1937
  Normal politics cohort: 1938-1947
  Baby boomers: 1948-1962
  Gen-Xers: 1963-

Chapter 8 (Martinez)
  Preboomers: up to 1942
  Early boomers: 1943-1957
  Late boomers: 1958-1971
  Gen-Xers: 1972-

---

*Intervals listed are the birth years for each cohort.

ditional research. They do not, however, represent the final word on any of the topics covered. In fact, we suspect that the debate over most of them has only begun.

Notes

1. As we explain later in the chapter, the turbulent 1960s were indeed "experienced" quite differently by those who went to college and those who did not (e.g., Kasschau et al. 1974; Thomas 1974).

2. Even longitudinal data do not provide a cure-all. Assume that in our previous example we found a strengthening of partisan ties over time among those who were young in 1996. Would this be due to the effects of aging or to a period effect that caused partisanship to become stronger among *all* cohorts? See Riley (1973); Glenn (1977).

3. For some good, mostly recent, discussion of issues related to generational research, see Jennings and Markus (1984); Billingsley and Tucker (1987); Schuman and Scott (1989); Beck and Jennings (1991); Braungart and Braungart (1991); Schuman and Rieger (1992); Rosenbaum and Button (1993); Scott and Zac (1993); Stoker and Jennings (1995); Dalhouse and Frideres (1996).

4. See, for example, Ladd with Hadley (1975); Converse et al. (1969); Kasschau et al. (1974); Light (1988).

5. These data were made available by the Inter-University Consortium for Political and Social Research. Neither the Consortium nor the original collectors of the data bear any responsibility for the analyses and interpretations presented here. See the Appendix for question wordings.

6. For this analysis, we will use the cohort breakdown discussed by Bennett and Rademacher in Chapter 2. Early boomers include those born between 1946 and 1954, late boomers between 1955 and 1964, and gen-Xers between 1965 and 1978. For comparative purposes, we also will examine "cold warriors" (born between 1930 and 1945) and "pre–cold warriors" (born prior to 1930).

7. See Chapter 7 for a longer-term (and not very optimistic) view of the economic future that Xers, as well as succeeding generations, may face as a result of political leaders' failure to deal with the problem of expanding national debt.

8. Except for the pre–cold warrior group, 44 to 49 percent expect the standard of living to be worse; 30 to 33 percent expect it to be better; and 16 to 17 percent say it will be about the same. The oldest cohort differs only in that slightly fewer expect the standard of living to decline (36 percent) and slightly more have no opinion (12 percent, compared with 4 to 6 percent of the remaining cohorts).

9. As noted by Craig and Halfacre in Chapter 4 (see note 6), Inglehart did not believe the United States was necessarily the best setting in which to test his theory.

2

The "Age of Indifference" Revisited: Patterns of Political Interest, Media Exposure, and Knowledge among Generation X

Stephen Earl Bennett and Eric W. Rademacher

In his famous essay *Democracy in America*, Alexis de Tocqueville (1945, 425–6) observed that the United States was "constantly" changing. In fact, one source of change in every society is the inevitable process of generational turnover. As older generations are replaced by younger ones, the latter's members may bring with them a different mix of attitudes, beliefs, lifestyles, and values. Actions taken by individuals on behalf of distinct, sometimes conflicting, generational perspectives thus have the potential to alter the social and political landscape in dramatic ways. Beginning about thirty years ago, the arrival into adulthood of post–World War II baby boomers was thought by many to have just such potential (e.g., Reich 1970).

Whether or not boomers have had the impact that observers in the late 1960s and early 1970s expected is not our focus in this chapter. Instead, we are intrigued by the fact that boomers today find themselves in the ironic position of being challenged by a new generation, many of whose members seem determined to implement change on behalf of their own world view. Variously labeled postboomers, twentysomethings, baby busters, or Generation X, the roughly 50 million Americans born between 1965 and 1978 have attracted the attention of demographers, journalists, marketing experts, and novelists who are trying to learn more about what makes them tick (e.g., Barna 1994; Coupland 1991; Dunn 1993; Howe and Strauss 1992; Crispell 1993; Isreal 1993). Any number of generalizations—not always very flattering—have sought to characterize the newly emerging birth cohort. Media accounts, for example, have noted their alleged "whining" (complaining about impoverished job and career opportunities), poor academic performance, and withdrawal from society in general and public affairs in particular.

Political scientists are only now beginning to explore patterns of attitude and behavior among these young citizens (e.g., Ladd 1993; MacManus 1996; Medvic 1994). Drawing on American National Election Study (ANES) surveys between 1972 and 1994, as well as several polls conducted on behalf of the Times Mirror/Pew Research Center for the People and the Press,[1] we will examine the level of involvement in politics that is evident among members of Generation X. Active engagement in and knowledge about the political process are essential features of democratic citizenship (Thompson 1970). It is our goal to ascertain how well gen-Xers fulfill these fundamental citizenship obligations.

An obvious question for students of generational change has to do with how different Xers are from earlier birth cohorts when the latter first came of age. Political apathy among young people would not, in and of itself, be anything new. Previous cohorts also have been relatively apathetic while in their twenties (Bennett 1986; Converse with Niemi 1971). If some accounts of Generation X are accurate, however, then it would appear that its members' indifference to public affairs, withdrawal from participation, and general lack of awareness of things political are unusually pronounced (see Times Mirror 1990a).

We intend to pursue several tacks in an effort to better understand Generation X's seemingly endemic political apathy. First, we will draw upon a measure of psychological involvement in public affairs, known as the Political Apathy Index (Bennett 1986), to determine whether gen-Xers are as disengaged as they are thought to be—and whether their disinterest is any more pronounced than that of earlier birth cohorts at a comparable period in their lives. Second, we will look at Xers' patterns of exposure to the mass media, including both entertainment and news outlets. Are younger Americans primarily "couch potatoes" addicted to MTV, or do they follow news accounts of current affairs to a greater degree than is generally believed? This last point is especially important because, unlike most previous studies of media exposure among the young, we plan to explore Xers' reports of how often they rely not only on traditional sources but also on newer media such as talk shows and the electronic bulletin boards that can be accessed through microcomputers. Finally, we will investigate what gen-Xers know about the political world. Once again, popular accounts suggest that young adults have very little knowledge of politics and government. We want to know if this is true and, if so, why.

No analysis of a given birth cohort makes sense unless it is in some sense comparative. We intend to look at Generation X in a double comparative perspective: First, what do data from previous birth cohorts of young citizens tell us about today's youth? Second, how do young Americans today compare with their same-age birth cohort abroad?

We believe our project is noteworthy for at least two reasons. In the first place, it is our view that social scientists should move aggressively to test propositions that acquire substantial currency in popular culture. About thirty years ago, the notion of a "generation gap" pitting young people against older citizens was widely believed, and social scientists only belatedly moved to test many facets of this purported gap with empirical data. When their research was completed (e.g., see Rosenberg et al. 1970), the gap thesis rightfully lost much of its intellectual force. Yet stories about generation gaps continued to play in the popular media, contributing to a distorted view of reality and perhaps affecting political decisions made on the basis of misleading information.[2]

The second reason for probing manifestations of political apathy among today's youth is more important: An understanding of contemporary political orientations can provide scholars with useful clues as to what lies ahead. If popular notions of Generation X's psychological withdrawal from public affairs are borne out by poll data, then concern for the future health of democracy in America may be warranted. As already noted, however, political scientists have long been aware of young people's tendency to be politically disconnected. Faced with a broad range of compelling personal challenges (finishing school, getting established in a job or career, seeking a mate), young adults tend to have little psychic energy left over for external matters such as public affairs. They also are more likely than older citizens to move from place to place, and residential mobility is another factor contributing to lower rates of civic involvement (Squire et al. 1987). Thus, if it is true that gen-Xers are relatively uninterested in politics, it may be that they are simply repeating a pattern typical of earlier birth cohorts during their own youths and that no threat to the future of democracy should be inferred.

A Short Note on Birth Cohorts

Those who write about generations as if their members were all of one mind engage in risky business.[3] Karl Mannheim warned against overuse of the concept of "generation" because "individuals of the same age . . . [are] only united as an actual generation in so far as they participate in the characteristic social and intellectual currents of their society and period, and in so far as they have an active or passive experience of the interactions of forces which made up the new situation" (Mannheim 1974, 8). As outlined in Chapter 1, Mannheim defined a more cohesive "generation unit" involving individuals bonded together by concrete experiences that cement the group in conscious identification. Although the baby boomers' experience with Vietnam comes to mind as a promising example, recent studies have stressed the diversity of economic circumstances and political outlooks existing even among young people who came of age during that tumultuous era (Delli

Carpini 1986; Light 1988). Mannheim probably would not be surprised by these results.[4]

We therefore are more comfortable with the term *birth cohort* rather than *generation* when describing boomers, Xers, and occasionally older age groups as well.[5] As Norval Glenn (1977, 8) explained, the boundaries of a cohort can be somewhat arbitrary, but they usually identify individuals "who experienced a common significant life event within a period of from one to 10 years." Some of the birth cohorts we will describe exceed ten years because the significant life event involved had sufficient impact as to justify incorporating a longer time frame. While some events such as Vietnam or the Great Depression undoubtedly affected more than one cohort, we have tried to define cohorts in terms of those who came of age during a given period. Of course, "coming of age" is itself a vague notion. Our intent is to recognize the impact of history on young adults—sometimes as young as sixteen or seventeen—whose lives would presumably have been most directly shaped by the key social and political developments of the day.

For the remainder of the chapter, we focus on three birth cohorts: the baby boomers, who are divided into early and late waves, and gen-Xers, a.k.a. postboomers, baby busters, or twentysomethings. At times, we refer to those whom Bennett and Bennett (1990) labeled cold warriors (born between 1930 and 1945), the so-called Silent Generation that immediately preceded the earliest of the baby boomers. The oldest cold warriors came of age just after World War II ended, when national and international events were dominated by fears of Soviet expansion and nuclear war. The youngest members of this cohort reached maturity under Presidents Eisenhower and Kennedy. At bottom, the cold warriors' political outlooks and behavior patterns were shaped by the events of what historian John Patrick Diggins (1988) called "the proud decades."

Although many writers treat boomers as if they were a single birth cohort (e.g., Delli Carpini 1986; Jones 1980; Light 1988), we adopt Bennett and Bennett's (1990) decision to divide them into two categories. Early boomers were born between 1946 and 1954, late boomers between 1955 and 1964. The reason for making this distinction is that the men in the first wave were subject to the Vietnam draft, while those in the second wave were not. As Jones (1980, 106) pointed out, "for [those] . . . born between 1946 and 1954, Vietnam and the draft were the most cauterizing events of their young lives." Still, the Bennetts (1990, 114) have argued that "Vietnam was only part of the social activism of the period." Before Vietnam, the civil rights movement activated many early boomers; in later years, the Free Speech movement on the campus of the University of California at Berkeley came to symbolize a youthful commitment to political activism—a commitment that began to wane by 1973, just as late boomers were coming of age (Jennings and Niemi 1981; also see Blum 1991).

If early boomers had Vietnam, late boomers had Watergate and Richard Nixon's resignation, economic stagflation (high unemployment combined with high inflation and high interest rates), and Jimmy Carter's national "malaise" (Bennett and Bennett 1990, 114–15; see also Craig 1993, 1–5). While their older brothers and sisters majored in sociology and political science, late boomers were more inclined to study business and economics. As late boomers reached adulthood, there were signs of lessened interest in public affairs, and popular culture rang with characterizations of what eventually came to be known as the Me Decade (see Jennings and Niemi 1981).

Finally, we come to Generation X. The oldest Xers came of age during the early years of Ronald Reagan's presidency, the youngest during the final days of George Bush and the initial stages of the Clinton administration. Although at first blush one is hard-pressed to determine what people born between 1965 and 1978 might have in common, Susan Littwin (1986) has established that in many respects they constitute the "Postponed Genera-tion." In other words, they appear to be taking longer to grow up—marrying later, taking longer to leave the parental nest (often in order to avoid paying rent from meager salaries in service-industry jobs), and returning home when confronted with a life crisis (such as divorce). When interviewing Xers, Littwin found a mixture of entitlement and frustration, perhaps born out of the fact that the world they had entered was less economically hospita-ble than that known by the early boomers and, to some extent, even late boomers (see Chapters 1 and 7). Since economic insecurities and delayed assumption of complete adult social roles are frequently accompanied by a lack of involvement in public affairs, Littwin's observations provide insight into why many gen-Xers might be politically disengaged. Someone con-fronting the types of personal problems she describes is unlikely to possess the reserves of time and energy needed to fulfill his or her citizenship re-sponsibilities.

We have, then, three birth cohorts whose political orientations and be-haviors we seek to chart. In addition, we will juxtapose our findings with the patterns observed among so-called cold warriors, the Silent Generation of the 1950s and 1960s. The main focus, however, is on citizens born after 1945. In looking at cold warriors and, on occasion, their generational prede-cessors (see Bennett and Bennett 1990 for a more precise breakdown of these older cohorts),[6] our intent is primarily to lend perspective to whatever traits are found to predominate among Xers and boomers.

Cohorts and Political Interest

If it is true that gen-Xers face relatively hard economic times in the 1990s (MacManus 1996; Penny and Schier 1996), and if it is also true that economic dislocations and political disengagement tend to go hand in hand, then can we assume that Xers will generally refrain from any sort of active involvement in public affairs? Apathy is a charge commonly leveled against members of Generation X, who supposedly would rather watch MTV than pay heed to the goings-on in government and politics. One study of Xers' political dispositions and behavior patterns concluded that although "the level of [campaign] interest for Generation X does not meet that of the Baby Boomers when they were in their twenties, this evidence [from ANES data] seems to contradict the notion that today's young adults could not be less interested about politics" (Medvic 1994, 17).

Unfortunately, Medvic's analysis was based entirely on survey questions dealing with respondents' attentiveness to election campaigns—a notoriously slippery indicator of one's interest in politics as a whole (see Bennett and Bennett 1989). What do we find when a "new and improved" measure of interest is employed? Such a measure was developed by Bennett (1986) who, following guidelines initially set forth by Almond and Verba (1963), combined the core ANES question on campaign interest with a second item tapping the amount of attention given by individuals to public affairs in general (see Appendix for wordings). The result was a valid and reliable measure that Bennett called the Political Apathy Index.[7] Figure 2.1 depicts the index scores registered by our five cohorts (including cold warriors and pre–cold warriors) from 1972 to 1994.

Looking at trends in political apathy between 1960 and 1984, Bennett (1986) concluded that young Americans have consistently paid less attention to public affairs than either the middle-aged or (in most cases) the elderly, despite having the advantage of more years of formal schooling (a factor that is strongly and inversely related to apathy). In the main, the data in Figure 2.1 confirm that same pattern: Over a twenty-two-year period, the two oldest birth cohorts (cold warriors and pre–cold warriors) almost invariably registered higher—often much higher—levels of attentiveness than did the three youngest cohorts (early boomers, late boomers, and Xers). The data also are consistent with prior research showing that as people age, they tend to become more interested in public affairs.

One noteworthy finding has to do with the gap in interest between early and late boomers, with the former being more attentive to politics in every survey since the latter first became eligible to vote in 1976. This confirms a discovery by Jennings and Niemi (1981), who found a difference between the high school class of 1965 and their counterparts in the class of 1973—in short, early and late boomers. After looking at the two groups, Jennings and Niemi concluded that in comparison to the class of 1965, "we can categorize the 1973 cohort as distinctly less imbued with the traditional virtues associated with civic training. Politics was less central in their lives and the partici-

Figure 2.1
Net Scores on Political Apathy Index by Cohort, 1972–1994.

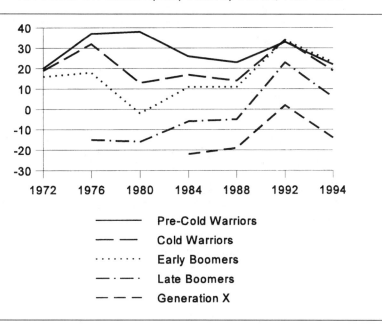

```
            Pre-Cold Warriors
  — —       Cold Warriors
  ·······   Early Boomers
  — · — ·   Late Boomers
  — — —     Generation X
```

Scores are calculated as percent interested minus percent apathetic within a particular age group (see note 7).
Source: American National Election Studies, 1972–1994.

pant culture was less valued. Indeed, one sees signs of withdrawal, of a turning inward" (Jennings and Niemi 1981, 225).

What apparently began among some late boomers has become even more common among gen-Xers, who exhibit higher levels of political apathy than any of the other four cohorts represented in Figure 2.1. If the results from 1988 and 1992 are to be credited, Xers shared in the general surge of political interest that occurred during those presidential election years, and in time they may yet overcome the images of apathy that dominate popular accounts of their political dispositions. It is important, however, to note that Xers remained less attentive even in 1992 than early boomers had been in the early 1970s (at a comparable age), although more involved than late boomers were in the late 1970s and early 1980s (a period of rising indifference to politics among the public as a whole).

What accounts for Generation X's relatively high degree of political apathy? Are the forces responsible any different from those that have produced higher apathy among young people in the past (see Converse with Niemi 1971; Bennett 1986)? To provide an answer, we performed separate regression analyses for (1) early boomers (using 1972 data, when the cohort was between eighteen and twenty-six years of age); (2) late boomers (1980 data, when they were also eighteen to twenty-six); and (3) gen-Xers (1992 data, when the youngest group was eighteen to twenty-seven). We employed the same procedure on each occasion, regressing the Political Apathy Index on eight variables usually thought to affect interest in public affairs: race, gender, marital status, education, occupation, income, strength of partisan identification, and concern about which party would win the election (see Bennett 1986 for the rationale behind this particular model). In addition, to capture the possibility that group identification may heighten or diminish one's interest in politics, we included a dummy variable coded 1 for those who identified most closely with young people and 0 for those who did not.[8]

Since the interpretation of regression analyses is fairly technical,[9] only general summaries will be provided here. Three major messages are communicated by our findings. First, only one independent variable accounts for all three cohorts' general interest in politics: education. Students of apathy among young people have long pointed to education as the key factor (Converse with Niemi 1971; Bennett 1986), and our analyses are consistent with that interpretation.

Second, and more importantly, we do find differences in the relative impact of variables across cohorts. For example, although gender is typically an important element in accounting for political interest (Bennett and Bennett 1989), it was not a statistically significant predictor for early boomers in 1972. This was a time when the second wave of the women's movement succeeded in mobilizing many younger women, and our results are perhaps a reflection of that success. Another interesting finding is that strength of partisanship (strong, weak, leaning, or none; see the Appendix for question wording) and concern about the election outcome were significant predictors of interest among early boomers and Xers, but not late boomers. Jennings and Niemi (1981), in their analysis of changes between the high school classes of 1965 and 1973, found a distinct pulling away from intense partisanship among the latter group, who would have been numbered among the late boomers, and that may account for the pattern witnessed here.

Third, and most intriguing of all, the data show that identification with "young people" was not a significant predictor of political interest among early or late boomers—but it was among Generation X. Moreover, in contrast to past studies which have found that a sense of group identification usually stimulates political involvement (Miller et al. 1981), the identification of Xers with their own age group worked to *depress* interest in 1992. There may be, as some have suggested, a tendency for those who feel "close" to this particular cohort of young Americans to withdraw from social and political involvement.[10]

Cohorts and Voting in National Elections

Previous research indicates that gen-Xers are not only indifferent to public affairs, but they are also disinclined to vote (Medvic 1994). In one sense, this finding merely confirms the well-known propensity for young adults to vote at lower rates than older citizens do (Converse with Niemi 1971; Teixeira 1987; Wolfinger and Rosenstone 1980). For example, 36 percent of early boomers reported abstaining from voting in 1972, the first year that a significant number of them were eligible to vote in presidential elections; the comparable figures were 54 percent for late boomers in 1976 and 53 percent for Xers in 1984. What, though, do we make of the fact that initial turnout rates were so much higher among early boomers than among either of their successor cohorts? Part of the difference can be traced to the nationwide turnout decline between 1972 and 1988.[11] Yet national rates jumped sharply in 1992, and that did little to lift Xers to anywhere near the level achieved by early boomers twenty years earlier.

Data from the 1992 and 1994 ANES surveys, shown in Figure 2.2, reveal substantial differences in turnout across our five cohorts.[12] As we would have predicted, participation rates were highest among cold warriors and pre–cold warriors—though early boomers (aged between thirty-eight and forty-six in 1992, and between forty and forty-eight in 1994) were at roughly the same level as these two older groups in both elections. By the 1990s, early boomers had entered into the "peak" years for voting. Fears expressed a decade or two ago that they would not follow in the path trod by their elders apparently can now be put to rest.

Reports of voting begin to sag a bit with the late boomers (aged twenty-eight to thirty-seven in 1992, and thirty to thirty-nine in 1994) and to plummet with gen-Xers (eighteen to twenty-seven, and eighteen to twenty-nine, respectively). Even though late boomers were still less likely to vote than early boomers, it is premature to conclude that their lower rates of turnout constitute a cohort effect. Another ten years or so must pass before such a conclusion would be warranted. The same cautionary note applies to Xers as well. It is possible that, with the passage of time, their participation rates will approach those among older cohorts. Nevertheless, one can hardly be impressed by the fact that only three-fifths of gen-Xers claimed to have voted in 1992—following a presidential campaign in which the winning candidate made a concerted effort to mobilize support among younger Americans. Two years later, in the 1994 off-year election, for every member of Generation X who reported going to the polls, two others admitted to staying home.

Figure 2.2
Reported Turnout by Cohort, 1992 and 1994.

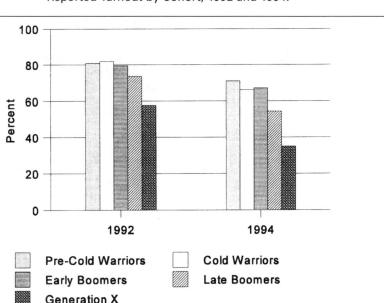

Figures indicate the proportion of each cohort who reported voting in the 1992 and 1994 general elections.
Source: American National Election Studies, 1992 and 1994.

Perhaps the unusually low first-time voting rates among Xers mentioned earlier (especially compared with early boomers in 1972) truly are a harbinger of things to come.

The reasons turnout is lower among young people are fairly well understood: they tend to be single, mobile, and preoccupied with finishing school and beginning a job or career (Teixeira 1992). The 1992 and 1994 ANES surveys show that, among gen-Xers, the single most important factor affecting turnout is education.[13] Only 19 percent of Xers who failed to complete high school reported voting in 1992 (13 percent in 1994), compared with roughly 80 percent (55 percent in 1994) of college graduates. Looking ahead, the Census Bureau (U.S. Department of Commerce 1993) estimates that Generation X is unlikely to achieve the high numbers of advanced college degrees earned by the two baby-boom cohorts, especially early boomers. If that projection proves accurate, we will probably not see the same levels of turnout in the future among Xers that we are now seeing among boomers.

There also is good reason to doubt that gen-Xers will ever match the older cohorts in terms of their participation in other modes of conventional political activity. According to the 1992 and 1994 ANES surveys, Xers are far less likely to report engaging in campaign-related behaviors such as trying to influence how people vote, attending a campaign meeting or rally, or working for a candidate or political party. Moreover, two Times Mirror Center polls, one from October 1994 and the second from May 1995, reveal that fewer members of Generation X are apt to have contacted a public official concerning an issue or problem or to express an opinion.[14]

It is too soon, of course, to write off Generation X in terms of their potential for becoming active participants in the political arena. As we have stressed repeatedly, the process of aging is known to result in, among other things, higher levels of participation. The problem is that Xers start off at such a low base—even compared with previous cohorts when they were young—that one can reasonably wonder what the future might hold. This becomes more of a concern when we look at the media habits of younger citizens.

Media Usage among American Birth Cohorts

Numerous studies have provided evidence that limited reliance on traditional media coverage of politics is typical among Xers, especially relative to older cohorts (e.g., MacManus 1996). Perhaps the most detailed study was done by the Times Mirror Center for the People and the Press, based on monthly polls conducted between January and April 1990. The Times Mirror Center, and the Pew Research Center that succeeded it, commissioned several surveys of Americans' patterns of media exposure between 1990 and 1996. We draw on data from these surveys to explore gen-Xers' reliance on mass media for public affairs information, and to compare their media usage with that of their elders.

Figure 2.3 presents a first look at respondents' reports concerning their use of so-called mainstream media to obtain information about public affairs. The data are from the Times Mirror Center's poll of February 1990, which was part of a sequence of surveys done for the Center's comprehensive analysis of Americans' media habits early in that year.[15] The figure depicts answers by members of five cohorts, beginning with those born before 1930 and ending with Generation X, to questions about whether they had read a daily newspaper, watched the news on television, or listened to the news on radio the day before they were interviewed.[16]

There are three aspects of Figure 2.3 that we want to stress. First, with the exception of radio (where they lagged behind by a smaller margin), gen-Xers reported far lower rates of exposure to mainstream media than did the older cohorts. In the case of newspapers and TV, drop-off among Xers was

Figure 2.3
Exposure to Mainstream Media by Cohort, 1990.

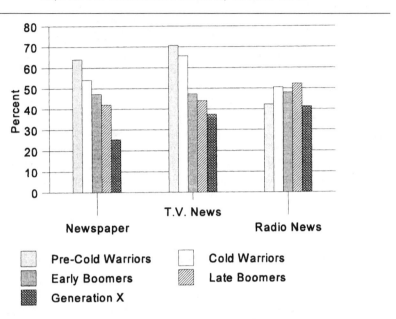

Figures indicate the proportion of each cohort who reported reading a newspaper, watching T.V. news, or listening to radio news on the day before the interview.
Source: Times Mirror Center for the People and the Press, February 1990.

dramatic. Indeed, only about one-quarter claimed to have read a newspaper the day before being interviewed, compared with nearly two-thirds of the oldest age group and slightly over half of the cold warriors.

Second, less than half of the three youngest birth cohorts—boomers *and* gen-Xers—said they had looked at a newspaper or watched a TV newscast the day before being polled. Communications researchers have long noted a tendency for fewer and fewer Americans to read a daily newspaper, and recent studies document a sharp decline in the proportion of the public watching the network newscasts on a regular basis (e.g., Pew Center 1996). The data shown here confirm these trends. Worse, from the perspective of newspapers and TV news, we may see even more serious declines in public exposure as the older birth cohorts die out and are replaced by younger ones with relatively sparse records of exposure to mainstream media.

The third message contained in Figure 2.3 is that, as we pointed out earlier, patterns of listening to the news on radio are rather different from those for newspapers and TV. One's birth cohort has only limited impact on the likelihood of one's listening to radio news, in contrast to the other media. As a result, the future for news on radio may not be quite as bleak as it appears to be for newspapers and TV news shows.

We can learn more about current media habits by examining the February 1990 Times Mirror survey, which contained questions dealing with citizens' exposure to different types of print and electronic media. Respondents were asked how often they read, watched, or listened to (1) newsmagazines such as *Time, Newsweek,* or *U.S. News and World Report*; (2) Sunday morning interview programs such as *This Week with David Brinkley* or *Face the Nation*; (3) *The MacNeil-Lehrer News Hour*; (4) National Public Radio; (5) the Cable News Network (CNN); and a variety of other publications and programs that are not known for their coverage of government and public affairs. There were four possible answers to each question, although we have collapsed them into two for ease of presentation (regularly/sometimes and hardly ever/never).

The distribution of responses outlined in Table 2.1 demonstrates that, in general, gen-Xers are less likely to report using these media than are older people (especially cold warriors and pre–cold warriors). The pattern is especially pronounced for the Sunday morning shows and for *MacNeil-Lehrer*— precisely the kind of in-depth program that might be expected to convey the richest blend of news about politics. On the other hand, there are only small age-related differences with regard to newsmagazines and CNN (see Mac-Manus 1996); Xers, in particular, compare fairly well with the four older cohorts in each of these two areas.[17]

The results in Table 2.1 dovetail nicely with the findings of a more recent study done by the Pew Research Center for the People and the Press. Based on a poll from April 1996, the Center reported that Americans under age thirty—that is, gen-Xers—were less likely than older citizens (especially those over fifty) to read newspapers and to watch the network newscasts or CNN. Xers were, however, *more* likely to watch MTV and the late-night TV shows—and almost as many reported listening to radio talk shows (Pew Research Center 1996). Young adults, who attend less often to the traditional, mainstream media, apparently are more inclined to draw upon newer, "alternative" media as a source of information about public affairs.

We can test this notion further with data from a Pew Research Center poll conducted in February 1996. Respondents were asked, first, how often they listened to radio or TV programs that invite people to call in and express their views. Although the results (not shown) indicate that early boomers are slightly more likely than other cohorts to report regular exposure to talk shows, variation from cohort to cohort—including the youngest—is rather modest. While only about one-sixth (15 percent) of Xers count themselves

Table 2.1
Exposure to Different Types of Media by Cohort, 1990*

	Pre-Cold Warriors	Cold Warriors	Early Boomers	Late Boomers	Generation X
Newsmagazines					
Never/hardly ever	51%	44%	42%	42%	44%
Sometimes/regularly	49	56	59	59	55
Sunday Interview Shows					
Never/hardly ever	55%	58%	68%	72%	77%
Sometimes/regularly	46	42	32	29	23
MacNeil-Lehrer					
Never/hardly ever	72%	74%	73%	76%	92%
Sometimes/regularly	29	27	27	25	9
National Public Radio					
Never/hardly ever	83%	84%	79%	77%	85%
Sometimes/regularly	18	15	20	23	14
Cable News Network (CNN)					
Never/hardly ever	50%	48%	42%	45%	46%
Sometimes/regularly	50	52	58	55	54
Sample N =	222	277	256	329	150

*See text for a discussion of question content. Table entries are column percentages, adding to 100% (respondents with missing values are excluded).
Source: Times Mirror Center for The People & The Press, 1990.

as regulars among the talk-show audience, more than half watch or listen at least occasionally.

Talk shows are usually considered to be a "new" form of media, but in fact they have been part of the radio/TV mixture of broadcasting for several decades. The same cannot be said about one of the fastest-growing forms of mass media in the 1990s: the computer-based "information superhighway" about which we have heard so much in recent years. The Pew Research Center's February 1996 poll asked respondents if they ever used a computer (at home, work, or school) to access electronic bulletin boards, information services such as America Online or Prodigy, or other computers via the Internet for news and information about public affairs. It also asked if these sources were being accessed specifically for information about the 1996 political campaign (at that point still in its early stages). Looking at Figure 2.4, one immediately notices the relatively low percentages at all age levels: When it comes to exploiting this emerging vehicle as a source of public affairs information, the overwhelming majority of citizens remain "off-line."[18]

There are, however, some small but interesting differences as we move from cohort to cohort. The oldest Americans, born long before computers of any kind became widespread, are virtually excluded from on-line technology, and cold warriors do not fare much better. Early boomers (who came of age along with the advent of old-fashioned mainframes) and late boomers (who probably recall and may have learned to use the first generation of personal computers) are considerably more likely to utilize computer technology for information about government and politics—yet fewer than one in five actually said they did so (less than 5 percent for information pertaining to the 1996 campaign).

And what about gen-Xers? Like the older cohorts, most Xers did not report using their computers for access to information about either politics in general or the 1996 campaign in particular. Yet they were more likely to have done so at least once (22 percent and 9 percent, respectively) than any other age group. This leaves us with the puzzle of whether to judge the glass half empty or half full. Young people are generally thought to be more adaptable than their elders; it is therefore possible that, if they do develop their computer skills more fully (and if information about public affairs can be readily accessed on-line, which clearly is the case now), we may see Xers—or perhaps the better-educated among them (Pew Research Center 1996)—build an even greater advantage over older cohorts than they have today.

It would be wrong, however, to assume that large numbers of gen-Xers will begin utilizing media for information about politics in the near future. Two Times Mirror polls, one in 1994 and the other in 1995, suggest otherwise. On each occasion, respondents were asked if they (1) would miss a

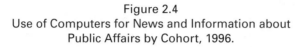

Figure 2.4
Use of Computers for News and Information about
Public Affairs by Cohort, 1996.

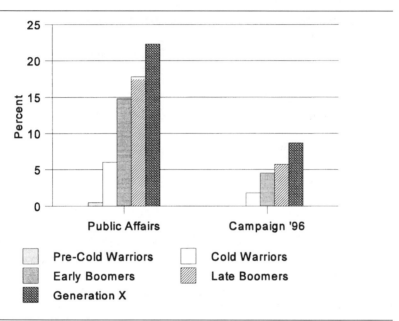

Figures indicate the proportion of each cohort who reported having used the computer to access information about public affairs generally, or about the 1996 campaign in particular.
Source: Pew Research Center for the People and the Press, February 1996.

daily newspaper should one suddenly not be available, and (2) enjoyed keeping up with news about public affairs. The results were identical in both surveys: Xers were less likely to say they would miss having the daily paper "a lot" (56 percent in 1995, compared with roughly two-thirds of boomers and three-quarters of older citizens), and less likely to say that they enjoyed keeping up with the news (38 percent in 1995, compared with about 55 percent of boomers and over two-thirds of cold warriors and pre–cold warriors).

These data are chilling to those who feel that citizens have an obligation to stay abreast of what is happening in the world of politics and government. Two polls taken a year apart cannot tell us if we are witnessing a generational phenomenon that will remain intact as members of a birth cohort pass through the life cycle, or if we are merely seeing the latest case of traditional youthful indifference toward public affairs. It will be necessary to track these questions and related behaviors over an extended period in order to resolve that quandary. However, one thing we can say for certain is that an overall lack of interest in public affairs and a tendency not to follow media accounts of politics have left many gen-Xers woefully ignorant about the world in which they live.

Birth Cohorts and Political Information

A core tenet of democratic theory holds that effective citizenship requires people to be well informed about public affairs (see Thompson 1970). Citizens cannot perform their most basic duties—voting, holding politicians accountable for their actions, and so on—when they are largely oblivious to the people and activities that constitute the public realm. How, then, do Xers perform on tests of what Americans know about public affairs?[19] Unfortunately, not very well. In a recent review of available evidence on the subject, Delli Carpini and Keeter (1996, 200–3) cited numerous polls indicating that younger Americans—gen-Xers—were much less knowledgeable than older citizens about key facts and personalities connected to politics, despite the former's relatively high level of formal education (at least compared to those born prior to World War II).

The discovery that younger people are less knowledgeable is hardly earth-shattering news. Converse and Niemi (1971) noted a similar pattern in surveys from the 1950s and 1960s; they explained that even though members of older cohorts did not have the educational advantages enjoyed by younger adults (and this observation was made before most baby boomers had come of age), the process of aging was itself associated with a higher rate of learning about public affairs.[20] In addition, older citizens who have directly experienced important events and been exposed to major personalities have a decided edge when pollsters ask questions with a historical context, for example, who was U.S. president during World War II? Were the United States and Japan allies or enemies in that war (Jennings 1996)?

Yet a Times Mirror (1990b) study, based on an examination of surveys dating back to the 1940s, concluded that the "knowledge gap" between young and old, at one time not that great, has actually widened over the years (also see Delli Carpini and Keeter 1996). A measure of political information constructed from variables in the 1994 ANES survey confirms that although none of our five cohorts was very well informed, Xers were much less knowledgeable than older people on matters relating to Congress, presidential candidates, the political parties, public policies, and various constitutional features of U.S. government (for example, who nominates federal judges).[21]

Data from other sources tell the same story. A survey done by Times Mirror in 1994, for example, found Xers getting an average of only 1.2 correct out of 5 questions that measured respondents' knowledge of foreign affairs (Bennett et al. 1996). Members of the four older cohorts averaged about 1.8 items correct—not a stellar performance, but certainly better than Xers. Likewise, a Pew Research Center poll from early 1996 revealed Xers to be less knowledgeable about domestic politics (an average score of 0.8 out of 2.0, compared with about 1.1 for the other cohorts). Finally, we should bear in mind that younger Americans would appear even more poorly informed than they do if it were not for their relatively high degree of educational attainment (Delli Carpini and Keeter 1996; Jennings 1996).

A Comparative Perspective

The portrait of Generation X presented thus far suggests that its members are, on balance, indifferent to public affairs, unlikely to vote or to take part in other kinds of political activities, disinclined to follow media accounts of public affairs, and generally uninformed about government and politics. In fact, a variety of evidence seems to indicate that apathy and disengagement are even more pronounced among Xers than among young people in years past, including both sets of boomers.

How do Xers in the United States compare with young people in other countries? A lack of appropriate data[22] makes it difficult to answer this question in terms of overall psychological involvement in politics. However, the Times Mirror's 1994 "International Media Monitor" study does permit a comparison of young citizens' reliance on newspapers, television (including CNN), and radio for public affairs information, and their knowledge about international politics, in five countries: Canada, France, Germany, Great Britain, and the United States (see Bennett et al. 1996). Our analysis was limited to those born between 1965 and 1978, aged between sixteen and twenty-nine at the time of the survey.

Results from the study are mixed. American Xers are less likely than their counterparts in the other four countries to rely on newspapers as a source of public affairs information, but they reported using electronic media (TV and radio) at a similar rate. And while only one in four said that they regularly watched CNN, this was about the same as in Canada—and a higher percentage than was found among the young in Britain, France, and Germany.[23] But when it came to knowledge of foreign affairs, American Xers did not fare nearly as well: an average score of just 1.2 correct out of 5 information questions relating to international politics (Bennett et al. 1996), compared with an average of 1.4 in Canada, 1.9 in Britain and France, and 3.5 in Germany. This may not be a completely fair test of political information, since Americans are less inclined than citizens of other countries to pay attention to news from abroad. Nevertheless, given the increasing importance to the United States of events beyond our borders, the ignorance exhibited by Xers when asked relatively easy questions about current events elsewhere in the world is hardly reassuring.

Conclusion

Everett Carll Ladd began his review of the latest wave of generational research with a scathing observation: "Social analysis and commentary has many shortcomings, but few of its chapters are as persistently wrong-headed as those on the generations and generational change. This literature abounds with hyperbole and unsubstantiated leaps from available data" (Ladd 1993, 14). We want to stress Ladd's final point, especially as it pertains to media commentaries on baby boomers in the 1960s and Generation X today: Too often, anecdotal evidence has been accepted as if it were proof that the patterns observed were typical among young people.

When scholars turn to Census Bureau and survey data, the portrait of Generation X that emerges bears only a scant resemblance to these caricatures. To the contrary, Xers' political tendencies do not, with a few exceptions such as ideological proclivities and possibly partisan leanings (Medvic 1994; see also Chapters 3 and 4), mark them as much different from earlier cohorts, including baby boomers, when they were young. Although sizable percentages of Xers eschew civic involvement, in this regard, as in so many others, they tread paths well worn by their generational predecessors.

At the same time, we have discovered some disturbing tendencies among younger citizens: They seldom engage in conventional forms of political participation (voting, contacting public officials, taking part in election campaigns, and so on). Their greater willingness to "surf the Net" notwithstanding, most Xers do not utilize mainstream or any other media as a source of information about public affairs. One consequence of such lack of attentiveness is massive ignorance, which may be the most unsettling aspect of Generation X reported in this chapter. Thomas Jefferson once noted that there never has been, nor ever will be, a people who are at once both politically ignorant and free. If so, we can legitimately wonder what the future holds if Xers remain as uninformed as they are about government and public affairs.

Like previous attempts to identify political patterns among Generation X, ours is an exploratory study. Much remains unknown about young Americans today, and the list of topics calling for further research is long indeed. We close, then, by noting two topics that we believe are particularly in need of clarification: First, what impact does Xers' tendency to remain single have on their political dispositions and behavior patterns? Second, it has been said that Xers are unusually cynical toward government and doubt-ful of their fellow humans' trustworthiness in general. Surveys do not really set gen-Xers apart from other cohorts in terms of political cynicism (see Chapter 5), yet we are uncertain whether they manifest dark suspicions of other people and, if they do, what impact that has on their political tenden-cies.[24]

Notes

1. The ANES surveys were made available by the Inter-University Consortium for Political and Social Research. The Times Mirror/Pew Center data were released directly to Bennett; we wish to thank Carol Bowman, formerly director of research at the Center, and Margaret Petrella, currently research analyst, for their kind help. We, of course, are responsible for all analyses and interpretations presented here.

2. For example, some Democratic party activists believed in 1972 that the recently ratified Twenty-Sixth Amendment to the Constitution, which lowered the minimum voting age to eighteen, would swell the ranks of voters sufficiently to elect George McGovern president. Nothing of the sort happened in large part because McGovern's popularity among young voters was not nearly as great as had been anticipated.

3. For good scholarly treatments of the various problems and pitfalls associated with generational analysis, see Abramson (1975, 1983); Braungart and Braungart (1987); Converse (1976); Glenn (1977); Jennings and Niemi (1974, 1981).

4. In his words, "Youth experiencing the same concrete historical problems may be said to be part of the same actual generation; while those groups within the same actual generation which work up the material of their common experiences in different specific ways, constitute separate generation units" (Mannheim 1974, 9).

5. The following discussion borrows heavily from Bennett and Bennett (1990, 1996).

6. The group we call pre–cold warriors were born prior to 1930.

7. The index (Cronbach's alpha = .69) initially divides people into five categories: very apathetic, slightly apathetic, neutral, slightly interested, and very interested. For Figure 2.1, (1) the percentage "very apathetic" and "slightly apathetic" are added together; (2) the percentage "very interested" and "slightly interested" are added together; and (3) the former is subtracted from the latter. When a cohort falls below the 0 percent line in Figure 2.1, that means more people are apathetic than are interested.

8. Respondents were presented with a list of different social groups and asked to indicate which groups they felt "particularly close to—people who are most like you in their ideas and interests and feelings about things." One group on the list was "young people"; others included "labor unions," "liberals," "the elderly," "southerners," "women," and "middle-class people."

9. Regression is a multivariate statistical technique that provides researchers with two types of information about a set of data. First, when a dependent variable, in this case the Political Apathy Index, is regressed on several independent variables—race, education, etc.—the regression coefficients tell us how much impact each independent variable has on the dependent variable *once the effects of all other independent variables have been taken into account.* Second, regression also provides an estimate of something called model fit, which is the combined effect that *all* independent variables have on the dependent variable. More detailed information concerning the results reported here can be obtained upon request from the authors.

10. Tests indicate that our overall regression model provides a satisfactory fit with the data for all three birth cohorts (i.e., explaining a reasonably high proportion of variance in the dependent variable), though it is better for Xers than for either early or late boomers.

11. The decline actually began following the 1960 election. See Luttbeg and Gant (1995).

12. Figure 2.2 is based on self-reports of voting rather than an actual check of voting records. We know from experience that some survey respondents tell interviewers that they voted in an election when in fact they did not, probably because they are embarrassed and want to appear to be "good citizens." There is no evidence, however, that age is very closely related to such misreporting; it occurs at about the same rate in every cohort.

13. Although the same is true at all age levels, the "turnout gap" between various education categories is larger for Xers than it is for older cohorts.

14. In 1994, 14 percent of Xers claimed to have contacted a public official in the last year; that number dropped to just 6 percent seven months later. These figures are derived from our own analysis of the Times Mirror data (see note 1).

15. We will not provide detailed results from the remaining surveys since they look much like the findings in Figure 2.3.

16. The questions were worded as follows: (1) "Did things come up that kept you from reading a paper yesterday, or did you get a chance to read a daily newspaper yesterday?"; (2) "Did things come up that prevented you from watching any TV news programs yesterday, or did you watch the news or a news program on television yesterday?"; (3) "About how much time, if any, did you spend listening to any news on the radio yesterday, or didn't you happen to listen to the news on the radio yesterday?" These same questions appeared in each of the Center's polls from January to March 1990. In the April 1990 survey, respondents were asked only if they got a daily newspaper, watched any TV news shows, or listened to the radio regularly—a type of question that leads to much higher reports of media usage.

17. For CNN, however, only 19 percent of Xers (versus 23 to 31 percent of their elders) said they watched on a regular basis.

18. The percentages in Figure 2.4 combine those who said they used a computer to access political information every day, three to five days a week, one to two days a week, or once every few weeks, and omit only those who said they "never" did so.

19. Here we encounter a debate between students of public opinion over how best to measure citizens' knowledge about politics. Some scholars contend either that the kinds of measures typically used in surveys to assay political information are "the wrong questions" and therefore get "the wrong answers" (e.g., Graber 1994, 1996; Popkin 1994), or that citizens can perform basic civic duties even though they may score poorly on standard tests of political information (Page and Shapiro 1992). Others disagree, arguing that "good decisions require good information" (Converse 1990, 372); if individuals lack essential information about politics, they are therefore ill prepared to conduct themselves as democratic citizens (also see Delli Carpini and Keeter 1996). This debate cannot be resolved here. Suffice it to say that we agree with the latter argument.

20. Converse and Niemi point out that age is often a substitute for formal schooling, especially with regard to what Delli Carpini and Keeter (1996) call "surveillance facts"— information about current events that can be picked up by following media news accounts. Take two individuals, one in her early seventies with an eighth-grade education and the other in his early twenties but with a high-school diploma. Ask the first person to name the man who led Yugoslavia after World War II, and she is likely to answer correctly because she recalls hearing about Marshal Tito on radio, seeing him on television, and/or reading about him in the print media. Ask the young man and he probably hasn't a clue, since Tito died before he came of age. (See Jennings 1996 for additional examples.) Of course, if we switched from public affairs to popular culture—e.g., who is Snoop Doggy Dogg?—the situa-

tion might well be reversed. It is therefore important to realize that when we say that aging is associated with "a higher rate of learning," we are talking about the learning of information about public affairs, not learning of all types. It is also important to distinguish between (1) the relationship involving aging and the acquisition of surveillance facts and (2) the well-known tendency for older people to become progressively less receptive to new values, life-styles, and so on (see Chapter 6). As scholars such as Converse and Niemi are aware, aging tends to harden attitudes and values, from party allegiance to beliefs about morality and a number of points in between.

21. This is based on the Political Information Index constructed by S. Bennett (1996). With scores ranging from 0 to 32, the mean for each cohort is as follows: gen-Xers (12.19), late boomers (15.04), early boomers (16.11), cold warriors (14.28), and pre–cold warriors (13.87).

22. Van Deth's (1989) analysis of Europe and the United States favors the conclusion that younger citizens are less attentive to politics on both sides of the Atlantic Ocean. Still, given polling differences from country to country, his comparison can only be regarded as suggestive.

23. This is probably because access to cable programming is much more widespread in Canada and the United States than in Europe.

24. The 1992 ANES shows that Xers are more misanthropic than their elders. Pinpointing the reasons for postboomers' tendency to mistrust other people will require another study.

3

The Partisanship Puzzle: Identification and Attitudes of Generation X

Jack Dennis and Diana Owen

During the 1996 presidential campaign, political parties and candidates worked hard to court young voters even before the nominating conventions were held. Polling data indicated that the eighteen-to-thirty-year-old vote was up for grabs—in part, it was said, because members of Generation X tend to make their choices based more on issues than on traditional partisan cues (Eilperin 1996a; Schalch 1996). In fact, far from being wedded to either Bill Clinton or Bob Dole, many gen-Xers declared that they would be happy to support a third-party alternative in 1996 if an appealing candidate were to enter the race.

The Democratic and Republican parties responded by launching creative campaigns to bring Xers into their ranks and to enhance the group's turnout in the upcoming election. Second Lady Tipper Gore hosted tea parties at the vice presidential mansion. House Speaker Newt Gingrich and Minority Leader Richard Gephardt turned out for beer bashes at trendy brew pubs (Eilperin 1996b). Other members of Congress performed with rock bands at MTV-sponsored events that encouraged young people to vote. The Congressional Internet Caucus launched an on-line voter registration drive, NetVote '96, targeting Xers with a press conference and a rally featuring Grammy Award–winning singer Sheryl Crow (Eilperin 1996a). Seventy-two-year-old Bob Dole traveled on MTV's "Rock the Vote" bus and was interviewed by popular gen-X correspondent Tabitha Soren.

After years of virtually discounting the nation's youngest voting cohort, politicians began to prepare for the possibility that Generation X might finally be ready, willing, and able to exercise some political clout. The first Xers became eligible to vote in a national election only in 1980, but by the late 1990s this age group—defined here as consisting of people born between 1961 and 1981 constituted one of America's largest voting blocs (Howe and Strauss 1993a). Generation X has been slow, however, to capitalize on its political potential. Younger citizens have a somewhat well-de-served reputation for being politically ambivalent, uninformed, and inactive (see Chapter 2). While their turnout rate improved slightly in the 1992 presidential race compared with four years earlier, less than 20 percent of genXers participated in the 1994 midterm elections (Rothenberg 1996). On the other hand, it is perhaps worth noting that a record number of Xers *ran* for federal office in 1996; close to three dozen twentysomething candidates waged congressional campaigns after winning their party's nomination in primary elections (Van Dongen 1996).

To a large extent, the political identity of Generation X remains amorphous. Gen-X's political attitudes and behavior have been rather unstable over time, although this is not atypical for young people (Rice and Hilton 1996). One potential source of this variability might be the cohort's professed estrangement from formal political institutions, including political parties. The two major parties, even as their importance to voters in general has diminished, offer individuals a conduit to the political world and provide cues for political decision making. If they do not identify strongly with parties, and especially if they harbor negative feelings about parties, gen-Xers are likely to be less anchored in the political world than their generational predecessors.

This chapter examines the partisan identification of Generation X. We will explore how Xers differ from prior generations[1] in their partisan preferences and offer some possible explanations for these differences. Specifically, we will address the following questions: To what extent does Generation X affiliate with political parties? What kinds of attitudes toward political parties do gen-Xers hold? What factors influence the development of Generation X's partisan identification?

Our analysis begins by examining Xers' partisan attachments. We then discuss two explanations that might account for the differences found between Generation X and prior cohorts: a *socialization* explanation and a political *alienation* explanation. The process of political socialization, through which partisan identification and other orientations are conveyed from parents to children, has been somewhat different for gen-Xers than it was for their elders. Strong political moorings, for example, are less likely to be rooted in the family than in the past. In addition, anti-institutional and, more specifically, antiparty attitudes have had a deleterious effect on the development of partisan attachments among the American public generally and younger people in particular.

Partisan Identification

The general inclination of Generation X is to think and operate farther outside the context of formal political institutions than has been true of earlier cohorts. This extrainstitutional orientation is reflected in a variety of ways, including the fact that Xers' sense of attachment to parties is less robust than that of older citizens. Not only are the former less likely to identify strongly with either the Republicans or the Democrats, but they also exhibit a relatively high degree of volatility in their partisan affiliations. Consider, by way of illustration, some of the data gathered during the 1996 presidential campaign. One survey reported rather dramatically that no more than one-third of Xers identified with either party and that very few expressed strong support for their preferred choice; moreover, there was evidence that only about one-quarter of Xers normally voted a straight party ticket at election time (Eilperin 1996b; Jutkowitz and Pollock 1996).

Other polls, though, produced estimates suggesting that young voters were a good bit more partisan than these figures might lead one to believe. One survey from early 1996 showed less than 30 percent of young adults calling themselves independents (versus 38 percent Democrats and 30 percent Republicans; see Dewar and Edsall 1996). Yet there also were indications that a substantial number of gen-Xers have difficulty selecting from the response categories provided by traditional party identification questions. A Global Strategy Group survey of eighteen- to-thirty-year-olds revealed that 24 percent considered themselves Republicans, 23 percent Democrats, 28 percent independents—and 24 percent did not know or refused to answer (*Public Perspective* 1996).

In order to take a closer look at the recent partisan preferences of Generation X, we have employed data from the 1994 American National Election Study (ANES).[2] Our results seem to confirm that Xers are more likely than not to identify with a political party, but the strength of their attachments is fairly weak. We also should point out, however, that the partisan profile of gen-Xers closely resembles that of the baby boomers who directly preceded them (see Chapter 4).

This resemblance is clear from the results presented in Table 3.1, which is a cohort-by-cohort breakdown of responses to the ANES seven-point party identification scale (see Appendix for wording). Reading right to left, we see that the percentage of strong Democrats increases as one moves from young to old: 11 percent of gen-Xers, 14 percent of baby boomers, 19 percent of the Silent Generation, and 23 percent of the G.I. Generation. Although slightly higher among older Americans, there is little difference in the proportion of weak Democratic identifiers across cohorts. Cross-generational similarities are found on the other side of the aisle as well. Boomers and members of the Silent Generation are somewhat more inclined to be strong Republicans, while the percentage of Xers in the weak Republican category is marginally higher than for the remaining three cohorts. Still, cohort differences on the whole are modest and, for the most part, not statistically significant.

Table 3.1
Party Identification by Cohort, 1994

	G.I. Generation	*Silent Generation*	*Baby Boomers*	*Generation X*
Strong Democrat	23%	19%	14%	11%
Weak Democrat	22	18	18	19
Independent Democrat	7	9	14	17
Independent	10	8	11	11
Independent Republican	9	16	12	9
Weak Republican	15	12	14	18
Strong Republican	13	17	18	14
Total	99%	99%	101%	99%
N =	243	388	636	497

*See Appendix for question wording. Table entries are column percentages (respondents with missing data omitted), which may not add to 100% due to rounding.
Source: American National Election Study, 1994.

The fact that Generation X's identification with political parties is weaker than that of preceding generations becomes more apparent when we examine the data only for people who identify with one of the major parties (i.e., excluding independents). Just 41 percent of Xer identifiers—compared with 55 percent of the Silent Generation and roughly half of boomers and the G.I. cohort—feel a strong attachment to their party of choice. Yet when we consider the extent to which Xers tend to think of themselves as political independents, the evidence is less than impressive. There is, for example, no meaningful difference between Xers and either boomers or members of the G.I. Generation in the proportion of "pure" independents (referring to those who do not lean one way or the other). And when pure independents are combined with independent "leaners," Xers and boomers both register at 37 percent, with the Silent Generation not too far behind (33 percent).

An interesting pattern is revealed by responses to two ANES 1993 Pilot Study items that asked specifically about political independence. In answer to the question "Do you ever think of yourself as an Independent in politics, or does being a political Independent not really apply to the way you think of yourself?" Forty-six percent of gen-Xers replied in the affirmative, compared with 56 to 59 percent of the older cohorts (see Table 3.2). Moreover, just 39 percent of Xers who *did* say they were independents considered themselves *strong* independents; this is in sharp contrast to the 46 percent of boomers, 61 percent of the Silent Generation, and 69 percent of the G.I. Generation that claimed strong independent identification. It may be that the independent label simply does not resonate with younger Americans. In other words, instead of viewing themselves explicitly as independents, Xers (by preferring not to rely on traditional labels) are perhaps exhibiting a lack of attachment to the party system in general. We will return to this point later in our discussion.

In sum, the findings reported here build upon a large body of prior research in demonstrating that affiliation with the political parties and, especially, strongly held partisan convictions are on the decline, most obviously among the younger generations (notwithstanding the apparent anomalies just noted). In the next section we will offer several explanations for why stable and deeply held partisan attachments are becoming increasingly uncommon in American society. We also will discuss a variety of reasons that might help to explain why partisanship is, at least in certain respects, weaker for Generation X than for its predecessors.

Table 3.2
Political Independence by Cohort, 1993

	G. I. Generation	Silent Generation	Baby Boomers	Generation X
1. "Do you ever think of yourself as an Independent in politics, or does being a political Independent not really apply to the way you think of yourself?"				
Yes	59%	56%	56%	46%
No	41	44	44	54
Total	100%	100%	100%	100%
N =	87	135	240	156
2. (If yes to question 1) "Do you think of yourself as a strong Independent or a not so strong Independent?"				
Strong	69%	61%	46%	39%
Not so strong	31	39	54	61
Total	100%	100%	100%	100%
N =	51	76	134	72

*Table entries are column percentages, adding to 100% (respondents with missing data are not included in the calculations).
Source: American National Election Study, 1993 Pilot Study.

The Decline in Partisan Attachments

As recently as the 1950s and early 1960s, it was possible to take for granted the existence of a robust collective sense of partisanship in the United States. At the time of the early empirical political socialization studies (e.g., Hyman 1959; Greenstein 1969; Hess and Torney 1967; Easton and Dennis 1969), the overwhelming majority of mature Americans seemed to hold clear partisan preferences (Dennis 1975, 1980). This conclusion was reinforced by contemporaneous scholarly research on vote choice, much of which suggested that deep-seated and enduring political "brand loyalties" often influenced other forms of political behavior (e.g., Berelson et al. 1954; Campbell et al. 1960). Those who investigated life span–related patterns of political learning believed that most people would eventually come to hold partisan attitudes—attitudes that, in most cases, were established in childhood. Thus, the main questions guiding research concerned not *whether* but *when* individuals typically formed partisan attitudes and under what circumstances.

Citizens today, however, are much less inclined than in the past to develop a secure sense of partisan identification. And individuals who do call themselves Democrats or Republicans are not always inclined to attach a high level of cognitive focus or affective involvement to this identity. Where they develop at all, partisan self-images therefore may develop slowly and sporadically during an era that is often labeled "antiparty" in mood (Owen and Dennis 1996).

The current literature on partisan decomposition among the general public confirms that neither the incidence of partisanship nor the influence of party identification on other political behavior (such as voting) is a given in contemporary U.S. politics (Dennis 1966, 1975, 1980, 1986; Burnham 1970; Wattenberg 1994). Partisan instability has in fact become the rule, with a majority of citizens, especially young adults (Rice and Hilton 1996), being likely to change their position on partisanship scales with some frequency. Indeed, our analysis supports the contention made by numerous scholars that each successive age cohort has, over the past several decades, manifested less collective partisan consciousness relative to the partisanship of generations that preceded it (see Beck 1984; Miller 1991). Only slightly more than half of the electorate in the 1990s are partisans, compared with nearly 80 percent of those who entered the electorate in the pre–New Deal era.

Political Culture and Socialization

One possible explanation for the decline in mass partisanship is that the broader political culture has changed significantly since the Silent and G.I.

generations entered the electorate (Bellah et al. 1985). For example, the political fabric of American society has, over time, become highly atomized. Traditionally strong societal institutions such as the family have become fragmented, and individuals' connections to larger communities have weakened. The mass media contribute to this collective sense of anomie and isolation by substituting indirect, global communication for local and more personal forms of interaction (Kornhauser 1959). Such cultural disintegration of personal ties is reflected in citizens' reduced inclination to form strong political identities; it also contributes to their estrangement from governmental institutions.

The transmission of a nation's political culture from generation to generation is accomplished via the process of *politicization*. As people become politicized, they develop a growing sense of politics as a distinct realm of human experience and acquire the necessary motivations to participate in the political order. Seminal research has posited that politicization usually begins early in the United States. Although the process continues in one form or another throughout an individual's lifetime, the foundations of political learning and political identity are thought to be established during the childhood years (e.g., see Hyman, 1959; Greenstein, 1969; Dawson and Prewitt, 1969; Easton and Dennis, 1969).

Early socialization studies determined that the family (along with school and peer groups) was most instrumental in instilling lifelong political orientations—identities, attitudes, values, and behaviors—in children. But socialization models that assume the primacy of early learning and the importance of personal agencies of socialization, such as the family, are more successfully applied to earlier cohorts than to Generation X. The changing structure and cohesiveness of the American family (especially as the divorce rate escalated, single-parent households multiplied, and two-income families grew in number; see Cutler 1989) mitigated the leverage that parents in earlier eras apparently had in politicizing their children. Parents were left with less time and perhaps less inclination to teach their progeny about politics. As a result, gen-Xers often received fewer, less direct, and less homogeneous political cues from family members over the course of their preadult political development.

Changes taking place within the institution of the family have some obvious implications for political learning in relation to Generation X (see Easterlin and Crimmins 1991). For one thing, Xers are less likely to be highly politicized by the time they reach voting age; they also are less apt to have fully developed and stable political identities, attitudes, and behavioral orientations than members of past generations. Still, socialization research on prior cohorts indicates that family may take a strong role in transferring *partisan* identities to younger citizens—even if it is no longer as central as it once was in other areas of preadult political socialization (Alwin et al.

1991). Jennings and Niemi (1974, 1981) found that, aside from candidate choice in particular elections, party identification is the area of greatest parent-child correspondence in political attitudes.

But has the family continued to exert a major influence on the development of party identification for Generation X? The parents of gen-Xers, many of whom are baby boomers, do not hold strong partisan attachments themselves. In addition, political socialization has become largely depersonalized for Xers, who rely to an unprecedented degree on electronic intervention for access to political information. For younger Americans, the mass media are generally more influential conduits for learning political attitudes, such as political tolerance (see Chapters 2 and 6; also see MacManus 1996), and for gaining information about the political world than are personal agencies (Owen and Dennis 1987, 1988, 1992).

In fact, data from a Wisconsin statewide survey of preadult gen-Xers, conducted in 1980–81 and described in greater detail below, indicated that 30 percent of the sample obtained most of its information about politics from television and 28 percent from newspapers; just 16 percent said they were informed about politics principally by their parents, 14 percent by teachers, 2 percent by friends, and 10 percent by other agents. This pattern apparently has continued into adulthood. Global Strategy Group data from 1996 revealed that the largest percentage (54 percent) of gen-Xers received a majority of their political information from television; 19 percent of the sample got most of its information from newspapers, 5 percent on-line from computers, 4 percent from radio, and 3 percent from magazines. Far fewer Xers cited personal agencies as their most important sources of information: 6 percent said parents, 2 percent friends, 5 percent college, 3 percent high school, and 3 percent teachers in general (*Public Perspective* 1996). Nevertheless, there may be exceptions to these overall tendencies for specific dimensions of politicization. It is possible, for example, that parental influence remains crucial for the transmission of basic political identifications (including partisanship) even though the identifications in question are not as strongly held as they are among older cohorts.

We can utilize the 1980–81 Wisconsin study[3] to explore more fully the socialization bases of party identification for members of Generation X.[4] For this survey, a statewide sample of preadults ranging from ten to seventeen years old—along with one parent of each respondent—was interviewed by telephone. The first set of interviews was completed in early 1980 before the presidential primaries, the second just prior to the presidential election, and the final one in November 1981, about one year after the election. Born between 1963 and 1970, and questioned at a much earlier stage of the life cycle than is typical in adult surveys, the children here are situated at the heart of the 1961–1981 birth cohort identified earlier as constituting Generation X.

Before examining the impact of parental partisanship, let us consider the extent to which gen-Xers identified with political parties during their preadult years. Two different measures of partisan affiliation are employed in our analysis. The first is the traditional seven-point party identification index (TPI) discussed earlier (see Table 3.1), while the second was developed by Jack Dennis for the 1980 ANES survey. Unlike the TPI, which assumes that independence represents the zero point along a bipolar continuum of identification with the Democratic Party on one end and the Republican Party on the other, this measure—the Partisan Supporter Typology (PST)—allows someone to be *both* partisan *and* independent at the same time, or *neither*.[5] In short, it is possible for individuals to be completely unattached to political parties. The PST is especially well suited for probing the partisanship of Generation X, given what appear to be that group's anti-institutional proclivities. As the Global Strategy Group data presented earlier demonstrate, some Xers would rather not respond to the party identification question at all than to characterize themselves in terms of the traditional categories of Democrat, Republican, or independent.

Table 3.3 compares parents and children in Wisconsin using both the seven-point party identification measure and the Partisan Supporter Typology. With the traditional partisanship index (TPI), there is nothing to suggest that gen-Xers at the early stage of their development were less attached to political parties than were their parents. In fact, we find a slightly *higher* incidence of identification in 1981—be it strong or weak—among children (70 percent) than among parents (65 percent). However, it is our belief that by forcing respondents to be either partisans or independents, the TPI has the potential to exaggerate the extent of partisan affiliation.

The PST measure yields quite different results. When the question was framed in terms of support rather than of identification, far fewer of our respondents overall reported an affiliation with the Democratic or Republican parties. More to the point, the intergenerational pattern observed for the TPI is reversed: a smaller proportion of children (56 percent) than parents (60 percent) presented themselves as party supporters. We also see evidence of many Xers' reluctance, very early in the life span, to associate themselves in any way with the party system: 19 percent of children were totally "unattached" (neither party supporter nor independent), compared with just 10 percent of parents. Adults, however, were somewhat more likely than their children to be classified as Ordinary Independents not leaning toward a party (30 percent versus 25 percent, respectively).

Within the Wisconsin sample, we calculated partisanship levels for younger (ages ten to thirteen) and older (ages fourteen to seventeen) preadults using both TPI and PST. The age-related variations are complex, but some distinct patterns (not shown) can be discerned. For example, there is no indication that gen-Xers develop closer ties to partisan institutions as they

Table 3.3
Party Identification of Parents and Their Children

	Children	Parents
A. Traditional Partisan Index (TPI)		
Strong Democrat	5%	10%
Weak Democrat	24	20
Independent Democrat	8	13
Independent	5	8
Independent Republican	17	14
Weak Republican	30	23
Strong Republican	11	12
Not ascertained/Don't know	50	31
Sample N =	366	366
B. Partisan Supporter Typology (PST)		
Ordinary Democrat	12%	12%
Independent Democrat	11	15
Unattached	19	10
Ordinary Independent	25	30
Independent Republican	13	22
Ordinary Republican	20	11
Not ascertained/Don't know	37	37
Sample N =	366	366

*See Appendix (TPI) and note 5 (PST) for question wordings. Table entries are column percentages, adding to 100% (respondents with missing data are not included in the calculations). Children in the sample were aged between ten and seventeen in 1980.
Source: Wisconsin Parent-Child Socialization Study, 1980–81.

grow older; to the contrary, older children were clearly *more* detached from the parties than were their younger counterparts. This is evident with the traditional partisanship index (36 percent older versus 24 percent younger labeling themselves as pure or leaning independents), as well as with the Partisan Supporter Typology (25 percent older versus 41 percent younger being Ordinary Republicans or Ordinary Democrats). On our PST measure, older Xers also were considerably more likely (33 percent versus 16 percent) to be Ordinary Independents—though younger respondents did have a modest edge (22 percent versus 16 percent older) among the unattached (those who reject both partisanship and independence).

Recall that, according to the Partisan Supporter Typology (if not the traditional partisanship index), gen-Xers as preadults were at least slightly less partisan than their parents. Let us close our analysis of the Wisconsin data by considering the relationship between parents' and children's party identification. In other words, are the children of Democratic (or Republican or independent) parents disproportionately Democratic (or Republican or independent) themselves? To answer this question, we computed simple bivariate correlations (Pearson's r) between the two generations' partisanship scores.[6] Our findings suggest that parental influence is substantial, but less than overwhelming, in passing along one's partisan preferences to members of Generation X. The correlation coefficient is a fairly strong r = .42 for TPI and a weaker, though statistically significant, r = .23 for our PST measure.

Parental socialization continues to play an important role in the transmission of party identification from parents to children. The partisan cues being conveyed by parents are, however, less powerful than was typically the case in the past. Thus, to a significant degree, early political socialization may have inhibited the development of party loyalties among today's young adults. In the following section we will examine some additional factors that could help to explain the decline of partisanship in the United States.

Attitudes toward Partisan Institutions

A second possible explanation for the erosion of mass partisanship is that each generation has become more disillusioned with, or at least less favorably disposed toward, partisan institutions in general. This might be part of a broad sense of mistrust directed at politics and government as a whole (Craig 1993) or, alternatively, the result of negative attitudes toward a specific institution (such as Congress; see Hibbing and Theiss-Morse 1995). As parental influence on socialization processes has diminished, the capacity of nonpersonal agencies to shape the development of political attitudes has naturally increased. We noted earlier that the mass media—and television most of all—are of central importance to Xers as a source of information about politics. In effect, for many Xers the media have become a proxy for face-to-face discussion with family members, teachers, and peers.

It is no wonder, then, that recent trends in mass communications are frequently blamed for undermining the legitimacy of partisanship among the public and among younger citizens above all. Investigative journalism, as it has evolved since the days of Vietnam and Watergate, tends to present partisan politics in an unflattering light and therefore contributes to a collective sense of partisan alienation within the electorate (L. Bennett 1996; Patterson 1993; Sabato 1991). If the message is commonly and persistently conveyed via mass media that the two major parties provide neither clear and attractive programmatic alternatives nor meaningful leadership options, then some degree of institutional delegitimation will almost inevitably result. Further, as a growing number of citizens come to regard the parties as ineffective, the idea may spread that perhaps we can do without political parties altogether.

One symptom of partisan alienation at the institutional level is the erosion of partisanship among individuals who are just entering the adult world of politics. As feelings of hostility (Craig 1985) and/or indifference (Wattenberg 1994) are reinforced by the media—and by other cue givers—over time, the macro-level consequence may ultimately be some form of partisan *de*alignment characterized by increased ticket splitting, electoral volatility, and voter abstention (see Beck 1974, 1984; Aldrich and Niemi 1995).

Looking to the future, we think it is useful to consider whether Generation X exhibits signs of broadly based partisan alienation—or whether its lack of strong party ties is simply a maturational phenomenon that is likely to disappear as this cohort grows older. In other words, is it true that gen-Xers have not had enough reinforcing partisan experiences (or been exposed to enough reinforcing partisan communications) to produce at least average levels of party identification compared to the population as a whole? To see if there is evidence of either (1) anti-institutional attitudes toward parties or (2) feelings of indifference about the institution of parties, we will examine a number of survey questions that deal with people's beliefs and feelings about the nature and role of parties in American politics.

One such question is drawn from the 1993 ANES Pilot Study, in which respondents were asked whether we still need political parties in the United States or whether, by implication, we could get along just as well without them.[7] Although gen-Xers were the most prone to say that parties are no longer needed (36 percent agree strongly or somewhat), they were followed closely in this regard by the baby-boom (34 percent) and G.I. (33 percent) generations; only members of the Silent Generation (27 percent) stood out in their relative support for the institution of parties. While admittedly small and statistically insignificant, these differences do run in the same direction as our hypothesis, that is, Xers are the least resistant of all four cohorts to the prospect of abolishing political parties.

Age-based differences are again modest on a second question that taps sentiments of approval or disapproval of the American party system. Our measure here is the feeling thermometer, on which respondents are asked to express their feelings about various political objects on a scale ranging from 0 (indicating a "very cold" or negative evaluation) to 100 (indicating a "very warm" or positive assessment; see Appendix for wording). In part A of Table 3.4, we see that in 1994 Xers *and* boomers provided evaluations of "political parties in general" that were less positive (very or moderately warm) and more negative (very or moderately cold) than were those of either the Silent or G.I. generations—especially the latter. Thus, in considering the public's global orientation toward the institution of parties, the sharpest contrasts

Table 3.4
Feeling Thermometers by Cohort, 1994

	G.I. Generation	Silent Generation	Baby Boomers	Generation X
A. Political Parties in General				
Very warm	19%	13%	8%	8%
Moderately warm	19	14	13	10
Neutral	44	52	45	50
Moderately cold	14	13	23	22
Very cold	4	9	10	10
Total	100%	101%	99%	100%
N =	249	390	642	505
B. Democratic Party				
Very warm	24%	23%	13%	15%
Moderately warm	19	16	19	18
Neutral	37	29	35	37
Moderately cold	15	24	20	21
Very cold	5	8	13	10
Total	100%	100%	100%	101%
N =	249	390	642	505
C. Republican Party				
Very warm	23%	20%	16%	18%
Moderately warm	19	19	18	16
Neutral	36	44	38	42
Moderately cold	16	10	20	16
Very cold	6	8	8	7
Total	100%	101%	100%	99%
N =	249	390	642	505

*See Appendix for question wordings. Individual scores have been recoded as 81–100 = very warm; 61–80 = moderately warm; 40–60 = neutral; 20–39 = moderately cold; and 0–19 = very cold. Table entries are column percentages, adding to 100% (respondents with missing data are not included in the calculations).
Source: American National Election Study, 1994.

appear to be, first, between the two youngest and the two oldest cohorts (see Chapter 4) and, second, between the G.I. Generation and everybody else.

A similar pattern is observed in parts B and C of Table 3.4, which display 1994 thermometer scores for the Democratic and Republican parties. As before, the ratings of gen-Xers and baby boomers were less generous than those of older citizens—though at the negative end of the scale it is actually boomers (33 percent very or moderately cold toward Democrats, 28 percent toward Republicans), not Xers (31 percent and 23 percent, respectively), whose attitudes were least supportive. And with a single exception (its 22 percent negative on the GOP thermometer, exceeding the Silent Generation's 18 percent and virtually matching Xers' 23 percent), the G.I. Generation once again emerges as the most favorably disposed toward the two principal partisan contenders in U.S. electoral politics.

Next, we turn to a more cognitively focused evaluation of the two major parties. Respondents in 1994 were asked whether they perceived differences between the parties, both overall and in a number of specific policy areas. Interestingly, in all but one of the categories (handling the economy) shown in Table 3.5, it is the oldest cohort, not the youngest, that is the most likely to believe there are no important programmatic differences between the Republicans and the Democrats. One might argue that this finding is evidence of experience being the teacher. Of all the cohorts, the G.I. Generation is the most tuned in to political parties; they also have greater knowledge of and longer experience with the American party system. Thus, if it is true that there really is not much to choose from between Republicans and Democrats in most of these areas, then older citizens should be more likely to recognize that fact—and their failure to differentiate would not necessarily reflect negative attitudes toward the parties or the party system as a whole.

Alternatively, the pattern we see here may derive more from political history and change than from the relative experience levels of our four cohorts. In an earlier era, when members of the G.I. and Silent generations were socialized, the parties were *not* always very distinctive in their policy stands; they generally placed greater emphasis on organizational incentives (such as patronage) than on issue articulation (see Eldersveld 1964; Rossiter 1960). Since the 1960s, however, there has emerged a "new breed" of party activists whose participation is more often motivated by substantive policy concerns than by the prospect of tangible rewards. The major parties, while still fairly close to each other in terms of global left/right ideology, have therefore developed rhetorically sharp differences of emphasis on a wide range of concrete policy issues (Bruce et al. 1991; Stone et al. 1994; Aldrich 1995). And as the parties' respective images have become more policy centered, it is natural that younger citizens—boomers and gen-Xers, both socialized during the period of transformation—would be more likely than their elders to believe that the parties really do stand for something different.[8]

This does not, of course, automatically make the parties more attractive to voters who have recently entered the electorate. Xers and boomers may view much of the controversy as unnecessary (see Chapter 4), or they may feel that both parties stand for things that would only incrementally change the underlying New Deal and cold war compromises that continue to domi-

Table 3.5
Difference between Parties by Cohort, 1994

	G.I. Generation	Silent Generation	Baby Boomers	Generation X
In general	52%	44%	39%	47%
Raise taxes	65%	62%	57%	57%
Handle economy	52%	51%	49%	54%
Handle pollution	62%	58%	45%	48%
Handle crime	54%	52%	46%	39%
Foreign affairs	47%	45%	39%	39%
Health care	42%	38%	35%	31%
Welfare	41%	38%	33%	34%
N =	246	379	640	499

*Questions: "Do you think there are any important differences in what the Republicans and Democrats stand for? (yes or no) Which party is more likely to raise taxes—the Democrats, the Republicans, or wouldn't there be much difference between them? Which party do you think would do a better job of (a) handling the nation's economy, (b) handling the problem of pollution and protecting the environment, (c) dealing with the crime problem, (d) handling foreign affairs, (e) making health care more affordable, (f) reforming the welfare system—the Democrats, the Republicans, or wouldn't there be much difference between them?" Table entries indicate the proportion of each cohort (based on 100%, respondents with missing data excluded) who felt that the parties did not offer voters much of a choice.
Source: American National Election Study, 1994.

nate the political landscape. Either way, our findings in Table 3.5 are inconclusive as to whether younger people are more or less favorably disposed toward the institution of political parties.

An area where gen-Xers do appear to be more clearly antiparty is indicated by an ANES Pilot Study question asking respondents whether they had ever supported Ross Perot or his organization, United We Stand America. The data (not shown) reveal that, as of 1993, at least two-thirds of each cohort had thus far managed to resist this particular third-party appeal. It is nevertheless telling, and consistent with our earlier findings, that support for Perot was slightly higher among Xers (33 percent) and boomers (31 percent) than among members of the G.I. (23 percent) or Silent (27 percent) generations. One might expect that in the 1996 presidential election Perot's Reform Party will fare better with younger voters who are less enamored of the options offered by the two major parties and, for that matter, of the two-party system in general.[9]

When 1993 Pilot Study respondents were presented with a wider set of options relating to the future of the U.S. party system, their overall anti-institutional bias, varying by age stratum, became more conspicuous. Table 3.6 shows that gen-Xers were the least enthusiastic about maintaining the present two-party system (29 percent versus 36 percent for boomers, 45 percent for the Silent Generation, and 58 percent for the G.I. Generation) and the most likely to favor candidates running not on party tickets but as individuals (45 percent versus 40 percent, 33 percent, and 22 percent, respectively). Cohort differences were less pronounced on the desirability of having new political parties, though here again it is Xers (26 percent), along with boomers (25 percent), who most often seemed to be searching for alternatives to the status quo. Coming on top of the results presented earlier concerning whether we "need political parties in America anymore," these findings reinforce the impression that younger voters are prepared to endorse basic changes in the existing party system.

Table 3.6
Support for Party System by Cohort, 1994

	G.I. Generation	Silent Generation	Baby Boomers	Generation X
Continue two-party system	58%	45%	36%	29%
Candidates run as individuals	22	33	40	45
Growth of more parties	20	22	25	26
Total	100%	100%	101%	100%
N =	231	382	630	493

*Question: "Which of the following would you prefer: A continuation of the two-party system of Democrats and Republicans; or, Elections in which candidates run as individuals without party labels; or, The growth of one or more new parties that could effectively challenge the Democrats and the Republicans?" Table entries are column percentages, adding to 100% (respondents with missing data are not included in the calculations).
Source: American National Election Study, 1994.

Conclusion

It is an important fact of American political life that citizens' attachments to the two major parties have weakened over the past few decades. This trend began with the dealignment of postwar baby boomers in the 1960s and continued—perhaps even accelerated—during the 1980s and 1990s with the coming of age of Generation X. Earlier cohorts experienced a more robust form of institutional socialization, and thus legitimation, that led them to exhibit greater support for the parties and the party system as a whole; indeed, members of the G.I. and Silent generations (more the former than the latter) maintain relatively strong partisan identities today.

But the socialization of younger Americans, especially gen-Xers, has been very different. In an era of fragmented families and pervasive mass communication, it is far more difficult for strong and unambiguous (as well as positive)[10] partisan cues to be disseminated to young people. Television in particular filled the vacuum of informing citizens about politics as the family's role diminished. Unfortunately, such influence did not result in greater partisan affiliation or respect for the critical linkage role that parties play in democratic politics. It is therefore not surprising that Generation X has a more detached partisan orientation than do previous cohorts—more detached even than boomers, in whose footsteps they so conspicuously follow.

Given the inverse relationship between age and strength of party identification which appears to be characteristic of any political era (see note 9), Generation X's weak partisan ties cannot yet be taken as a permanent feature of the American political landscape. Our data show that Xers are not so different from boomers in their overall partisan profile, and over time it is possible that the attachments of Xers may actually come to exceed those of their immediate generational predecessors. It is in the area of support for—or alienation from—traditional partisan institutions that gen-Xers are more distinctive. For example, Xers are the cohort least likely to reject strongly the proposition that "we probably don't need political parties in America anymore" and the one least inclined to support continuation of the two-party system in its present form (Table 3.6). If the "none of the above" movement ever takes hold, Xers' stated preference for candidates running without party labels leads us to believe that they would be numbered disproportionately in its ranks.

But there is more. Statistically speaking, Xers are no more likely than boomers to describe themselves as independents on traditional measures of party identification (Tables 3.1 and 3.3), and they lag behind *all* other cohorts in their propensity to say that they think of themselves as political independents (Table 3.2). We have presented evidence, however, which suggests that the distinction between Democrats, Republicans, and independents simply does not resonate with Xers they way it does with older Americans; Xers seem to have weaker attachments to the party system as a whole and to the labels normally associated with it (bottom half of Table 3.3; see also *Public Perspective* 1996). Our youngest citizens do not "dislike" political parties to an unusual degree, and yet they show many signs of estrangement from them. Even the one instance in which Xers look to be less antiparty than their elders—in their cognitive assessments of whether there are important differences between the Republicans and the Democrats (Table 3.5)—can be seen as a possible warning sign: If important differences are thought to exist but are viewed as either excessive or irrelevant to solving people's everyday problems, then popular support for the party system will almost certainly continue to decline. Based on what we have seen here, this may very well be what is happening among gen-Xers.

In sum, Xers have yet to be mobilized by the parties in any definite or ongoing fashion. Despite the best efforts of Republican and Democratic party organizations and their standard-bearers during the 1996 campaign, it will be a formidable task to bring these young recruits into the fold. In order to do so, party leaders must first persuade Xers that political parties have a constructive role to play in a representative democracy such as the United States. This is more easily said than done. In an antiparty age, gen-Xers are the most antiparty of all the present age strata within the American adult population. It remains to be seen, as the next group of Xers reaches voting age in 1998, whether the generation will once again baffle pollsters with its partisan volatility or whether, as its members reach greater political and biological maturity, Generation X will at last find its collective political identity.

Notes

The authors would like to acknowledge the National Science Foundation (grant #SES–791343522), whose support made collection of the Wisconsin data base possible. We also would like to thank Steve Farnsworth for his invaluable assistance in the preparation of this chapter.

1. We employ the generational breakdowns defined by Howe and Strauss (1993a). These are as follows: Generation X (born between 1961 and 1981), the baby boom generation (1943–1960), the Silent Generation (1925–1942), and the G.I. Generation (1901–1924).

2. These data were made available by the Inter-University Consortium for Political and Social Research. Neither the Consortium nor the original collectors of the data bear any responsibility for the analyses and interpretations presented here.

3. The study, funded by the National Science Foundation and executed by Jack Dennis, Steven H. Chaffee, and David O. Sears, was entitled "Election Campaigns and Preadult Political Socialization." The Wisconsin Survey Research Laboratory conducted the interviews and coded the data. The original sample contained approximately 700 child-parent pairs. A total

of 366 child-parent pairs completed all three waves of the panel interviews. It is this portion of the study whose responses we analyze here. While the attrition rate for the survey is nearly 50 percent, an analysis of demographic, political, and communication variables by Steven H. Chaffee uncovered no apparent evidence of systematic response bias.

4.–See note 1. Aged between twenty-four and thirty-one at the time of the 1994 election, these individuals are somewhat older than the twentysomething generation as a whole.

5. The Partisan Supporter Typology is constructed, first, by asking respondents, "In your own mind, do you think of yourself as a supporter of one of the political parties, or not?" Those who profess support are then asked to identify their preferred party and to indicate their "closeness" to it on a scale of one to seven. Those who initially shy away from the self-image as a party supporter are asked whether "you ever think of yourself as closer to one of the two major parties, or not"; if so, the same seven-point closeness scale is employed. Step two in building the PST involves asking all respondents, "Do you ever think of yourself as a political independent, or not?" Those who reply in the affirmative are asked to assess the strength of their independence on a scale that again ranges from one (not very strongly) to seven (very strongly).

The PST categories shown in Table 3.3 are determined as follows: Ordinary Democrats/Republicans (yes to being a party supporter, no to being an independent); Independent Democrats/Republicans (yes to being both a party supporter and an independent); Ordinary Independents (no to being a party supporter, yes to being an independent); and Unattached (no to both). For a more complete discussion, see Dennis (1988).

6. Correlation coefficients range between 0.0 (no relationship) and plus or minus 1.0 (a perfect relationship). A coefficient of plus or minus 1.0 means that knowing a respondent's relative score on the first variable allows one to predict, with perfect accuracy, his or her relative score on the second variable. A score of 0.0 means that there is no tendency at all for high (or low) scores on one variable to occur among individuals who score high (or low) on the other. For the relationships examined here, high positive scores mean that children *tend* to have the same partisan identity as their parents.

7. Specifically, respondents were asked to agree or disagree (strongly or somewhat) with the following statement: "The truth is we probably don't need political parties in America anymore."

8. Yet another possibility has to do with the fact that people with higher levels of education are more likely to perceive differences between the parties (Bennett 1995). Since Xers and boomers have had more formal schooling than their elders, this should contribute to the former's ability to discern whatever true differences, large or small, may exist.

9. Admittedly, this is not a very bold prediction since younger people in any political era tend to have relatively weak partisan loyalties (Converse 1969, 1976; Fiorina 1981; Cassel 1993) and hence are more inclined to vote for independent or third-party candidates (Converse et al. 1969). See Owen and Dennis (1996) and Dennis (1994) for an account of age differences in 1992 and other bases of support for Perot.

10. On the negative tone of political news coverage and its impact on citizen attitudes, see Sabato (1991); Neuman et al. (1992); Fallows (1996).

4

Political Issues and Political Choice: Belief Systems, Generations, and the Potential for Realignment in American Politics

Stephen C. Craig and Angela C. Halfacre

Considerable effort, scholarly and otherwise, has been expended in careful examination of the post–World War II birth cohort and its impact on U.S. politics. Looking at some of the ways in which this group's policy views, partisan preferences, and patterns of participation diverged at least for a time from those of Americans who entered the electorate before, during, and shortly after the Great Depression, many analysts concluded that a new political age was dawning. Especially during the late 1960s and early 1970s, generational change seemed to be a driving force behind the increasing pressures for *party realignment*.[1] Not only did younger citizens, in the aggregate, exhibit an unusually low level of partisan attachment (presumably leaving them "ripe" for mobilization into a new alignment; see Beck 1974); they also appeared to be making policy demands that were qualitatively different from those expressed by older cohorts. Rather than organizing their political identities around the traditional government management/social welfare issues that arose in the 1930s and 1940s, young adults were often portrayed as insisting that government respond to problems relating to the "quality of life" in America (e.g., Inglehart 1977; Miller and Levitin 1976).

In the end, of course, nothing approximating a "classic" realignment occurred (but see Aldrich and Niemi 1995); that is, there was no clear-cut alteration of the political agenda accompanied by a sharp and durable shift in the distribution of party loyalties in the electorate. Newer issues (race, crime, abortion, the environment) became salient to young and old alike, as did newer forms of economic conflict (inflation, energy, international trade), without necessarily displacing the long-standing clash between society's haves and have-nots which gave shape to the party system in place since the Roosevelt years. And even though the character of mass partisanship did change in some fairly significant ways—largely as a result of heightened independence among postwar baby boomers (Jennings and Markus 1984)—neither party emerged as a clear winner as had the Democrats during the New Deal. Moreover, it is noteworthy that voters of *all* ages began during this same period to express doubts about whether U.S. parties were even capable of dealing with the most important problems facing the nation (Wattenberg 1994).

In the 1990s, a new generation of Americans is being subjected to scrutiny. The partisan orientations of these young citizens are examined elsewhere in this book (see Chapter 3), so the focus here will be less on realignment per se than on what we believe to be, at least potentially, the attitudinal foundations and attachments upon which age-related partisan change in the current era might be based. Before pursuing this idea, however, let us review the concept of a *political generation*.

Political Generations and Political Change

Although the idea of generations has existed for centuries, its central reference point for many contemporary discussions in sociology and politics is the work of Karl Mannheim (1952). Mannheim wrote of the ever-changing character of society, with new participants constantly entering the cultural process to replace older participants who have dominated that process for decades. These new participants are characterized by a "fresh contact" with society, and as a result they bring the potential for change and innovation—a potential that evolves from shared experiences. Membership in the same generation presumably endows individuals with "a common location in the social and historical process, and thereby [limits them] to a specific range of potential experience, predisposing them for a certain characteristic mode of thought and experience, and a characteristic type of historically relevant action" (Mannheim 1952, 291). The realization of a generation's potential is said to depend in large measure on the quickening "tempo of social change" which can render "traditional patterns of experience, thought, and expression" obsolete (309).[2]

It is therefore in response and adaptation to dramatic social and political events (transformations) that a distinctive generational outlook seems likely to emerge. Nevertheless, even if the current historical period can be characterized as one in which the "tempo of social change" has been accelerated, one might wonder whether these events—especially when they are experienced directly or vicariously by all or most members of society—do not have a similar impact upon people of different ages. In some cases, this may be true: Political learning can occur at any stage of a person's life, with attitudinal change a possible outcome of that learning.[3] Yet the concept of generation presumes that there is something unusually meaningful about the learning that occurs during an individual's formative years. "Early impressions," said Mannheim (1952, 298; emphasis in original), "tend to coalesce into a *natural view* of the world. All later experiences then tend to receive their meaning from this original set, whether they appear as that set's verification and fulfillment or as its negation and antithesis." Thus, the generational approach assumes that (1) youth are particularly susceptible to the shaping forces of the environment and (2) the resulting learning is likely to *persist* and to *structure* later experiences and later learning (see Searing et al. 1973).

As noted earlier, the empirical study of political generations gained momentum during the late 1960s and early 1970s, in large part because of scholarly fascination with the process of partisan realignment, in which younger voters are understood to play a crucial role. Age is a variable that is strongly associated with the *strength* of partisan attachment among voters;[4] in other words, there appears to be a hardening of attachment over the life span such that older citizens are "immunized" from the effects of contemporary events (some of which might otherwise draw them toward modes of behavior at odds with their existing partisan orientations; McPhee and Ferguson 1962). In contrast, younger voters have limited electoral experience, their resistance to the pull of events is relatively weak, and therefore it is they who should provide disproportionate support for whatever political tides are dominant at a given moment. We do not mean to imply, of course, that older voters are entirely immune to the forces of change, rather that the susceptibility to change (according to generational theory) varies with age.[5]

To be sure, realignment sequences in American politics are always marked by the defection of some party identifiers whose allegiances cannot inoculate them completely against the effects of dramatic new issues and catalyzing events. But for many older citizens, defections of this sort apparently do not signal any long-term change in party affiliation; instead, they represent deviations from traditional voting patterns which are stimulated by societal forces too strong to ignore (Converse 1975). It is among the younger segments of the population that analysts have found the response that gives a realignment its durability. The political (including partisan) identities of younger cohorts supposedly are shaped by changes in the political environment, if these occur at a period of the life cycle when young people are most receptive to them. Over time, and consistent with the concept of immunization, identities harden and the social and political cleavages that have survived the earlier turmoil become the foundation for a new, stable era of partisan competition.

What kinds of "societal forces" are powerful enough to cause major movement in mass partisanship? At least in the classic case (Sundquist 1983), a realignment involves the emergence of new, cross-cutting issues that cleave the electorate in ways different from the conflicts upon which the prevailing alignment is based. As these issues become increasingly important to citizens, and as the traditional party system is (initially) unable to accommodate the distribution of preferences on them, one or both parties are likely to experience serious internal divisions. However, when new issues supersede the old in their salience for many groups—and when party leaders finally do step forward to give them voice—the result is an alteration of the parties' support coalitions and a readjustment of voter loyalties that signals the beginning of a new period (historically, about thirty to forty years long) of electoral stability.

Generational theory suggests once again that younger voters are at the heart of this process; it is therefore not surprising that a good deal of research conducted in the 1960s and 1970s uncovered evidence of what appeared to be the changing value priorities and policy expectations of postwar baby boomers. For example, Ronald Inglehart (1977; cf. Inglehart 1990) described a gradual reduction in the centrality of sustenance and physical safety needs among people living in affluent Western nations. With these needs (which are believed to be the most salient in all cultures, so long as they remain in short supply) now met for most citizens, popular demands were said by Inglehart to have embraced a variety of social and self-actualization (or postmaterialist) values. More to the point, the burgeoning demands of postindustrial society in the United States and elsewhere were strongest among younger cohorts, that is, those whose formative experiences occurred during the prosperous and relatively peaceful years following World War II.[6]

Focusing solely on U.S. politics, Warren Miller and Teresa Levitin (1976) characterized the early 1970s as a time when the agenda was coming to be dominated by a new dimension of conflict involving such issues as the counterculture and divergent lifestyles, the growth of political protest, law and order (mixed with race), and the tension between social control and individual freedom. Preferences on these New Politics issues were said to be crystallized and polarized for a growing segment of the population, especially the young, who were more liberal than other age groups.[7] Less dramatic but along the same lines, an examination of citizens' policy views by Gerald Pomper (1975) indicated that the attitudes of younger people were more clearly crystallized on issues having to do with lifestyle, social equality, and war; older Americans, in contrast, seemed to place greater emphasis on matters of race and economic opportunity. Alden Raine likewise maintained that social and cultural issues had assumed a dominant position in the belief systems of youth by the early 1970s. Not only were the young more inclined to define their ideological self-perceptions (as liberals or conservatives) in terms of these issues, but Raine concluded that "the economic debate so central to the most recent American party alignment is simply not an important feature in the attitude structure of the newer voters" (Raine 1977, 39–40).

It eventually became obvious that the policy views and belief structures of baby boomers were not nearly as distinctive as they appeared at the time (Delli Carpini 1986). As a consequence, later studies dealt less with the prospects for an age-based agenda shift than with the complex mix of attitudes and issue priorities among different groups in society which made realignment in the classic sense very difficult to achieve within a two-party framework (Maddox and Lilie 1984; Ornstein et al. 1988; Black and Black 1994; Shafer and Claggett 1995; Greenberg 1995).[8] Yet the search for political generations persisted, and the postwar cohort in particular continued to provide good copy for analysts of social change.

For example, according to Paul Light (1988, 223), baby boomers' preferences are "based on a constellation of issues that no longer fit the traditional liberal/conservative rhetoric." Although rejecting the rather bold claim (see Maddox and Lilie 1984) that "the baby boom and libertarianism [a combination of opposition to government intervention in the economy and support for the expansion of personal freedoms] may soon be synonymous" (225), Light conceded that "some of the old liberalism [of the 1960s] is gone" (227) and that many boomers exhibit a blend of opinions—left, right, and various positions in between—that defy efforts by party leaders to secure their loyalties. Going further, Light argued that among the principal traits of the boomer cohort is its electoral and attitudinal *volatility* (owing to weakened party loyalties and accumulated feelings of mistrust toward Democrats and Republicans alike). Such volatility also stems from *ambivalence* on key policy issues (reflecting the repeated failures of governance at both ends of the partisan/ideological spectrum) and from *pragmatism* (indicating a rejection of ideology based on these same failures, as well as some boomers' exaggerated sense of individualism—their commitment "to taking care of number one, and number one alone"; see Light 1988, 225).[9]

Despite an alleged antipathy toward their parents' generation,[10] today's young adults—Generation X—are often depicted in similar terms. Nearly three decades ago, Jones and Demarest (1967, 20) said of youth in the 1960s that "if they have one ideal, it is pragmatism." More recently, Susan Mitchell (1993, 50) suggested that Xers "may turn out to be the most pragmatic of the lot," and Jon Meacham (1995, 21) described them as "shrewd, pragmatic, anti-government" (the latter representing less a philosophical outlook than a long-term performance judgment).[11] Neil Howe and William Strauss (1992, 75) have portrayed Xers as believing that "America's greatest need . . . is to clear out the underbrush of name-calling and ideology so that simple things can work again"; holding a pessimistic view of the country's future, they think of themselves as "the clean-up crew, [sensing] that their role in history will be sacrificial—that whatever comeuppance America has to face, they'll bear more than their share of the burden."

Another common theme in analyses of the two postwar generations is that they share, in certain respects, a particular set of cultural orientations. Echoing Light's notion that boomers are committed to "taking care of number one," Cheryl Russell (1993, 30) traced the tearing of our nation's social fabric to this cohort's passage into adulthood beginning in the late 1960s. Specifically, Russell observed, "Baby boomers' parents raised their children to think for and of themselves. Studies of child-rearing practices show that parents of the 1950s and 1960s . . . . [indulged] their children as never before. They invested in their children's skills by sending them to college. They encouraged their children to succeed in a job market that rewarded competitive drive more than cooperative spirit, and individual skills more than teamwork."

A well-honed sense of *individualism* is sometimes attributed to Xers as well, partly because of circumstances quite different from those that faced boomers: economic hard times. According to Howe and Strauss (1992, 78), "the overall stagnation in American economic progress [since the early 1970s] has masked some vastly unequal changes in living standards by phase of life. Older people have prospered. Boomers have barely held their own, and Thirteeners [that is, Xers] have fallen off a cliff." Indeed, we are told, "There can't be that much question . . . as to whether there is as much 'opportunity' for [young people today] as there has been in the past. There isn't" (Lipsky and Abrams 1994, 168; see Chapter 7 in this volume). And "[w]orry about jobs and debt feeds skepticism; if people don't think they are getting ahead, then they are unlikely to be very interested in improving something as seemingly vague as 'the country' " (Meacham 1995, 23).

By the same token, individualistic attitudes, whatever their source, may help to account not only for the economic conservatism of younger citizens, but also for their relatively liberal opinions on many social, moral, and lifestyle issues (though not all; see Chapter 6) such as homosexual rights, gender equality, and interracial dating. What we are describing here, of course, are the libertarian preferences that are frequently attributed to both baby boomers (Light 1988) and, perhaps to an even greater degree, gen-Xers (Mitchell 1993). In reference to the cluster of traits culled earlier from Light's analysis, it would not be surprising to learn that their libertarian leanings are one important factor contributing to the volatility and lack of partisan moorings evident among voters who entered the electorate since the early 1960s. In other words, even if (1) concern about the country's economic future, combined with growing doubts about the government's ability to play a constructive role in shaping that future, lead boomers and Xers to be generally sympathetic to Republican appeals, (2) the GOP's rightward tilt on social and moral issues makes an enduring alliance with either cohort problematic.

Alternatively, it could be ambivalence more than a commitment to libertarian values that lies at the root of younger Americans' discomfort with the existing two-party system. Carll Ladd observed several years ago (1981, 21; see Feldman and Zaller 1992) that citizens "of all classes and most social positions [have] come to accept two basic propositions: first, that there is no alternative to a major role by government in regulating the economy, providing social services, and assuring economic progress; and second, that these generally desired interventions by the state frequently cause problems." Thus, according to James Sundquist (paraphrased in Light 1988, 228), people today "want less government, but also say government should guarantee a job to everyone who wants to work"; "say government should do more for the poor, but not for people on welfare"; "say they favor lower taxes, but support a balanced budget"; "want to protect the environment, but not if it costs jobs—conversely, they want new jobs, but not if it hurts the environment"; "want the courts to be tough on criminals, but want to protect the innocent"; and so on.[12] What remains to be seen is whether such ambivalence is more prevalent among boomers and/or Xers than among the population as a whole. And if it is, how much of a stretch would we be making to suggest that these cohorts form the core of what is increasingly known as the "radical middle" in contemporary American politics (e.g., Black and Black 1994; Klein 1995)?

Limited space and the absence of appropriate data preclude any effort to tie these various strands together into a comprehensive generational portrait.[13] Our focus in the remainder of the chapter is therefore on issue beliefs and attitude structures and on the ways in which the patterns we find are related to different aspects of political choice and evaluation among young people today. As already noted, we are especially interested in the degree to which some of the key conditions for partisan realignment—or, alternatively, for partisan disarray—are present in the policy views of gen-Xers. At the same time, however, we want to take at least a tentative look at a few of the broader orientations discussed above and to determine as best we can whether Xers are as distinctive from both boomers and other birth cohorts as they are occasionally said to be.

Generations: Issues, Attitudes, and Behavior

The following analysis is based on data from the 1992 American National Election Study.[14] We segmented the nationally representative ANES sample into six age categories, first, by identifying age seventeen as the approximate point of an individual's maximum suggestibility to changes in the sociopolitical environment (Mannheim 1952; also see Schuman and Scott 1989) and, second, by dividing recent U.S. history into different eras based on pivotal events and the overall tenor of the times. Our six cohorts are those who reached the age of seventeen (1) from 1980 to 1992: the contemporary era, beginning with Ronald Reagan's election as president;[15] (2) from 1965 to 1979: a tumultuous period featuring civil rights protests and urban riots, Vietnam, Watergate, energy shortages, and the economic stagflation of the late 1970s that helped put Reagan in the White House; (3) from 1955 to 1964: a time of more or less "normal politics" marked by relative tranquillity and broad public consensus about important national goals; (4) from 1940 to 1954: an "internationalist" era during which the most burning issues usually had to do with war, defense preparedness, and national security; (5) from 1929 to 1939: the era of the Great Depression and Franklin Roosevelt's New Deal; and (6) before 1929.

To repeat an earlier point: Generational scholars have hypothesized that partisan realignments are most likely to occur whenever a new, cross-cutting dimension of conflict comes to dominate the political identities of young Americans (and when, in turn, party leaders respond to the new issues in a suitable manner). Setting the latter question aside for now, we begin our investigation by utilizing the strategy recommended by Kristi Andersen (1978, 664): to identify the "issues which were particularly important during the formative years of a generation, and to see whether those issues are more salient to the members of that generation and whether their attitudes on those issues are more closely related to their political behavior . . . than is true for citizens in other age groups." For a variety of fairly obvious reasons, it is doubtful that the political events and social transformations of the past several decades have been experienced in identical ways by all Americans. Because of these differences and their probable effect on patterns of generational change—and, as a practical matter, because the small number of black and other minority respondents in ANES surveys makes age-based comparisons inadvisable—we restrict our analysis to whites only.

Belief Structures and Political Choice

By way of introduction to their study of attitudes among citizens and elites in the former Soviet Union, Arthur Miller and his colleagues (1995, 2) observed:

> If political leaders are to associate meaningfully with citizens, and vice versa, these two sets of political actors must share a common understanding of political symbols, articulate similar sets of values and preferences on issues, view the same groups and individuals as friends or enemies, see similar connections

between various political stimuli, and be moved by the same hopes and fears of tomorrow. In short, they must share a commonly constructed sense of social and political reality, or belief system, from which they derive their own individual social and political identities (also see Converse 1964, 1975).

This is also true within the mass public itself. If gen-Xers and/or baby boomers are thinking and speaking in a fundamentally different language (or languages) from their elders, then the pressures on existing parties and on the parties' electoral support coalitions would seem to be considerable—and the prospects for partisan upheaval greatly enhanced.

Although the details might have varied from one study to the next, research done in the late 1960s and early 1970s frequently identified four interrelated yet distinct dimensions of policy opinion among the American public. These involved (1) traditional social welfare and government management issues; (2) social issues (including race and civil rights); (3) lifestyle issues (especially dealing with women's rights and the sixties counterculture); and (4) issues of national defense generally and the Vietnam war in particular (e.g., Miller et al. 1976). To the extent that baby boomers, in the aggregate, were thought to hold an "agenda" at odds with that of the prevailing New Deal party system (Pomper 1975; Raine 1977), it was not simply because they were more liberal or more conservative than older citizens on matters of public concern; above all, it was because the priorities and preferences attributed to them appeared to reflect different ways of thinking about politics and political conflict. For this reason, boomers were seen as having the potential to induce changes in a party system that many believed had run its course.

If such potential was never fully realized for the postwar cohort, perhaps gen-Xers will prove to be more potent. The initial stage in our own investigation was to inspect the belief structures (or patterns of ideological "constraint"; see Converse 1964) evidenced by all white respondents and by whites in each of the six age groups. Using factor analysis (principal components) to explore the linkages among a broad range of policy and group affect questions asked in the 1992 ANES,[16] we looked primarily for any of three possible solutions:

- A two-dimensional space defined by attitudes on social welfare and civil rights/civil liberties issues (Maddox and Lilie 1984);
- A four-dimensional space defined by attitudes on social welfare, race and civil rights, lifestyle issues, and national security (Miller et al. 1976; also Craig and Hurley 1984); and
- A six-dimensional space defined by attitudes on social welfare, social insurance (including health care and Social Security), civil rights,

civil liberties, foreign relations, and cultural issues (homosexuality, abortion, and school prayer; see Shafer and Claggett 1995).

As always with factor analysis, results depend entirely upon the nature of the raw data being processed. We therefore need to be cautious in drawing conclusions, if only because a different mix of questions might—and in some of our preliminary work did—yield a somewhat different factor structure.

With this in mind, a few tentative observations can nevertheless be made. First, the policy views of white respondents as a whole were organized around five underlying dimensions: *cultural issues* (abortion, attitudes toward homosexuals, role of women in society), *social welfare* (spending levels for social programs, health care, guarantee of a good job and standard of living), *race* (affirmative action, government programs aimed at helping black people), *national security* (strong military, defense spending, use of military force), and issues related to the *family* (government assistance and spending levels for child care by the government, leave time for parents of newborn or adopted children). Two issues that we examined in depth (school prayer and the death penalty) did not load at an acceptable level on any dimension. For the most part—with the notable addition of family as a distinct area of citizen concern—the configuration here is roughly comparable to the four-dimensional space uncovered in a number of studies since the 1960s.

As for our birth cohorts, the two oldest (Great Depression, aged seventy to eighty in 1992, and pre-Depression, aged eighty-one and over) have been omitted from Table 4.1, largely because of small N's (sixty-five and twenty-one, respectively, based on listwise deletion of missing data[17]) that contributed to belief structures that were peculiar and difficult to interpret. Looking across the remaining four groups, we find many more similarities than differences. The cultural dimension is more central and broader in scope for baby boomers than for any of the others, while the same can (perhaps surprisingly) be said of race among those who achieved maximum suggestibility during and shortly after World War II. In general, though, there is little in our findings to support the argument that younger citizens tend to think about politics in a substantially different way from those who were socialized during earlier periods.

What about the possibility that certain types of issues—however conceptualized within the context of individuals' larger belief systems or ideological frameworks—may play a disproportionate role in shaping the political attitudes and behavior of young people today (see Andersen 1978)? To answer this question, we created six indices measuring respondents' policy preferences: the cultural dimension shown in Table 4.1 was broken down into its two main components (abortion and homosexual rights); child care

Table 4.1
Factor Structure by Age Cohort (whites only), 1992

Generation X (age 17-29, N=155, 63.1% of variance explained)
1. Race (quotas, affirmative action, assist blacks, spend blacks)
2. Social welfare (guaranteed job, spend poor people, services, health care)
3. National security (strong military, defense spending, military force)
4. Cultural 1 (abortion, fund abortions, homosexuals thermometer, gay rights, gays military)
5. Child care/Cultural 2 (child care assist and spend, death penalty)
6. Cultural 3 (school prayer, gays military)
7. Working women (women, parental leave)
Note: "gays military" fits about equally well on factors 4 and 6

Baby Boomers (age 30-44, N=301, 59.3% of variance explained)
1. Cultural (abortion, fund abortion, gays military, gay rights, homosexuals thermometer, Women, school prayer)
2. Social welfare (services, health care, guaranteed job, spending poor people)
3. Race (quotas, affirmative action, assist blacks, spend blacks)
4. National security/Crime (defense spending, strong military, military force, death penalty)
5. Child care (child care assist and spend)
Other issues: parental leave

Normal Politics Cohort (age 45-54, N=126, 61.9% of variance explained)
1. Race (quotas, affirmative action, spend blacks, death penalty)
2. Cultural 1 (gay rights, gays military, homosexuals thermometer, spend poor people)
3. Cultural 2 (abortion, women, fund abortions)
4. Social welfare/Child care (child care assist & spend, health care, services)
5. National security (strong military, defense spending, military force)
6. Social welfare/Cultural 3 (guaranteed job, parental leave, school prayer)
Other issues: assist blacks

World War II/Cold War Cohort (age 55-69, N=120, 66.1% of variance explained)
1. Race (death penalty, affirmative action, quotas, spend poor people, spend blacks, assist blacks)
2. Cultural 1 (gays military, gay rights, homosexuals thermometer)
3. National security (strong military, military force, defense spending)
4. Social services (child care assist & spend, fund abortions, government services)
5. Social welfare (health care, guaranteed job, government services)
6. Cultural 2 (women, abortion)
7. Cultural 3 (school prayer)
Other issues: parental leave
Note: "government services" fits about equally well on factors 4 and 5

*See Appendix for question wordings. Results are from a principal-components factor analysis, varimax rotation, listwise deletion of missing data.
Source: American National Election Study, 1992.

was kept distinct from other categories of government social services (and did not include parental leave);[18] the traditional social welfare cluster was left intact (services, poor people, jobs, health care); racial issues were limited to affirmative action (in hiring and promotion and in college admissions); and two items were used to gauge national security concerns (defense spending and whether the United States should remain the world's foremost military power). Correlations between these indices and several measures of political choice and evaluation were then calculated.[19] Our assumption was that a high degree of internal consistency (strong relationships) could be taken as evidence of the centrality or salience of particular issues to particular cohorts (Converse 1964).

Given the nature of partisan conflict during the New Deal period, we might hypothesize that (1) social welfare issues are (even in the 1990s) a cornerstone of the political identities of older Americans, especially those in the Depression cohort, who reached the age of maximum suggestibility between 1929 and 1939; similarly, (2) issues of national security should be most salient to citizens coming of age during World War II and its cold war aftermath; (3) cultural issues and perhaps race (though not necessarily affirmative action, which is rather different from the 1960s struggle to achieve basic legal and political rights for blacks), as well as child care (due to changes in the nuclear family), should stand out among baby boomers; and (4) reflecting uncertainty about their and the nation's economic future, social welfare (along with child care) presumably will take center stage among gen-Xers.

In fact, when examining the correlations between policy views and a broad sampling of dependent variables[20] (results not shown), one searches in vain for any sort of clear-cut generational pattern. Overall, issues play a consistent and relatively substantial role only in the shaping of one's ideological and partisan attachments. As for intercohort differences, there are few worth noting. Probably the most significant is the modest tendency for issues in general to be less fully integrated into the liberal-conservative identities of gen-Xers, especially as compared with the boomer and postwar (normal politics) age groups.[21] Yet it seems likely that this is at least partly a lifecycle rather than a generational phenomenon.

A final option that we explored had to do with the mix of views expressed by citizens across policy domains. It is by now widely recognized that public opinion is multidimensional and that many Americans hold well-considered beliefs that are liberal (or middle-of-the-road) in certain respects and conservative (or middle-of-the-road) in others. Gen-Xers and baby boomers, for example, are sometimes thought to have pronounced *libertarian* leanings, that is, they supposedly are uncomfortable not only with the social welfare liberalism that dominated U.S. politics for several decades following the Great Depression, but also with the willingness of cultural conservatives to let society impose limits on personal freedom in such areas as abortion, sexual orientation, and artistic as well as political expression. On the other side of the coin, there are individuals—once a fairly sizable group, especially among Democrats (Shafer and Claggett 1995, 48–49), but today maybe less so—who favor both economic interventionism and government efforts to promote so-called traditional values. Borrowing from Maddox and Lilie (1984), we will call these people *populists*.

In order to assess the prevalence of ideological "mismatches" in the 1992 ANES, respondents were divided into liberals (everyone scoring below the midpoint of our index) and conservatives (everyone scoring above the midpoint) for (1) social welfare issues (government services, health care, guaranteed jobs) and (2) both sets of cultural issues discussed earlier: abortion (pro-choice versus pro-life, government funding for abortions) and homosexual rights (protection against discrimination, military service, the feeling thermometer for "gay men and lesbians"). To complicate matters slightly, we also compared social welfare attitudes with preferences on national security issues (scores once again trichotomized), another policy area in which many Americans hold views that may at first glance seem at odds with their other beliefs. For convenience, the two groups of principal interest have been labeled *New Deal hawks* (left of center on social welfare, favoring a strong military and high levels of defense spending) and *laissez-faire doves* (right of center on social welfare, less supportive of U.S. military power and defense spending).

From the figures in Table 4.2, it appears that roughly one-third of white Americans hold inconsistent views on each of the three pairs of issues shown.[22] There is, however, nothing in the data to suggest that inconsistency in general, or libertarian preferences in particular, are appreciably more common among gen-Xers or boomers than other cohorts. If anything, Xers show signs of being slightly *less* libertarian (and/or slightly more populist) than some of their elders, especially on the social welfare/abortion pair. Still, the safest conclusion that can be drawn from these data is that neither Xers nor boomers stand out in their tendency to favor limited government in all spheres.

Volatility

Attitudinal inconsistency (in the context of a predominantly two-party system) might help to explain the high levels of electoral volatility observed among younger voters since the 1960s. That is, people who are liberal on some issues but conservative on others may exhibit a corresponding behavioral inconsistency when choosing between parties and candidates with whom they differ on key issues—for example, splitting their ballots across offices in the same election or switching their votes back and forth over

Table 4.2
Ideological Inconsistency by Age Cohort (whites only), 1992

	Generation X	Baby Boomers	Normal Politics	World War II/ Cold War	Great Depression	Pre-Depression
Social welfare and abortion						
Populists	17.9%	13.1%	13.4%	16.5%	8.7%	11.1%
Libertarians	13.2%	16.4%	17.6%	13.3%	22.8%	13.9%
Combined	31.1%	29.5%	31.0%	29.8%	31.5%	25.0%
tau-b =	.15	.21	.16	.15	.08	.32
N =	273	505	239	218	127	36
Social welfare and homosexuals						
Populists	20.4%	13.8%	13.8%	21.1%	17.5%	35.3%
Libertarians	14.2%	13.8%	12.8%	8.8%	16.5%	8.8%
Combined	34.6%	27.6%	26.6%	29.9%	34.0%	44.1%
tau-b =	.15	.31	.34	.29	.15	-.05
N =	240	458	203	194	103	34
Social welfare and national security						
New Deal hawks	28.0%	25.8%	26.3%	30.1%	23.8%	36.8%
Laissez-faire doves	8.7%	10.2%	4.8%	10.0%	10.7%	13.2%
Combined	36.7%	36.0%	31.1%	40.1%	34.5%	50.0%
tau-b =	.22	.19	.32	.10	.13	-.22
N =	275	511	228	219	122	38

*See Appendix for question wordings. Table entries indicate the total percentage of a cohort (except for those with missing values on one or more index items) who fall into a particular category. Populists/New Deal hawks are liberal on social welfare but (1) conservative on abortion and homosexual issues or (2) supportive of a strong U.S. military. Libertarians/laissez-faire doves are conservative on social welfare but (3) culturally liberal or (4) less supportive of a strong U.S. military. Correlation coefficients (tau-b) are based on the trichotomized issue scales rather than on the full range of responses.
Source: American National Election Study, 1992.

time. Although this argument cannot be adequately tested with data from a single survey, we did attempt to measure *potential* volatility in three ways: (1) independent partisanship;[23] (2) voting for Ross Perot in the 1992 presidential race; and (3) the belief that it is better when control of the presidency and Congress is split between Republicans and Democrats. Our assumption is that each of these traits indicates an increased likelihood that one will support candidates of different parties in different elections, depending (among other things) on the candidates' personal qualities and on the issues that are most salient to the individual when the vote decision is made.

As it happens, both libertarians and populists are somewhat more likely than other whites to have voted for Perot, but (1) only populists scored above average in their preference for divided government (46 percent, compared with 40 percent overall), and (2) the two groups hover at or slightly below the figure for whites as a whole (40 percent) in their tendency to identify as partisan independents. A similar pattern is evident for New Deal hawks and laissez-faire doves. None of this really matters for purposes of our analysis, of course, since the four types of inconsistency cited in Table 4.2 are not substantially more common among Xers or boomers.

However, we did investigate a second probable source of electoral volatility in the 1992 ANES. Respondents were asked whether they felt that one party would do a better job than the other at handling the economy, managing foreign affairs, dealing with poverty, and making health care more affordable; they also were asked whether George Bush or Bill Clinton would do a better job in the same four policy areas plus two others (protecting the environment and reducing the budget deficit). Separate measures of partisan and candidate consistency were created according to whether people favored one side in most instances, waffled back and forth, or indicated with some regularity that there was not much difference between the two. While the latter reflects indifference more than inconsistency, we thought it best to simplify our presentation by combining all those who displayed a *lack* of consistency into a single grouping.[24] The results are shown in Table 4.3.

What we find is a modest tendency for gen-Xers and boomers to have the least consistent preferences with regard to the parties (though the normal politics cohort is not far behind) and their 1992 standard-bearers.[25] In addition, as might be expected, inconsistency/indifference is associated with (1) substantially higher levels of independence and Perot voting and (2) a slight bias in favor of divided government. These findings certainly do not break new ground. In a sense, we are doing little more than confirming the already well known tendency for younger voters to be less partisan and hence more volatile (less behaviorally consistent) than other age groups. Nevertheless, the data presented here do a couple of things. First, they help to flesh out our understanding of *why* so many young people today have yet to find a partisan home. Second, they serve as a reminder that the independent streak long exhibited by citizens who entered the electorate during the 1960s and 1970s has managed to survive into the 1990s.

Ambivalence

It is one thing when citizens have divergent views across a range of issues. It is something else altogether when they have inconsistent or uncertain views within the same issue domain. We are not talking about "nonattitudes" (survey respondents expressing opinions on subjects about which they have given little thought) but rather about the genuine ambivalence that many Americans feel on important political issues (Zaller and Feldman 1992; Zaller 1992). Open-ended interviews have repeatedly demonstrated

Table 4.3
Partisan and Candidate Inconsistency by Age Cohort (whites only), 1992

	Generation X	Baby Boomers	Normal Politics	World War II/ Cold War	Great Depression	Pre- Depression
Partisan:						
Consistent	51.4%	52.9%	56.1%	62.3%	63.3%	67.2%
Inconsistent/ Indifferent	48.6	47.1	43.9	37.7%	36.7	32.8
N =	395	680	303	337	188	67
C/I difference^X on						
Independent ID	-30.7	-19.3	-23.7	-13.9	-36.1	-20.9
Perot voting	-11.3	-15.1	-13.9	-11.9	- 9.9	-38.5
Divided government	- 7.4	+ 2.0	- 7.0	- 3.2	- 9.9	-13.7
Candidate:						
Consistent	54.5%	54.1%	61.3%	66.9%	66.5%	76.7%
Inconsistent/ indifferent	45.5	45.9	38.7	33.1	33.5	23.3
N =	382	634	282	311	170	60
C/I difference^X on						
Independent ID	-14.0	- 8.0	-21.0	-17.0	-13.6	-21.2
Perot voting	-18.8	-15.9	-24.0	-12.4	-15.4	-16.8
Divided government	- 1.6	- 3.8	-13.9	- 6.7	- 7.1	-19.3

*See Appendix for question wordings. Table entries are column percentages, adding to 100% (respondents with missing values on any index item are excluded). Inconsistent/indifferent respondents are those who either (1) tended to name different parties/candidates as being better able to handle various national problems, or (2) frequently said there would be no difference between the two; especially on candidate items, the later group includes a handful of individuals who felt that Perot would do a better job than his major-party rivals. ^{X}C/I difference is the percentage of consistent minus the percentage of inconsistent respondents who profess no party allegiance ("leaners" are counted as independents), report voting for Ross Perot in 1992, or say that it is better when the presidency and Congress are controlled by different parties.
Source: American National Election Study, 1992.

that, "given the opportunity, people do not make simple statements; they shade, modulate, deny, retract, or just grind to a halt in frustration. . . . [In other words,] people are seldom as certain of their opinions as their bald summary statements imply. We all know that and none more than survey researchers who must work around this fact" (Hochschild 1981, 238; also see Craig 1993). As survey researchers, we recognize the problem. Our challenge for this study, then, was to find examples of forced-choice questions in the 1992 ANES that permitted us to make a realistic assessment as to whether ambivalence is (as some analysts believe; see Light 1988) more typical of baby boomers and/or gen-Xers than of the public as a whole.

The results in Table 4.4 are based on responses to four pairs of items:

Table 4.4
Issue Ambivalence by Age Cohort (whites only), 1992*

	Generation X	Baby Boomers	Normal Politics	World War II/ Cold War	Great Depression	Pre- Depression
Strong military power/ Willing to use force						
Stay powerful/no force	6.4%	6.9%	10.1%	9.4%	8.5%	10.8%
Less powerful/use force	1.5%	1.7%	1.9%	2.6%	2.0%	3.1%
N =	409	699	317	341	199	65
Racial discrimination/ Government assist blacks						
Blacks not hurt/programs	3.9%	2.4%	2.2%	3.7%	7.4%	3.6%
Blacks hurt/no programs	16.5%	20.9%	19.9%	19.5%	22.7%	25.0%
N =	334	584	271	272	163	56
Government power/ More or less government						
Too powerful/do more things	40.4%	31.6%	17.7%	26.4%	31.3%	20.0%
Not too strong/less gov't	2.7%	7.9%	5.4%	4.6%	6.1%	11.4%
N =	183	367	186	197	115	35
Willing to pay taxes/ Government services						
Same tax/more services	25.0%	17.2%	13.3%	14.8%	13.6%	12.5%
Pay more/fewer services	5.4%	5.4%	6.4%	4.9%	7.1%	6.3%
N =	296	551	249	244	140	48

*See Appendix for question wordings. Table entries indicate the total percentage of a cohort (except for those with missing values on one or both items) who answer as shown.
Source: American National Election Study, 1992.

one involving foreign policy (whether the United States should maintain its position as the world's strongest military power; the degree to which we should be willing to use that military force), another involving race (whether slavery and discrimination have made it difficult for blacks to work their way out of the lower class; whether the federal government should try to improve the social and economic position of black Americans), one relating to activist government in general (whether the federal government is becoming too powerful; whether government needs to be doing more than it is currently doing), and a final pair that connects taxes to spending (whether respondents are willing to pay higher taxes in order to support more spending in favored policy areas; whether it would be better to raise or to lower both taxes and the amount of government services).

Apart from any other measurement issues, we appreciate that the actual *level* of ambivalence is impossible to estimate using these kinds of survey questions. Is someone ambivalent, for example, if he or she feels that the United States should maintain its position as the world's strongest military power but then says that our leaders should be only "somewhat" (as opposed to "extremely" or "very") willing to apply that power in attempting to solve international problems? Conceding the arbitrariness of whatever decision rules might be used to resolve such matters, we will largely restrict our attention to the presence or absence of intercohort differences.[26]

One can see from Table 4.4 that differences are quite small on both the foreign policy and race issue pairs. Although the latter suggest that there are, in every cohort, more racial "liberals" who oppose policies designed to help blacks than there are racial "conservatives" who support such policies, we are reluctant to make too much of this, in part for the reasons just outlined. On the other hand, support for certain types of governmental activity and for the maintenance of certain social programs is a long-standing trait of the U.S. electorate (e.g., Free and Cantril 1967; Bennett and Bennett 1990). It is therefore not terribly surprising (and we are inclined here to believe that the percentages are substantively meaningful) to learn that respondents in 1992 frequently complained about "big government" and high taxes—and then in the next breath stated their desire for government to do "more things" and to provide additional services even at the cost of raising taxes. The data also make clear that ambivalent attitudes on these sorts of issues are especially common among gen-Xers and, to a lesser extent, baby boomers.[27] If the "radical middle" is indeed gaining strength in American politics today, we suspect that one reason can be found in the unsettled and sometimes contradictory views of people who have come of age since the mid–1960s.

Conclusion

Our main goal in this chapter has been to determine whether some of the elements thought to be among the necessary preconditions for partisan realignment are present in the policy views of young adults, or perhaps in the policy views of not-so-young adults, most notably the baby boomer cohort that has so fascinated social and political analysts for the past three decades. Although evidence from the 1992 ANES revealed relatively few age-related variations in belief structure, two of our findings do stand out. One is a bit of old news that bears repeating: neither Xers nor boomers (many of the latter now approaching age fifty) are entirely comfortable operating within the constraints imposed by America's two-party system. Further, we doubt that the recent shift in the balance of power between the parties is going to change that situation in any permanent way without a serious (and at the moment unlikely) reorientation of policy focus by one or both sets of contestants. Why not? At least part of the reason brings us to the second of our key findings: Ambivalent attitudes concerning the proper role of government are particularly widespread among citizens who have entered the electorate since 1965—and among Xers more than boomers.

A *Newsweek* article (Leland and McCormick 1996) focusing mainly on college students as "the children of gridlock" was published not long before the formal selection of Bill Clinton and Bob Dole as the major parties' presidential nominees in 1996. This article took note of an eighteen-year-old at Ohio State University who was impressed with the GOP's Contract with America even though she opposed many of its provisions ("They got something done"); and she indicated that she would consider voting for Dole even though she was a registered Democrat. Yet the young woman took both parties to task for their failure to represent the complexity of popular opinion in the United States in the 1990s. "I have a lot of conservative views; I have a lot of liberal views," she said. "If people would recognize that we're all like that, I'd have a lot more faith in our political system" (33). Until political leaders find an appropriate response to such concerns, public dissatisfaction with the political process will almost certainly continue to grow.

Notes

An earlier version of this chapter was presented at the 1995 Annual Meetings of the Southern Political Science Association, Tampa, Florida.

1. For our purposes, realignments such as those occurring in the 1860s, 1890s, and 1930s can be said to involve an adjustment in the coalitional bases of the political parties, as well as (in most instances) a subsequent shift in the balance of power between parties, all of which is organized around—and stimulated by—a crisis-induced change in the nation's political agenda. For various perspectives on the subject of realignment, see Key (1955, 1959); Burnham (1970); Ladd with Hadley (1975); Clubb et al. (1980); Petrocik (1981); Sundquist (1983); Shafer (1991); Aldrich (1995); Nardulli (1995).

2. Alternatively, Mannheim argued that such realization also may be inhibited when the pace of change is *too* rapid.

3. An example might be the development, or "learning," of cynicism and mistrust toward government since the 1960s (Markus 1979; Craig 1993).

4. Actually, it is the length of time that one has identified with a party, rather than age itself, that appears to be the stronger correlate of partisan strength; it just happens to be the young who are most likely to have a newly adopted partisan affiliation, or else no affiliation at all (see Chapter 3). With length of party membership held constant, the relationship between age and partisan strength is negative since faster rates of learning tend to occur among the young (see Converse 1969, 1976).

5. This is especially true since partisan loyalties often serve to "screen" dissonant stimuli that are inconsistent with those loyalties.

6. Inglehart felt that the United States was less prone to these changes, and thus to generational value shifts based on them, than were most nations of Western Europe (excepting Britain) because of (1) its relative economic prosperity throughout the twentieth century and (2) the physical security provided by its geographical isolation over the course of several wars.

7. As it happens, it was among New Liberals that one was most likely to find evidence of Inglehart's postmaterialist values orientation.

8. In addition, there is the even more basic question of whether political parties are so poorly regarded that they can no longer serve their historical role as institutions of democratic linkage in a representative system (Wattenberg 1994).

9. In fairness to Light, the three themes described here were woven throughout his account; our appropriation and interpretation of them for purposes of the analysis in this chapter inevitably involves a certain amount of oversimplification.

10. Susan Mitchell (1993, 51), for example, contended that Xers were resentful of baby boomers because in their eyes, "boomers had a party and didn't clean up the mess" (in terms of coming to grips with a faltering national economy, rising crime, the consequences of broken families and of changes in sexual mores, as well as various other social ills). See Howe and Strauss (1992); Lipsky and Abrams (1994). Feelings of resentment may, of course, run in the other direction as well (e.g., Giles 1994; also see Chapter 1).

11. As Meacham (23) pointed out, Xers "have never lived through a sustained time in which government was broadly effective." Even so, he greatly overstated the depth of antigovernment sentiment that exists among young adults (*American Enterprise* 1994, 96; also see Mitchell 1993 and Chapter 5 in this volume).

12. For a fairly recent illustration of this sort of thing, see Times Mirror (1994).

13. Gen-Xers (those under age thirty in 1992; see the following section for a breakdown of cohorts and a description of the data used in our analysis) are only slightly more *pessimistic* about the nation's long-term future than are older citizens: 51 percent (versus 49 percent of boomers, 43 to 46 percent of those aged between forty-five and eighty, and 33 percent of those over eighty) indicated in 1992 that "the standard of living for the people who are just children now" would worsen over the next twenty years. In the shorter term, age-related differences are negligible in terms of the belief that things in this country are "generally going in the right direction" versus their having "pretty seriously gotten off on the wrong track" (80 to 85 percent of each cohort said "wrong track"). There are no appropriate measures of *pragmatism* in the data set we employed, and commitment to the norm of *individualism* can be tapped only indirectly. On the latter, between 77 percent (boomers) and 87 percent (those who came of age during the Great Depression) endorsed the idea that one defining characteristic of a "true American" is "trying to get ahead on your own effort." On two questions regarding the qualities that children should have, the principal distinction was between respondents under age fifty-five (somewhat more likely to stress independence over respect for elders and self-reliance over obedience) and those aged fifty-five and over (just the reverse). Neither Xers nor boomers stood out on either item.

14. These data were made available by the Inter-University Consortium for Political and Social Research. Neither the Consortium nor the original collectors of the data bear any responsibility for the analyses and interpretations presented here.

15. Because citizens who did not turn eighteen until after the 1992 election fell outside the ANES sampling frame, our analysis necessarily excludes the very youngest group of gen-Xers.

16. Factor analysis works by obtaining the correlation (see note 19) between each variable and all other variables in the analysis, then uses a statistical algorithm to identify the dimension or dimensions that are initially hidden within the correlation matrix; see Kim and Mueller (1978a, 1978b) for a good discussion of the different types of factor analysis and their uses. Alternative procedures (maximum-likelihood extraction, oblique rotation, pairwise deletion of missing data) usually produced similar, though not always identical, results to those reported in the text and in Table 4.1. See the Appendix for question wordings.

17. This means that respondents who did not answer any one of the issue questions outlined in Table 4.1 were dropped from our calculations.

18. Parental leave clustered with the two child care items in the factor analysis for all whites but, oddly, it did not do so (instead loading either separately or with other issues) for *any* of the six cohorts.

19. Correlation coefficients, in this case tau-b, range between 0.0 (no relationship) and plus or minus 1.0 (a perfect relationship). A coefficient of plus or minus 1.0 means that knowing a respondent's relative score on the first variable allows one to predict, with perfect accuracy, his or her relative score on the second variable. A score of 0.0 means that there is no tendency at all for high (or low) scores on one variable to occur among individuals who score high (or low) on the other. See the footnote at the bottom of Table 4.2 for a brief explanation as to how the variables examined in this table were coded.

20. These included party identification, liberalism-conservatism, job performance ratings of elected officials, candidate and political party feeling thermometers, perceived differences between Republicans and Democrats, internal and external political efficacy, political and interpersonal trust, voting and campaign participation, and others.

21. As a rule, one should not compare correlation coefficients unless the item variances are roughly equivalent across populations (cohorts). With this caution in mind, we were interested to learn that the mean inter-item correlation (tau-b) for the six policy measures described in the preceding paragraph and seven selected dependent variables (partisan and ideological self-identification, approval scores for President Bush and for Congress, the "federal government" feeling thermometer, perceived differences between the parties, and voting participation in 1992) is as follows: .16 for gen-Xers, .21 for boomers, .22 for the Silent Generation, and .19 for the World War II/cold war cohort. The mean is lower (and some of the individual correlations are actually negative) for older respondents, where small N's again present problems of interpretation.

22. For whites as a whole, the numbers are 30.2 percent (social welfare/abortion), 30.1 percent (social welfare/homosexuals), and 36.2 percent (social welfare/national security). The exact percentages both here and in Table 4.2 depend, of course, on coding decisions made for each of the three indices—and especially on our decision to define *middle-of-the-road* in terms of the index midpoint (with scores even slightly on either side of the midpoint designated as left-leaning or right-leaning). In addition, we want to emphasize that these calculations are based on respondents who answered *all* questions in a given pair of issue batteries. It is therefore likely that the proportion of genuine populists, libertarians, New Deal hawks, and laissez-faire doves in the U.S. electorate is somewhat lower than our estimates might lead one to believe.

23. For the analysis here, independents include those who say they lean toward one party or the other.

24. Specifically, Democratic/Clinton responses were coded as 0, Republican/Bush responses as 1, and no difference (or Ross Perot) as 0.5. Respondents were classified as inconsistent or indifferent if they scored between 1.5 and 2.5 on the partisan index (43.8 percent for all whites versus 56.2 percent consistent), and between 2.0 and 4.0 on the candidate index (40.7 percent versus 59.3 percent).

25. Gen-Xers are a bit more distinctive when our partisan measure includes just the two items on handling the economy and managing foreign affairs: 39 percent inconsistent among Xers versus 28 to 30 percent for the next three age groups, 24 percent for the Depression cohort, and just 15 percent for those who came of age prior to 1929.

26. For the record, we trichotomized each variable with more than three response options, for example, (1) combining those who were "extremely" and "very" willing to use force, as well as those who were "not very" and "never" willing to do so; and (2) collapsing people on either side of the midpoint on the ANES seven-point government services question into "liberals" (scores of 1 through 3) and "conservatives" (scores of 5 through 7).

27. We found a similar pattern with several other item pairings. For example, gen-Xers were much more likely than other cohorts to (1) say that government has become too powerful but then agree that the reason government has become bigger is because the problems we face have become bigger (35 percent, 9 points higher than boomers and the World War II/cold war cohort); and (2) express opposition to higher taxes but also indicate that the federal government should see that every person has a job and a good standard of living (23 percent, 8 points higher than boomers and the pre-Depression age group).

5

Mixed Signals: Generation X's Attitudes toward the Political System

Diana Owen

It has become almost cliché to note that Americans' trust in their government reached precipitously low levels during the 1990s. Pollsters and reporters routinely cite statistics and make stock pronouncements about this sad state of affairs; pundits and politicians are quick to place blame on particular people, institutions, and sometimes even the public itself. But while the bad news that citizens have lost faith in their government is publicized almost to the point of triviality, the real causes and consequences of their doing so tend not to receive serious play in public discourse.

Recognizing that trust in government is close to an all-time low is one thing. Identifying the sources and underlying dynamics of this widespread discontent is another, more vital task. Scholars have isolated a variety of factors that contribute to the decline in support for government, political institutions, and elected leaders. Stephen Craig (1993, 3) got to the heart of the matter when he said, "Government in general, and the national government in particular, simply has not done a very good job of dealing with the country's most important problems." Since the early 1960s, American society has endured a cavalcade of divisive struggles such as the civil rights movement, protest over U.S. involvement in Vietnam, riots in many of our big cities, and political scandals ranging from Watergate to Iran-contra to Whitewater. Leaders have failed to make and implement policies that deal effectively with major problems such as unemployment, crime, and AIDS. They have not made good on sweeping proclamations such as President Clinton's promise to achieve fundamental institutional "change" and the Gingrich Congress's Contract with America (Craig 1993, 1996b; Hibbing and Theiss-Morse 1995; MacManus 1996). Citizens understandably feel that government officials are not responsive to their needs and demands. The situation is made worse by an increasing atmosphere of incivility that permeates the political realm today, with personal attacks rapidly becoming politicians' dominant modus operandi. Media reports tend to exacerbate, or at least reinforce, negative public attitudes by highlighting conflict and failure in government and by ignoring cooperation and success (L. Bennett 1996; Fallows 1996; Kerbel 1995).

The implications of such pervasive disillusionment are a matter of debate (e.g., see Citrin 1974; Miller 1974a, 1974b). Some analysts fear that a long-term drop in public support has potentially dangerous consequences in that it threatens the legitimacy of the political system and, in the process, weakens the ability of leaders and institutions to govern (Gamson 1968, 1971; Easton and Dennis 1969; Dennis 1970; Easton 1975; Finkel 1985). Moreover, a decline in support coincides with and supposedly contributes to an erosion of "civic community"—a broader loss of faith in one's fellow citizens (Putnam 1993a, 1993b, 1993c)—and these factors together may cause people to withdraw from politics and other aspects of public life. Lower voter turnout and a retreat from other types of active participation is one possible outgrowth of popular disenchantment with the political process (Rosenstone and Hansen 1993; Owen and Farnsworth 1995; MacManus 1996).

Others contend that diminished levels of public trust may not pose a serious threat to the established order at all; instead, we are told, this could stimulate citizens to exercise their political muscle and to work for change in both leadership and policy direction (Miller 1974a, 1974b; Barber 1984), for example, through support for outsider candidates such as Ross Perot (Atkeson et al. 1996). Alternatively, there is a third perspective which suggests that since politics is a low-salience domain for many people (as it does not often seem to directly affect their everyday lives), the so-called crisis of confidence is not likely to lead to significant political upheaval or change of any sort (see Craig 1993).

In short, the essence of the concept *political support* (or *political trust*)[1] is multifaceted—and the implications of its apparent disintegration are uncertain. This is unfortunate because, in my view, understanding the nature of support is truly central to comprehending the role of citizens in the American polity. Scholars have traditionally considered political support, as well as the related concepts of efficacy and patriotism, to be part of a core set of orientations that constitute the dominant "political culture" in the United States (Almond and Verba 1963; Inglehart 1990; Jackman and Miller 1996). The transmission of these orientations from generation to generation has therefore been a preoccupation of researchers who study the process by which new members of society are socialized into the political system. A case can be made, for example, that it is important for young people to develop positive attitudes toward politics and government early in life as a basis for learning strong citizenship orientations—including the belief that one should be attentive to public affairs and exercise one's right to vote in elections. It also may be beneficial (in terms of maintaining system stability) for younger cohorts to start off with a somewhat idealized view of government, since we know from prior research that good feelings tend to erode as children and adolescents move into adulthood (Jennings and Niemi 1981).

Generation X and Attitudes toward Government

Initial reports on Generation X, the most recent birth cohort to come of age politically in the United States, quickly set off alarms in certain quarters. As scholars, journalists, and social commentators became aware of the existence of a distinct new generation in the early 1990s, the portrait they painted stressed what seemed to be rampant cynicism—accompanied by various other negative orientations toward politics and government—among gen-Xers (e.g., Black 1990; Times Mirror 1991). This alleged mistrust, if it existed, was a clear departure from past patterns whereby young people were usually found to be *less* cynical than their elders. In their highly publicized book *Generations*, William Strauss and Neil Howe concluded, "Before 13ers [Xers] came along, postwar sociologists generally assumed that hardening cynicism was a function of advancing age. No longer. . . . In a late–1980s survey of 'Cynical Americans,' researchers noted that 'the biggest surprise' was how 'cynicism now seems to defy the traditional partnership of youth and idealism.' Today, cynicism is hitting hardest among young adolescents—more than half of those age 24 and under. . . . They think it's all bull" (Strauss and Howe 1991, 327–8). According to these early accounts, gen-Xers' disillusionment with government and politics was grounded in a more general sense of detachment and anomie (Coupland 1991); that is, Xers supposedly had been swept up in a broad secular trend toward greater interpersonal mistrust. Citizens not only were losing faith in government institutions and political leaders, but they also were becoming wary of people in nongovernmental roles. Gen-Xers were said to be especially cynical because their personal economic prospects appeared bleak (Howe and Strauss 1993a).

Related to its heightened suspicion of government—most notably, of national government—Generation X was also reported to hold weak feelings of political efficacy (the belief that one has the ability to effectively influence the political process through voting and other forms of active involvement). Young people, the argument went, simply could not find their comfort zone within the realm of national politics and had retreated to local community politics—when they took part at all (Strauss and Howe 1991; Howe and Strauss 1993a). Further, gen-Xers were described as viewing the government in Washington as dysfunctional: While problems such as the national debt were inherently solvable, politicians were too busy fighting among themselves to take positive action. Government, in the minds of gen-Xers, was not responsive to the needs and wishes of ordinary citizens, and young people least of all. Instead, it catered to the special interests (Booth 1994).

While this characterization caught the attention of the popular press, it has not gone unchallenged. Some preliminary empirical investigations using the standard American National Election Study (ANES) "trust in government" questions,[2] for example, revealed that Xers do *not* harbor extraordinarily strong feelings of political cynicism. To the contrary, data indicate that they may be somewhat less mistrustful of government than are older cohorts and, in relative terms, are no less trusting than were older Americans when the latter were young (e.g., Bennett and Rademacher 1994; Ladd 1994; Medvic 1994; Owen and Farnsworth 1995).[3] Finally, gen-Xers are fairly optimistic about the future and tend to believe they will be better off than their parents were when they reach the age of forty (see Chapter 1).[4]

In this chapter, I will take a closer look at the distribution of political trust and related attitudes (efficacy, perceptions of governmental responsiveness, patriotism) for Generation X and older birth cohorts. How do the different generations break down in terms of their beliefs and opinions concerning the political system as a whole, governmental institutions, and specific political leaders? In addition, I will consider some of the possible explanations for why gen-Xers (and their elders) feel the way they do about politics and government.

Political Support and Socialization:
Generation X and Baby Boomers

Much has been made of what some analysts see as important differences in the socialization experiences of gen-Xers and their immediate predecessors, the postwar baby-boom generation. In fact, Xers are frequently described as harboring resentment toward boomers (see Chapter 1), believing that the latter—by luck of the draw more than anything else—inherited a privileged position in the country's social and economic hierarchy. Making matters worse is the smugness exhibited by boomers, especially their tendency to exaggerate the level of political "commitment" among young people during the legendary 1960s antiwar era (Ratan 1993). As it happens, research on the political socialization of preadults was in its heyday when baby boomers were starting to move toward adulthood, which means that a good deal is known about their early orientations toward government and politics. Briefly contrasting the childhood politicization of Xers and boomers should thus provide a useful point of departure for a discussion of generational differences (or similarities, as the case may be) in feelings of support, efficacy, and patriotism.

In the halcyon days of the Eisenhower and Kennedy presidencies,

Americans had mixed but generally positive views about the political system (Nie et al. 1976)—a sort of rosy glow that was reflected in patterns of political learning among preadults during that period. Virtually all of the empirical work on socialization done in the late 1950s and early 1960s (or at least that which focused on "mainstream" white, urban, middle-class youth) indicated very high levels of support for political authorities, institutions, and the broad constitutional structure of U.S. government (see Greenstein 1969; Hess and Torney 1967; Easton and Dennis 1969). Nor is this surprising given that, despite an omnipresent fear of the atomic bomb and the emergence of the "rebel without a cause" as an icon of alienated youth culture, the critical agencies of socialization—families, schools, peer groups, the mass media— painted a mostly favorable picture of political institutions for preadults. Younger children (the baby boomers) tended, if anything, to overidealize visible authority figures such as the president (Greenstein 1960). In later years, of course, when events such as Vietnam and Watergate caused their youthful idealism to be shattered by perceptions that the system had become unresponsive, misguided, and corrupt, many rebelled. Yet even in the wake of these events, boomers continued to believe that the system "belonged" to them and that, with effort, they could correct its flaws (see Keniston 1971; Light 1988).

Eventually, however, that began to change. The dissatisfaction with government that first became evident in the mid- to late 1960s persisted and deepened throughout the 1970s, affecting citizens of all ages (see note 3). And while the public's mood did improve slightly during the early 1980s under President Ronald Reagan (Miller and Borrelli 1991), levels of discontent and disillusionment dropped once again during the Bush and Clinton administrations (Bennett and Bennett 1996; Craig 1996b). Thus, gen-Xers have lived their entire lives in an environment in which damning messages about government and its leaders are the norm. The tone of political discussion by parents, teachers, friends, and the media—amplified by the vitriolic discourse of talk radio and tabloid television—often is cynical, stressing the inability of average citizens to affect political affairs. Moreover, the life experiences of gen-Xers have tended to confirm this negative dialogue. Young Americans have in recent years been forced to adjust their lifestyles in order to contend with a litany of social problems ranging from a floundering educational system to joblessness and corporate downsizing to crime and drugs to AIDS. It is really not too difficult to imagine that, in an atmosphere of such extreme political negativism, very few Xers would be supportive, optimistic, or idealistic about government.

Equally predictable, perhaps, is that gen-Xers, rather than taking on the political system, making their voices heard, and promoting change, would remain ambivalent about the political world—about the kinds of things that government should and should not be doing. Political scientist Gregory Markus remarked that while Xers remain somewhat aloof from the political system, they also expect little from it. "Not only do most young Americans want little to do with government," said Markus, "they want government to have little to do with them in terms of obligations or responsibilities" (quoted in Morin 1994). Nevertheless, as Craig and Halfacre show in Chapter 4, young adults frequently complain about government being too powerful and taxes being too high while maintaining that government should be doing more things and providing more services, even if such efforts lead to higher taxes. As we shall see momentarily, gen-Xers are not entirely ready to abandon the premise that government can and should be made responsive to essential citizen needs and interests.

This ambivalence may stem at least partially from the fact that Generation X has had difficulty gaining access to national politics; that is, Xers have few identifiable political spokespersons and little representation in the national arena.[5] The problem is a typical one for youth cohorts, but Xers lack a significant mouthpiece possibly more than did previous generations because they do not yet have a solid political identity or a unifying issue agenda (see Chapter 7). During the 1960s, antiwar protest produced charismatic leaders such as Paul Rudd and Abbie Hoffman, who were promoted by the mass media and who politically galvanized at least some segments of the baby-boom cohort (Gitlin 1980). Describing the situation today, reporter Clay Chandler observed, "For anything to change, for the candidates to start including the young in this country's political discourse, Generation X had best find itself some level-headed torchbearers and soon. After all, it's not that the media aren't anxious to give this group air time, it's that they don't know where to point the camera" (quoted in Wood 1996).

Given gen-Xers' early socialization experiences and their current lack of political cohesion and direction, the speculation that they might exhibit distressingly low levels of support does not seem unreasonable (Strauss and Howe 1991). But do they? Are Xers less trusting of institutions and leaders, less efficacious, less patriotic, and less likely to believe that government pays attention to what they think than older cohorts who were socialized in an environment that was much more favorable to the established political order? The answers to these questions are not as cut and dried as one might expect.

Methodology: Concepts, Measures, and Data

Before proceeding with my analysis, I should acknowledge briefly the scholarly debate that has developed over how best to conceptualize and measure the attitudes studied here. First, *political trust* refers to citizens' beliefs about whether government is functioning in accordance with individual expectations (Miller 1974a). Researchers who employ either the ANES or some other measure of political trust often try to place it within the framework of David Easton's well-worn distinction between *diffuse* and *specific* support. Diffuse support is usually defined as representing the degree of confidence one has in the broader structural elements of the political system (for example, the regime or political community); specific support, in contrast, is concerned with assessments of the day-to-day performance of those in power in relation to what citizens want, need, or demand (see Easton 1965; Kornberg and Clarke 1992). The reservoir of goodwill that exists when diffuse support is high supposedly allows the political system as a whole to persist and provides incumbent authorities with the flexibility they need to do their jobs, even during periods when (specific) support for institutions and incumbent leaders is diminished. Following this logic, a serious erosion of diffuse support could lead to system collapse, especially if short-term government performance is judged unfavorably.

Craig (1993) has argued that the diffuse versus specific dichotomy is problematic because, as presented by Easton, it is tautological. Other scholars question whether specific support is really support at all (in the Eastonian sense) or merely a temporary, conditional expression of approval for some particular policy decision or decision maker (e.g., Hibbing and Theiss-Morse 1995). In an effort to avoid these conceptual problems, I will follow the lead of those who focus attention on the *objects* of political trust/support rather than trying to accommodate the diffuse versus specific support distinction (Craig 1993; Hibbing and Theiss-Morse 1995; Luttbeg and Gant 1995). Attitude objects ranging from the abstract (government in general) to the concrete (presidency, Congress, Supreme Court, President Clinton, and others) will be considered.

Political trust and *political efficacy* are companion constructs, each tapping different aspects of the relationship between citizens and their government. Efficacy refers to an individual's beliefs about whether he or she can have an impact on the political process; it is more closely tied to the likelihood of one's participating actively in politics than is trust (Craig et al. 1990). The concept of efficacy can be divided into separate internal and external dimensions. Internal efficacy refers to the perception that one either does or does not possess the skills and resources needed to be an effective political actor. External efficacy has to do with people's beliefs about whether government is responsive to attempts by ordinary citizens like themselves to affect the system (Craig et al. 1990). Although the usage of two dimensions is widely accepted, there is less agreement as to how internal and external efficacy should be measured. Thus, for purposes of this analysis, I will divide the available indicators into the categories of *political effectiveness* (the degree to which a person believes that she or he can personally influence politics) and *government responsiveness* (the degree to which a person accepts the proposition that political leaders pay attention to what citizens think).

Like political efficacy, *patriotism* is related to, but obviously separate from, political trust. And like efficacy (as well as trust), its definition and measurement is a matter of some dispute (see Sullivan et al. 1992). As used here, patriotism implies a particular type of deep-seated, instinctive support at the broadest level—a chauvinistic preference for one's own country and, in principle, form of government over all others. It also involves an acceptance, even veneration, of important national symbols such as the flag.

In order to examine intercohort differences in political support, I will employ data from the 1992 and 1994 ANES surveys.[6] In addition, data from the *Congress as Public Enemy* project conducted in 1992[7] by John Hibbing and Elizabeth Theiss-Morse (1995) will be explored for the insights they might be able to provide concerning some of the attitudes we have been considering. Finally, I will present findings obtained from the *1996 Youth Voices* study,[8] which was based on a national survey (supplemented by focus groups) of 1,200 citizens aged between eighteen and twenty-four years. In each instance, it is important to keep in mind that the data presented represent a snapshot in time. We know that evaluations of governmental institutions and political leaders fluctuate regularly, and cross-sectional analysis is unable to capture that fluctuation. However, my analysis centers mainly on overall trends and comparisons across generations—and previous research suggests that levels of trust and support tend to rise and fall in much the same way among people of all ages.

The comparisons that I will make are based on five birth cohorts: (1) Generation X, born 1965–1980; (2) late baby boomers, born 1955–1964; (3) early baby boomers, born 1946–1954; (4) the Silent Generation, born 1930–1945; and (5) the Oldest Generation, born 1901–1929.[9] Since the ANES only interviews individuals of voting age, the 1992 and 1994 samples of Xers includes those born from 1964–74 and 1964–76, respectively.

Attitudes toward Government, Institutions, and Leaders

Trust in Government

A good place to begin is with the long-running ANES trust in government questions, which more or less explicitly tap respondents' views about the performance of incumbent federal government officials. As can be seen in Table 5.1, none of our five birth cohorts had particularly high regard for the government in 1994. There is, however, no indication that Xers were more cynical than anyone else. On three of the four items (trust government, few big interests, how many are crooked), there is little variation from one

Table 5.1
Trust in Government by Cohort, 1994*

	Oldest Generation	Silent Generation	Early Boomers	Late Boomers	Generation X
1. "How much of the time do you think you can trust the government in Washington to do what is right?"					
Just about always	4%	2%	1%	1%	2%
Most of the time	23	17	17	19	21
Only some/none of the time	73	81	82	80	77
2. "Do you think that people in the government waste a lot of the money we pay in taxes, waste some of it, or don't waste very much of it?"					
Waste a lot	73%	79%	71%	70%	61%
Waste some	23	20	28	29	37
Don't waste much	4	1	1	1	2
3. "Would you say the government is pretty much run by a few big interests looking out for themselves or that it is run for the benefit of all the people?"					
Few big interests	79%	79%	80%	82%	79%
Benefit of all	21	21	20	18	21
4. "Do you think that quite a few of the people running the government are a little crooked, not very many are, or do you think hardly any of them are crooked at all?"					
Quite a few	48%	51%	50%	55%	53%
Not very many	42	44	40	38	38
Hardly any	10	5	10	7	9
Sample N =	353	338	299	454	312

*Table entries are column percentages adding to 100% (respondents with missing values are excluded).
Source: American National Election Study, 1994.

age group to the next. And for the question of government waste, Xers are actually *least* likely to attribute to elected officials a profligate approach toward spending taxpayers' dollars.

The *1996 Youth Voices* survey contained a question that followed along similar lines. Among gen-Xers, 52 percent indicated that the statement "Government can help people, and needs to be made to work for average working families" came closest to their own views, compared with just 38 percent who opted for the statement that "Government is the problem, not the solution to our problems."[10] Percentages for the total sample were 43 percent and 47 percent, respectively. Thus, based on these general and admittedly somewhat ambiguous measures of political trust, there is nothing to support the contention that gen-Xers are any more turned off or cynical than their elders. If anything, the opposite is true.

Attitudes toward Institutions

The *Congress as Public Enemy* data set permits us to explore people's attitudes toward government from a slightly different perspective. In fact, when the attitude objects are specific institutions and political actors, the story becomes a little more complex than we saw before: gen-Xers sometimes, but not always, fit the stereotype of an alienated generation. Table 5.2, for example, presents answers to a battery of questions asking respondents to express their approval or disapproval of major institutions *no matter who the actual incumbents happen to be.*

Results show, in the aggregate, overwhelming levels of support for the presidency (over 90 percent approve strongly or not strongly), Congress (between 83 percent and 91 percent), and the Supreme Court (over 90 percent) in each of the five birth cohorts. However, a closer look at the table reveals that gen-Xers are substantially less likely than any of the other age groups to register strong approval of the presidency (14 percent versus 24 to 34 percent for older respondents), and somewhat less likely to do the same for Congress (12 percent versus 16 to 21 percent). Although Xers stand out less clearly in terms of their attitudes toward the Supreme Court, they are in a virtual dead heat with the Oldest Generation here as well (22 percent strong approval versus 21 percent for the oldest and 25 to 28 percent for the others). It is interesting that for all three of these questions, Xers' evaluations more closely resemble those of the oldest cohort than they do either early or late boomers.

The final question presented in Table 5.2 deals with support for "the basic constitutional structure of the U.S. government." Once again, the prevailing view is extremely positive across the board, with between 85 percent and 96 percent registering approval. Yet a lower proportion of Xers than of any other cohort (26 percent versus 29 to 41 percent) approve strongly—and

Table 5.2
Approval of Institutions and Constitutional Structure by Cohort, 1992*

	Oldest Generation	Silent Generation	Early Boomers	Late Boomers	Generation X
1. "The institution of the presidency, no matter who is in office"					
Strongly approve	24%	34%	28%	31%	14%
Approve	71	63	69	65	79
Disapprove	5	3	3	4	5
Strongly disapprove	0	1	0	1	1
2. "The U.S. Congress, no matter who is in office"					
Strongly qpprove	16%	21%	21%	21%	12%
Approve	71	70	69	65	71
Disapprove	11	7	10	14	16
Strongly disapprove	1	2	1	1	1
3. "The Supreme Court, no matter who the justices are"					
Strongly approve	21%	28%	25%	27%	22%
Approve	69	65	71	71	71
Disapprove	10	6	4	2	7
Strongly disapprove	0	1	0	0	0
4. "The basic constitutional structure of the U.S. government"					
Strongly approve	29%	41%	39%	37%	26%
Approve	64	55	54	54	59
Disapprove	6	4	7	9	14
Strongly disapprove	1	1	0	0	1
Sample N =	270	272	310	364	215

*Respondents were asked the following: "I have a few questions about the institutions of the government of Washington. . . . In general, do you strongly approve, approve, disapprove, or disapprove of . . . ?" Table entries are column percentages, adding to 100% (respondents with missing values are excluded). Source: Congress as Public Enemy 1992 data base (see Hibbing and Theiss-Morse 1995).

a higher proportion express *disapproval* (15 percent versus 5 to 9 percent) at this most basic level. While younger Americans show few signs of being deeply disaffected from our governing institutions, the data suggest that they may be less fully committed to these institutions than their elders are.

A different slant on citizens' perceptions is captured by other items drawn from the *Congress as Public Enemy* survey. Respondents were asked whether they believed the presidency, Congress, and the Supreme Court (again, "no matter who is in office") have too much, not enough, or about the right amount of power. Results (not shown) vary from one question to the next. Gen-Xers are far more likely than any of the older cohorts to say that the institution of the presidency is too powerful (30 percent versus 15 to 19 percent for the older cohorts). It is people aged forty-seven and up, how-

ever (35 percent oldest, 32 percent Silent, versus 21 to 23 percent for everyone else), who most often see the U. S. Supreme Court as exercising too
much authority.[11]

As for Congress, generational differences are small. Each of the five
cohorts tends to believe that Congress, relative to the presidency and the
Supreme Court, has too much power. This supports the current view that
negative public sentiments in the United States today are directed first and
foremost at the legislative branch (Hibbing and Theiss-Morse 1995). What
is interesting about Xers is that the difference between their assessments of
the power of Congress and of the presidency are the smallest of any age
group. In other words, they are the most likely to indicate that *both* elected
branches are more powerful than they need to be.

We can take one final pass at institutional evaluations by looking at how
good a job respondents feel the president, Congress, and the Supreme Court
are doing on whatever has been identified as the single most important problem facing the country. According to the *Youth Voices* study, economic concerns (having a job that pays well, high taxes, health care benefits) as well
as crime, violence, gangs, and the quality and cost of education are among
the issues that preoccupy members of Generation X. Be that as it may, the
Congress as Public Enemy data (not shown) reveal that very few people in
any age category feel that the three principal institutions of our national
government are doing a good job at contending with major problems; only
for the Supreme Court do "good" and "fair" evaluations outnumber "poor"
responses, and in this instance there is no clear-cut generational pattern.
Whereas gen-Xers, relative to most of the other cohorts, tend to be slightly
more critical of the presidency and slightly less disparaging with regard to
Congress, their evaluations of the Court differ appreciably only from those
of the Oldest Generation (the former being less favorable).

Curiously, the 1994 American National Election Study included a question that tapped approval of the way Congress is doing its job without refer-
encing (or asking respondents to name) a specific problem,[12] and the results
are not altogether consistent with the *Congress as Public Enemy* study. According to the ANES measure, there is an almost linear decline in approval
of Congress with increasing age: 47 percent approval among Xers compared
with 32 percent for both boomer groups, 30 percent for the Silent Generation, and 25 percent of the Oldest Generation.

Taken as a whole, these two sets of findings point to an interesting dynamic in the nature of political support among members of Generation X.
When the issue of trust in government is posed in general terms (as with the
four-item index discussed earlier), Xers appear to be no more cynical than
older citizens. But when approval of specific institutions is solicited, Xers
are often, though not always, at least somewhat less supportive than their
elders. While Congress provides an exception to this pattern, the degree to

which Xers stand out depends on whether evaluations are (Xers only marginally less critical than most other cohorts) or are not (Xers much less critical) anchored to a concrete policy concern. Such differences say a lot about the importance of question wording to the study of mass political opinion. They also suggest that empirical estimates of gen-Xers' attitudes toward government in a *general* sense may be inflated on the positive side; that is, when Xers are asked to focus *specifically* on issues and objects of support, their views tend to be more negative.[13]

Approval of Political Leaders

Turning to performance ratings of incumbent leaders, the views of gen-Xers are not particularly distinctive. Judging from findings from the *Youth Voices* survey and focus groups, young Americans are basically no different from other age groups in terms of perceiving politicians as a self-interested elite. The *Youth Voices* report also indicates that most Xers do not identify with any current leader, not even Bill Clinton, despite his efforts to reach out to them during his 1992 campaign. In general, Xers (and others) tend to believe that politicians are inaccessible, out of touch, and corrupted by power. A theme that resonates throughout the study is that Xers often perceive leaders to be exceptionally affluent and therefore unable to relate to ordinary citizens or to understand their problems.

According to the *Congress as Public Enemy* 1992 survey (results not shown), Xers' evaluations of incumbent officials usually ranked in the middle (then-President Bush)[14] or slightly on the high side (Congress as a whole, congressional leaders, their own representative, the Supreme Court) compared with those of older cohorts.[15] One thing seen clearly here is the familiar tendency for people to be more favorably disposed toward their own member of Congress than toward either the U.S. House of Representatives itself or its remaining 434 members (or the 100 members of the Senate). For our purposes, though, the most important message in these data is the fact that gen-Xers do not differ in any systematic way from older citizens in their performance ratings of political leaders.

Political Effectiveness and Government Responsiveness

Gen-Xers (or those who claim to speak on their behalf) have been known to complain that their partisan, ideological, and policy concerns are seldom taken seriously by political decision makers (see Chapter 4). If this is indeed the case—and more the case for Xers than for older citizens—then we would expect to find a positive and perhaps fairly strong relationship between age and feelings of political effectiveness. From the 1994 ANES data presented in Table 5.3, however, we see that young people are *not* appre-

Table 5.3
Political Efficacy and Government Responsiveness by Cohort, 1994*

	Oldest Generation	Silent Generation	Early Boomers	Late Boomers	Generation X
1. "I don't think public officials care much about what people like me think."					
Agree	78%	66%	60%	64%	62%
Disagree	16	23	32	23	23
2. "People like me don't have any say about what the government does."					
Agree	66%	59%	48%	53%	50%
Disagree	19	36	46	37	35
3. "Sometimes politics and government seem so complicated that a person like me can't really understand what's going on."					
Agree	80%	68%	60%	61%	57%
Disagree	13	25	33	31	27
4. "Over the years, how much attention do you feel the government pays to what the people think when it decides what to do?"					
A good deal	17%	14%	16%	9%	10%
Some	54	63	65	64	64
Not much	29	23	19	27	26
5. "[H]ow much do you feel that having elections makes the government pay attention to what the people think?"					
A good deal	55%	47%	44%	46%	49%
Some	33	40	45	42	38
Not much	12	13	11	12	13
Sample N =	353	338	299	454	312

*Table entries are column percentages, with respondents who have missing values being excluded from the calculations. The total does not add to 100% for questions 1-3 because those who answered "neither agree nor disagree" are not shown.
Source: American National Election Study, 1994.

ciably less efficacious than older age cohorts. In fact, it is the Oldest Generation that stands out in terms of its belief that (1) public officials don't care
what people like them think (78 percent versus 62 percent for Xers and 60
to 66 percent for the middle three age groups); (2) people like themselves
don't have any say about what the government does (66 percent versus 50
percent and 48 to 59 percent, respectively); and (3) politics and government
are so complicated that they have trouble understanding what is going on
(80 percent versus 57 percent and 60 to 68 percent).

One possible explanation for this pattern is that the oldest Americans
are less well educated than their younger counterparts, and people with
higher levels of educational attainment tend to have a stronger sense of political effectiveness as measured by the first three items in Table 5.3. In addition, gen-Xers have not yet had the long-term opportunity for negative (or,
for that matter, positive; see Finkel 1985) experiences in the political arena
that might lead them to conclude that their effectiveness is limited. Finally,
Xers and boomers were socialized during the television age, which brought
about significant changes in the way politics is conducted in the United
States (see Patterson 1993). Younger generations may therefore regard the
world of government and politics as being less remote and feel that they can
better navigate the political waters, should they choose to do so, than those
who came of age under different circumstances.

Closely related to the notion of personal political effectiveness are one's
perceptions of government responsiveness. A clear finding of the *Youth
Voices* study is that gen-Xers believe they have been ignored by politicians.
For example, 72 percent agreed with the statement "Our generation has an
important voice but no one seems to hear it"; getting right to the bottom
line, 61 percent said, "Politicians and political leaders have failed my generation." Focus group participants echoed the same themes, many of them
claiming that the priorities of people in power are at odds with those of
Xers—and that the age gap between leaders and themselves made reconcilia-
tion of these differences impossible. Because politicians were not perceived
as paying attention to them, some participants insisted there was no need to
vote.

Judging from the 1994 ANES data, such complaints are not typical of
gen-Xers as a whole. The fourth and fifth entries in Table 5.3 indicate that
Xers are no more likely than older cohorts to believe that government is
unresponsive to their needs. Relatively few respondents in any of the age
groups said that government pays "a good deal" of attention to what the
people think, and those under age forty (Xers and late boomers) felt this way
least of all, but only by a small margin (roughly 10 percent versus 15 percent
for individuals aged forty and above). Moreover, Xers (49 percent) rank just
behind the Oldest Generation (55 percent versus 44 to 47 percent for the
middle three cohorts) in suggesting that elections do "a good deal" to make

government pay attention. Part of the discrepancy here may be due to the general wording of ANES questions versus the specific focus on generational concerns evident in the *Youth Voices* study. Still, there is little support from ANES for the claim that gen-Xers are more estranged from the political process than are older Americans.

Patriotism

Patriotism is a mark of individuals' identification with, and feelings about, their nation and political community (see Easton 1965). Looking at the 1992 ANES results presented in Table 5.4, we find something close to a linear decline in patriotic sentiments as we move from old to young. Asked how they feel when they see the American flag flying, only 35 percent of gen-Xers said "very good," compared with at least 43 percent in every other cohort (up to a high of 58 percent for the Oldest Generation). And when asked about the strength of their love for the country, just 41 percent of Xers responded "extremely strong" (versus 49 percent and above in other cohorts, 66 percent among those aged sixty-three and over). The data obviously do not demonstrate that Xers are unpatriotic, since more than two-thirds give positive answers to each of the two questions. Yet the gap between younger and older citizens is quite noticeable.

This divergence comes somewhat as a surprise, especially given the established lore from political socialization research that most citizens— Americans, certainly—learn to identify with their national community fairly early in life.[16] Such early identification supposedly establishes a pattern that is unlikely to be disturbed for the remainder of one's lifetime (Davies 1973). The lower levels of patriotism exhibited by gen-Xers may therefore be a genuine cohort effect rather than a maturational or life-cycle effect. And if they are, then it is conceivable that the process of generational replacement will eventually lead to increased disengagement from (and perhaps even resistance to) the political system and constitutional order.

What might account for the apparent generational decline in patriotic feelings? One possibility, suggested by the *Youth Voices* study, is that some gen-Xers have lost their sense of community and hence their ability to hold lofty ideals about the country.[17] On a more personal level, Xers are said to believe that forming lasting attachments is difficult; many of them allegedly are convinced that community is disappearing, that their ability to have a stable family life is in jeopardy, and that they may spend the rest of their lives moving from place to place and from job to job. It is unclear how common these beliefs are among the young. But if they are widely shared (an empirical question), we probably should not be surprised to discover that the misgivings they reflect tend to undermine Xers' feelings of national pride—all the more so when uncertainty happens to be coupled with the

Table 5.4
Patriotism by Cohort, 1992*

	Oldest Generation	Silent Generation	Early Boomers	Late Boomers	Generation X
1. "When you see the American flag flying, does it make you feel. . . ?"					
Extremely good	58%	53%	45%	43%	35%
Very good	38	30	29	33	35
Somewhat good	4	15	25	23	24
Not Very good	0	2	1	2	6
2. "How strong is your love for your country?"					
Extremely strong	66%	56%	55%	49%	41%
Very strong	31	35	33	40	35
Somewhat strong	3	8	9	10	19
Not Very strong	0	1	3	1	4
Sample N =	145	152	129	217	115

*Table entries are column percentages, adding to 100% (respondents with missing values are excluded).
Source: American National Election Study, 1992.

pervasive negative portrayal of government and politics that is present in most forms of popular communication in the 1990s.

Explaining Attitudes toward Government:
Is Generation X Different?

Gen-Xers voice many of the same complaints about government as older people: "It just doesn't work . . . Our political institutions are stymied by gridlock, unable to perform effectively in making good public policy . . . Politicians give lip service to voters at election time, only to ignore their concerns once in office . . . Government leaders have the wrong priorities, too often seeking quick fixes to complex social problems." Yet it is also true that at least some Xers have their own set of grievances: "We feel locked out of national politics . . . Those running the country are too old and out of touch to understand what young people are going through today . . . Our generation has been given a bad rap, written off by the politicians who don't think they need Xers' votes to get elected."

There is good cause, however, to suspect that gen-Xers' indictment of "politics as usual" is based—to a greater degree than that of older co-horts—on impressionistic evidence as opposed to hard information. Younger people are traditionally less inclined than their elders to attend to public affairs, and members of Generation X have been accused (not entirely without reason; see Chapter 2) of being even more uninterested and disengaged than other new generations in the past. The *Congress as Public Enemy* survey included four questions that were designed to tap some of the reasons people might have negative feelings about Congress. Specifically, respondents were asked whether (1) members' voting themselves a pay raise; (2) the Clarence Thomas–Anita Hill hearings; (3) overdrafts at the House bank; and (4) gridlock over the budget deficit contributed to their negative views.[18]

By a sizable margin in every case, gen-Xers were less likely than the other cohorts to claim that these actions exerted "a great deal" of influence on their evaluations of Congress (see Table 5.5). More telling, perhaps, is that Xers had by far the highest percentages saying they "didn't know" whether a particular issue shaped their opinions: 32 percent for the pay raise (versus 17 to 24 percent for older citizens), 39 percent for Hill-Thomas (versus 18 to 26 percent), 33 percent for overdrafts (versus 17 to 25 percent), and 32 percent for gridlock (versus 16 to 24 percent). Although this list obviously does not run the entire gamut of possible events and actions that might have led individuals to develop negative assessments, the data suggest that Xers often work with a limited awareness of specific issues, controversies, and scandals when they pass judgment on government institutions and incumbent leaders. If so, those judgments, like many of the political attitudes

Table 5.5
Reasons for Negative Feelings toward Congress by Cohort, 1992

	Oldest Generation	Silent Generation	Early Boomers	Late Boomers	Generation X
1. "Members of Congress voting for their own pay raise"					
A great deal	68%	71%	62%	63%	55%
Some/a little/ not at all	8	13	15	15	13
Don't know	24	17	23	22	32
2. "The Clarence Thomas-Anita Hill hearings"					
A great deal	58%	65%	53%	54%	39%
Some/a little/ not at all	15	16	21	21	22
Don't know	26	18	26	24	39
3. "The overdrafts at the House bank"					
A great deal	67%	71%	62%	66%	55%
Some/a little/ not at all	8	12	14	12	12
Don't know	25	17	23	22	33
4. "Gridlock over the budget deficit"					
A great deal	60%	68%	59%	63%	49%
Some/a little not at all	16	16	19	16	19
Don't know	24	16	22	21	32
Sample N =	270	272	310	364	215

Respondents were asked the following: "There are many reasons why people might have negative feelings toward Congress. I would like to know how much each of the following actions of Congress contribute to your negative feelings. Did the action contribute a great deal, some, a little, or not at all to your feelings?" Table entries are column percentages, adding to 100%; respondents who said "don't know" are included in the calculations, but those who refused to answer have been omitted.
Source: Congress as Public Enemy 1992 data base (see Hibbing and Theiss-Morse 1995).

expressed by young people in the past, may prove to be malleable, inconsistent, and subject to change with the passage of time.

Conclusion

The preceding analysis points to the complexities and nuances that appear to characterize gen-Xers' relationship to the American polity. First,

Xers are as fed up with government and politics as other citizens, but so far the evidence does not indicate any real cause for alarm. On general, abstract measures of political support, Xers tend to be slightly less cynical than older Americans. However, when asked to take a more focused look at the performance of specific institutions or to evaluate these institutions and incumbent leaders in terms of their impact on young people, Xers' judgments often become less generous. Which of the two sets of orientations is more valid? It is impossible to know for sure. Considering the limited degree to which many young citizens attend to, and are well informed about, public affairs, the safest conclusion is probably that Generation X is still very much a work in progress.

On the plus side, it is clear that Xers are not ready to give up on government altogether: Their feelings of political effectiveness are about as strong as anyone else's, and they rank relatively high among the cohorts in terms of their belief that elections are an effective means by which the general public can help to shape the direction of government policy. It is therefore much too early to conclude that Xers lack the potential to become more fully engaged participants as they mature. Their feelings of patriotism and national pride are not as strong as those of older Americans, and that may present problems later on if our political system and its leaders continue to be perceived, at least by many, as ineffective, unresponsive, and occasionally corrupt.

Even here, though, we should not lose sight of the fact that 70 percent or more of gen-Xers say they (1) feel extremely good or very good when they see the flag flying; (2) have an extremely strong or very strong love for their country; and (3) approve or strongly approve of the basic constitutional structure of the U.S. government. These are solid numbers that help to put the rest of our findings in perspective. While they may currently find fault with institutions and individual leaders who are not dealing effectively with the issues that trouble them most, Xers are a long way from abandoning or actively rebelling against the system. In fact, in light of what we have seen happen with other "alienated" generations in the past, it is likely that Xers will eventually find their political voice(s) and take their place, naturally enough, at the table of power. The irony is that when they do, they will almost certainly face criticism from some future generation of young people who don't believe that their own concerns are being addressed.

Notes

The author would like to extend special thanks to Virginia Dennis and Jack Dennis for their insights in the writing of this chapter.

1. Although political scientists sometimes attach slightly different meanings to these two concepts, I will use them more or less interchangeably.

2. See the Appendix for question wordings.

3. The "in relative terms" qualifier in this sentence is extremely important. Levels of trust have dropped sharply since the early 1960s among all categories of Americans (a period effect; see Chapter 1) including the young. Craig (1996b, 53), for example, showed that from 1964 and 1992, the proportion of those aged between seventeen and twenty-four years who were classified as "very mistrustful" on the ANES trust in government index jumped from 23.1 percent to 63.8 percent. Still, the seventeen-to-twenty-four group was the least mistrustful age cohort in both 1964 *and* 1992.

4. This finding is drawn from the *Youth Voices* study described later in the chapter (see note 8).

5. As one would expect, there are indications of change with Xers now beginning to mature. During the 1996 presidential contest, for example, both parties made an effort to showcase young people—including Michela Alioto, a twenty-six-year-old congressional candidate from California, who seconded Al Gore's nomination for vice president at the Democratic National Convention.

6. The ANES surveys were made available by the Inter-University Consortium for Political and Social Research. Neither the Consortium nor the original collectors of the data bear any responsibility for the analyses and interpretations presented here.

7. I would like to thank John Hibbing and Elizabeth Theiss-Morse for making their data set (a representative national sample, $N = 1432$) available to me. The *Congress as Public Enemy* project was funded by the National Science Foundation, grant #SES-91-22733.

8. The *Youth Voices* project was jointly sponsored by the Center for Policy Alternatives and *Who Cares* magazine. Data were collected by Lake Research, Research Strategy Management, and Buffalo Qualitative Research. The nationwide survey mentioned earlier included oversamples of African American and Hispanic youth. Focus groups involving several different types of young people were held in Los Angeles; Philadelphia; and Raleigh, North Carolina.

9. These categories are informed by, but do not replicate exactly, the generational breakdown employed by Bennett and Bennett (1990; also see Bennett and Rademacher 1994).

10. Unlike Table 5.1, the percentages here are calculated based on all respondents, i.e., those missing data have not been excluded.

11. This may be because older citizens remember, and their perceptions have been shaped by, some of the highly visible and activist Courts of years past (especially under liberal Chief Justice Earl Warren throughout most of the 1950s and 1960s, but perhaps also the Republican-dominated Court that caused such a stir during Franklin Roosevelt's first term as president in the 1930s).

12. "In general, do you approve or disapprove of the way the U.S. Congress has been handling its job?"

13. Alternatively, recall from Table 5.2 that Xers expressed the lowest level of strong support for "the basic constitutional structure of the U.S. government"—an indication that their negativism is not always tied to specific question referents.

14. The 1994 ANES asked the same question about President Clinton. By a negligible margin, Xers were more likely to approve (54 percent) of the president's job performance than were other cohorts (49 to 52 percent).

15. The question read as follows: "Thinking about people in government, please tell me if you strongly approve, approve, disapprove, or strongly disapprove of the way the people [President George Bush, the 535 members of Congress, the leaders of Congress, your own representative in the U.S. House of Representatives, the nine justices on the Supreme Court] are handling their jobs."

16. But also see Janowitz (1983), who suggests that this may no longer be the case due to changes in civic education during the period since the end of World War II.

17. Gen-Xers do participate more regularly in local affairs than at the state or national levels (e.g., People for the American Way 1990; Strauss and Howe 1991; Howe and Strauss 1993a).

18. One concern about these questions (see Table 5.5 for wording) is that they more or less assume respondents have a negative view of Congress. As we have seen, most Americans do—but not everyone.

6

Generations and Tolerance: Is Youth Really a Liberalizing Factor?

Kevin A. Hill

Since at least the 1950s, scholars have been seeking an answer to the following question: How politically and socially *tolerant* is the American public? That is, how willing are citizens to accord basic civil liberties (freedom of speech, press, assembly, worship, and so forth) to members of all groups regardless of those groups' political stances or lifestyles? The first in-depth study of tolerance, conducted by Samuel Stouffer (1955), gave little encouragement to those who perhaps hoped to learn that a respect for such freedoms pervaded society. However, later analyses by other researchers not only challenged the methodological assumptions on which Stouffer's work was based, but also suggested that levels of tolerance may have risen during the 1960s and 1970s largely as a result of (1) expanding educational attainment among the public at large and (2) the coming of age of a new generation—the post–World War II baby boomers.

The generations component of this argument is typically based on the assumption that youth, by its very nature, is causally related to heightened political and social tolerance. The hypothesis to be tested here proposes something rather different: that the perceived rise in tolerance may have been a cohort-based phenomenon triggered specifically by the baby-boom generation. If, as I contend, there is no inherent link between youth and tolerance,[1] then it would be wrong to expect that newer cohorts will inevitably be more tolerant than their elders. In fact, one of the things we will see is that the cohort commonly known as Generation X scores *lower* than boomers on some measures of political tolerance—most notably, tolerance of racial and ethnic minorities. Winston Churchill once quipped, "If a young man is not a socialist at twenty, he has no heart. If he is still a socialist at forty, he has no head." The following analysis provides an empirical test of this famous aphorism, to determine whether the relationship it describes applies to the American public in the 1990s.

The Link between Youth and Tolerance

The pioneering work on public opinion and political tolerance in the United States was Samuel Stouffer's (1955) *Communism, Conformity, and Civil Liberties.* Using questions from a national survey conducted in 1954, Stouffer measured respondents' attitudes toward Communism and their willingness to extend civil liberties protections to people who advocated pro-Communist positions. Further, the survey explored levels of public tolerance for two other "undesirable" out-groups of the period, Socialists and atheists. Examining a variety of items, Stouffer found that large majorities of those interviewed believed that Communists, Socialists, and atheists should not be allowed to make public speeches, teach in the public schools, or have their works placed in public libraries. There also was widespread support for government wiretapping of, and even for the arrest of, people suspected of being Communists. The obvious conclusion drawn from these results was that respect for the basic rights of other citizens fell far short of the democratic ideal. To the contrary, the American public seemed to be dangerously *intolerant* of certain unpopular groups.

All was not gloom and doom, however. Stouffer did find that higher levels of education were associated with greater tolerance (see Prothro and Grigg 1960; Jackman 1972), presumably because individuals who are exposed to alternative points of view tend to be more politically open-minded. In his original analysis, Stouffer also discovered large age-related differences in the attitudes that people held toward Communists, Socialists, and atheists; specifically, younger cohorts (aged twenty-one to twenty-nine) were more tolerant than older citizens (especially those aged sixty and over). Thus, as society became both better educated and younger—the latter due to the postwar baby boom—levels of tolerance should have increased accordingly.[2] Yet even in the early 1950s, age and education were so highly correlated[3] that the independent effects of the two variables on political tolerance were difficult to disentangle. Stouffer's efforts in this regard were not entirely convincing. While stressing the role of education in shaping tolerance, he believed that the aging process might be important as well, following the Churchillian view that the older one gets, the more conservative (intolerant) one becomes (also see Sears 1983).

There are, of course, other ways to account for Stouffer's findings. Cutler and Kaufman (1975) offered a generational interpretation: As new birth cohorts enter the electorate, they supposedly bring with them different "life experiences," and consequently each generation can be expected to develop a combination of beliefs, values, and attitudes that is at least somewhat different from those of its predecessors. Notice the underlying assumption here, that the "liberalizing" life experiences of newer generations cause them to be more politically tolerant than older cohorts. This assumption would obviously not be very credible if we were to learn that younger Americans today are in fact *less* tolerant.

The first real opportunity to observe changes over time in political tolerance came in 1972 and again in 1977, when the National Opinion Research Center replicated the Stouffer questions in its annual General Social Survey (GSS). In the wake of more than twenty years' worth of profound social and political transformations in the nation, scholars began to wonder whether the passage of time—and especially the epochal events of the 1960s and early 1970s (the civil rights and women's movements, Vietnam, the Watergate scandal, challenges to traditional values and lifestyles, and so on)—had had any measurable impact on aggregate levels of tolerance in the United States.

When James Davis (1975) used the first wave of GSS data to examine the period from 1954 to 1972, he found that tolerance had increased among *all* birth cohorts.[4] More to the point, although age and education were highly correlated, the independent effects of cohort on political tolerance were nonetheless significant. That is, while better-educated Americans exhibited greater tolerance, younger people as a whole—even setting aside their relative advantage in years of formal schooling—continued to be the most tolerant of all (as in Stouffer's study). This latter finding is actually consistent with either an aging or a generational interpretation, though Davis made little effort to determine which was more appropriate.

How, then, can we assess the effects of age on political tolerance? On the one hand, we have Stouffer's claim that the aging process itself leads a person to become more conservative (less tolerant) as he or she gets older. On the other hand, there is the generational argument which holds that different cohorts bring different life experiences and political expectations with them as they enter the electorate—and that younger people, in recent decades, have been more tolerant than their elders as a result of these experiences. Unfortunately, neither interpretation provides a very clear or theoretically sound rationale for understanding *why* age and tolerance should be linked. By what psychological process does conservatism/intolerance increase as one gets older? Or, alternatively, how have the distinctive life experiences of successive generations contributed (if indeed they have) to greater tolerance over the past thirty or forty or fifty years?

Clyde Nunn and his colleagues, reflecting on the social and political ferment that shook the country during the late 1960s and early 1970s, made an effort to tie some of these various themes together. Citing the important role played by education, they observed that "[c]onfronting the post–1945 world anew meant experiencing the exhilarating pace of change and massive change of scale; it meant that being a well-educated person was commonplace and that the experience of being a highly educated member of an educationally advanced society—surely a unique feature of the post–1945 world—was routine; it meant that living in cities amid many other persons and groups, all expressing a multiplicity of values, was the rule" (Nunn et al. 1978, 89). The authors went on to suggest, however, that not only rising education but also the civil rights movement, Vietnam, and other societal changes had strengthened the commitment of the American public to political tolerance (a period effect; see note 4), while affecting the youngest generation (baby boomers) most profoundly. The Vietnam war in particular raised a number of moral issues that elicited sharply differing points of view. Not surprisingly, the willingness to tolerate such diverse views appeared to be greatest among young people who at the time were questioning many of the assumptions about political life that their parents' generation had taught them. But what about individuals who have come of age *since* the early 1970s? Has the march of history been so uniformly "progressive" in its direction that we should expect members of Generation X to be more politically tolerant than even their baby-boom counterparts?

One must bear in mind that the Stouffer study, as well as most replications done by scholars in the 1970s, measured tolerance in terms of public attitudes toward three very specific groups: Communists, Socialists, and atheists. Each of these groups was ideologically left of center (and therefore a more likely target of intolerance among conservatives than among liberals), and two of the three were consistently portrayed by government leaders as especially undesirable elements in the aftermath of World War II and the beginning of the cold war. Sullivan, Piereson, and Marcus (1982) took a different approach, developing new survey questions that allowed respondents to pick their own "least-liked" groups and then to express feelings of tolerance or intolerance for those particular groups, for example, as to whether members should be allowed to teach in public schools or hold public rallies.[5] According to Sullivan et al., this method is better able to tap one's commitment to political tolerance in general[6] and, sure enough, their results showed substantially lower levels of tolerance in society than did research conducted using the Stouffer-type measures.

In addition to the work of Sullivan et al., there have been numerous attempts over the years to improve upon the ways in which political tolerance is conceptualized and measured.[7] Some studies, for example, have distinguished between support for democratic values in the abstract (equality of condition, freedom of speech, and so on) and support for the rights of unpopular groups to engage in certain acts intended to further their goals. Sniderman et al. (1989) concluded that overall levels of tolerance for various *groups* and for different peaceful *activities* do not vary much, no matter what the group or activity in question—and that, by implication, the American public is largely supportive of both democratic values and the expression of those values.[8] More recently, Chanley (1994) found that when people were allowed to choose their least-liked group, there seemed to be rather broad support for basic political freedoms; however, when the respondent's hometown was mentioned as the site of activity by a least-liked group, or when a relative was specifically named as being affected by that activity, tolerance (even holding education constant) dropped sharply. In other words, it is one thing for citizens to express support for the rights of out-groups— and quite another to do so when they feel personally threatened by those groups' activities.

The research reported in this chapter does not deal with tolerance for narrowly defined out-groups (such as Communists, Socialists, and atheists) at all, whether using the least-liked or any other approach. I focus instead on social and political tolerance in a broader and more exploratory fashion, with special attention given to the search for intergenerational differences. Many of the issues that appear to strain the borders of tolerance for today's youth—including affirmative action, immigration reform, and experimentation with "newer lifestyles"—cannot be adequately captured in a study of tolerance for a handful of specific interest or categorical groups, no matter how noxious the views of those groups may be. Nevertheless, although the conceptualization and measurement of political tolerance utilized here is not an exact replication of previous work on the subject, these findings should be read in the context of that literature.

Data and Conceptualization

The following analysis is based on data from the 1992 American National Election Study (ANES).[9] Because several items relate specifically to political and social tolerance for African Americans and Latinos, I will limit my discussion to the subsample of 1,924 non-Hispanic whites. Four birth cohorts are identified: (1) the G.I. Generation, born 1901–1924; (2) the Silent Generation, born 1925–1942; (3) the baby boom generation, born 1943– 1963; and (4) Generation X, born 1964–1981.[10] Since the ANES interviews only individuals of voting age, our 1992 sample of gen-Xers includes those who were born from 1964 to 1974.

As already noted, my conceptualization of tolerance is different from and somewhat broader than the targeted versions used by Stouffer (1955) and Sullivan et al. (1982). Here, I follow more closely upon Prothro and Grigg (1960), McClosky (1964), and Sniderman et al. (1989) in defining tolerance as support for general democratic norms such as equality of opportunity and privacy. Moreover, since this book is concerned primarily with the attitudes and behavior of gen-Xers, I also will examine measures of social and political tolerance for African Americans, Latinos, and "alternative lifestyles." Just as Vietnam and the civil rights movement were critical events for the baby-boom generation (e.g., Light 1988), more recent developments have made affirmative action, immigration, and unconventional lifestyles key issues of the 1980s and 1990s—precisely the years during which Xers came of age politically. The specific measurements employed for these variables will be discussed more fully as we proceed.

Finally, I have weighted the data so that (1) each respondent has a level of education equal to his or her cohort mean and (2) the entire sample has a mean of exactly twelve years of formal schooling, that is, a high school diploma. This strategy acknowledges that almost all prior research has found that education plays an important role in shaping feelings of political tolerance. Weighting the 1,924 respondents at the outset permits me to present results more simply than if I took the more conventional approach of controlling for arbitrary levels of education; the latter would lead to a proliferation of tables and figures, making the presentation unwieldy.[11]

Tolerance and Four Generations

Before continuing, let us examine the demographic profile of the entire ANES subsample of non-Hispanic whites (not shown). We find, first of all, that baby boomers are by far the largest of the four generations, constituting 44.6 percent of the total; they are followed at some distance by the Silent (21.7 percent) and G.I. (17.3 percent) generations, with gen-Xers[12] bringing up the rear (16.3 percent). A comparison of the mean number of years of formal schooling completed confirms the earlier point regarding the strong relationship between age and education: On average, members of the G.I. Generation—now mostly retirees—did not quite finish high school (11.7 years), while each of the two succeeding cohorts completed at least one year more than its immediate predecessor (12.8 and 13.9, respectively). The exception to this ascending pattern is Xers, who have a lower mean score (13.2 years) than boomers. We should not be terribly surprised, however, since Xers (many of whom are still in college or other tertiary institutions) average just twenty-four years of age.[13]

Median family income operates in much the same fashion. In general, we observe increasing affluence as one moves from older to younger cohorts—but Generation X once again provides an exception. Although a substantial portion of this variance is undoubtedly due to gen-Xers' still being in school or otherwise positioned early in their careers, the income gap between Xers and boomers is an important point that I will return to later.

Tolerance for the General Idea of Equality

In the late 1950s and early 1960s, both Prothro and Grigg (1960) and McClosky (1964) found that most citizens endorsed abstract democratic norms such as freedom of speech, voting rights, and the general ideas of equality of opportunity and equality before the law. The more recent study by Chanley (1994) likewise revealed widespread support for abstract principles, though there was considerably less tolerance of out-group activities that might affect one's family, friends, or local community. Aside from this important qualification, prior research suggests that we probably should expect to find a fairly high degree of "generic" tolerance among the American public as a whole.

Figure 6.1 presents findings from several additive indices constructed using items in the 1992 ANES survey. First, respondents were asked to agree (strongly or not strongly) or disagree (strongly or not strongly) with six statements concerning the importance of ensuring equal opportunity and equal rights for all citizens; index scores range from +12 to –12, with zero being a true neutral point.[14] The figure breaks down support for equality by

Figure 6.1
Support for Equality, Tolerance of Newer Lifestyles and Homosexual Rights, and Symbolic Racism by Cohort, 1992.

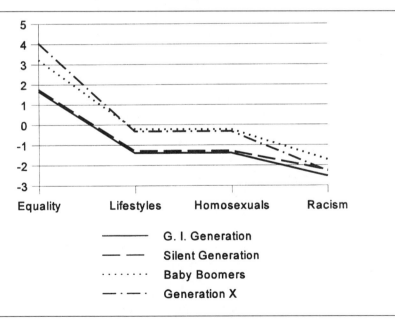

Figures are based on index scores for each age group, with higher values indicating greater tolerance; see text (including notes 14, 17, 19, and 23) for explanation and Appendix for question wordings.
Source: American National Election Study, 1992.

birth cohort, with an average (mean) score being represented as a point on the line. Readers should keep in mind that these data have been weighted so as to remove the effects of intercohort differences in education. Controlling for education is critical because of the consistency with which that variable has been found to be a powerful predictor of political tolerance, even with other independent variables held constant. Thus, if we discover any significant relationships between cohort and tolerance once the impact of education is taken into account (by imposing on each age group an identical mean of twelve years of formal schooling), our results can be taken more seriously as being consistent with the proposition that age does play a role in shaping the attitudes in question.

The mean score for all non-Hispanic whites on our equality scale is +2.77, indicating somewhat more support for equality in the abstract than opposition to it. Looking at the four cohorts, Figure 6.1 depicts an essentially linear pattern of increasing support as one moves from old to young (Xers being most supportive, the G.I. Generation least). The two oldest cohorts are statistically indistinguishable from one another, however, as are the two youngest. That is, the sharpest contrast is between boomers and Xers on the one hand (both relatively more supportive of equality), and the G.I. and Silent generations on the other (both relatively less supportive).[15] It is notable that this relationship persists even with controls for education.[16]

Tolerance for "Deviant Behavior"

The original Stouffer study and many of those that followed focused on Americans' tolerance for specific out-groups either identified by researchers or named by survey respondents themselves. The purpose was to assess the public's willingness to "put up with" various types of "deviant" behavior. At first this approach looked primarily at the activities of left-leaning groups, revolutionaries, and individuals or groups that expressed hostility toward religion. The measurement strategy developed by Sullivan et al. (1982) allowed respondents to select their own least-liked group(s) from a predetermined list, which made theoretical sense during an era when other deviant groups clearly had arisen to replace (or at least join) Communists, Socialists, and atheists in the public's collective mind.

The 1992 ANES included a battery of morality and lifestyle questions that can be used to construct an index of tolerance for deviant *behavior* if not deviant *groups*. These four questions, in the same agree-disagree format as before,[17] deal with the necessity of adjusting to the times one's view of what constitutes moral behavior, being tolerant of people whose standards are different from one's own, the importance of emphasizing traditional family ties, and one's feelings about whether "newer lifestyles" are contributing to the breakdown of society. Mean scores for each cohort, controlling for education, are again presented in Figure 6.1.

The mean for all respondents is −1.71, indicating that non-Hispanic whites tend to be more intolerant of newer lifestyles than tolerant of them. Generationally, the two older cohorts have virtually identical mean scores, as do the two younger groups. In line with the results reported earlier, however, there is a large gap between the two pairs, with younger citizens being significantly more tolerant. Xers, for example, are 1.6 points more tolerant than members of the G.I. generation on this 17-point scale. As before, our findings here are consistent with the hypothesis that youth—either in and of itself (aging), or because of the liberalizing life experiences of recent cohorts (generations)—is a source of increased social and political tolerance.[18]

In much the same vein, I also examined three ANES questions concerning the civil rights of homosexuals. Respondents were asked whether there should be laws to protect homosexuals from job discrimination, whether homosexuals should be allowed to serve in the armed forces, and whether gay or lesbian couples should be permitted to adopt children. These items were combined into an index with scores ranging from −6 to +6, higher values representing greater tolerance for homosexual rights.[19]

The mean score for all non-Hispanic whites is −0.67, which reflects a slight tilt toward intolerance but is nonetheless closer to the neutral point than was true for either equality or newer lifestyles. The cohort pattern depicted in Figure 6.1 is comparable to the other scales, however, with boomers and Xers (mean scores statistically equivalent) exhibiting much higher levels of tolerance than the G.I. and Silent generations (also statistically equivalent), even when education is controlled.[20] Once again, our results are generally consistent with the youthful-tolerance argument.

Tolerance for African Americans

One of the most hotly debated topics in political psychology over the past several years has to do with the proper conceptualization of citizens' attitudes about race. Taking their cue from Kinder and Sears (1981; also see Sears and Kinder 1985), some scholars contend that there are at least two separate dimensions to the antiblack sentiments held by white Americans. One dimension involves what is called *symbolic racism*—prejudice rooted less in the perception that blacks are innately inferior than in the belief that they are "unworthy" because of their failure to embrace "the kind of traditional [or conservative] American moral values embodied in the Protestant ethic" (Kinder and Sears 1981, 416). In short, African Americans are supposedly viewed as lazy, unmotivated violators of the work ethic who have not truly earned their place in American society. The second racial dimension deals with feelings of *racial threat* felt by whites who see themselves as vulnerable, especially to government policies thought to give blacks and other minorities preferential treatment. Thus, it is not racism per se so much as perceived threat that is said to be behind the opposition of many whites to welfare, affirmative action, and related programs.[21]

The 1992 ANES contained measures that appear to tap each of these dimensions, including three policy items pertinent to the notion of racial threat: quotas for black students at colleges and universities, preferential treatment for blacks in hiring and promotion, and, more generally, whether civil rights leaders have been pushing too fast to effect social change (see Appendix for question wordings). Looking at the data (not shown), one is immediately struck by the depth of resistance among non-Hispanic whites of *all* ages to both educational and job-related affirmative action. Opposition to college quotas for blacks is greatest among the two middle cohorts (79.9 percent boomers, 75.6 percent Silent Generation), with Xers and the G.I. Generation not far behind (68.3 and 62.4 percent, respectively). Despite the absence of a clear-cut pattern, it is probably no accident that quotas are especially unpopular among those in the middle of the age spectrum who are likely to have children in college or approaching college age. Opposition to preferential treatment in hiring and promotion is even more widespread (over 80 percent) and pretty much across the board.

When examining respondents' beliefs about the pace of civil rights reform efforts, we see faint echoes of the pattern that emerged earlier for equality and newer lifestyles: Xers and to a lesser extent boomers are marginally more tolerant (that is, more likely to say that civil rights leaders have been pushing too slowly and/or moving at about the right speed) than their G.I. and Silent Generation counterparts. But, as is also true for attitudes toward preferential treatment in hiring and promotion, a chi-square test indicates that there really are no statistically significant differences across the four cohorts. Taken together, these three items relating to racial threat provide little or no support for the argument that younger people are more tolerant.[22]

The second dimension of racial attitudes, called symbolic racism, is measured with an index built from four agree-disagree ANES items that invoke stereotypes and global judgments of one sort or another: that blacks should work their way up "without any special favors," that they have "gotten less than they deserve" in recent years, that they "could be as well off as whites" if they only tried harder, and that the legacy of slavery and discrimination has made it difficult for blacks "to work their way out of the lower class." Index scores range from -8 to $+8$, higher values denoting greater tolerance.[23] With an overall mean of -2.05 for the subsample of non-Hispanic whites, there seems to be more agreement than disagreement with negative racial stereotypes. The mean score for all four birth cohorts is negative as well.

In terms of generational differences, there is less here than initially meets the eye. Figure 6.1 reveals what appears to be a general although nonlinear pattern of increasing tolerance as one moves from old to young— roughly similar to the trend lines for newer lifestyles and homosexual rights. Before controlling for education, however, the only statistically significant cohort differences are between baby boomers on the one hand and all three other cohorts on the other. And when education (itself a highly significant predictor of symbolic racist attitudes) is controlled, even this distinction disappears. That is, once their relatively higher levels of schooling are taken into account, neither boomers nor Xers stand out as being more (or, for that matter, less) tolerant than older Americans. Our findings in this regard are again at odds with the hypothesis that youth contributes to greater tolerance.

Tolerance for Latinos

The striking results just reported would perhaps be only a curiosity were there not some way to assess their external validity. Fortunately, the 1992 ANES also asked a series of questions designed to capture citizens' attitudes toward Latinos in the United States. This allows us to determine, indirectly, whether the absence of generational differences is limited to whites' views of African Americans or whether it is evident in their attitudes toward racial and ethnic minorities in general. Three questions were analyzed (results not shown), having to do with respondents' beliefs that the "growing number of Hispanics" will or will not (1) take away jobs from people already in the country, (2) cause taxes to rise due to increased demand for public services, and (3) improve our culture with new ideas and customs.[24]

Overall, the non-Hispanic white public is moderately supportive of the proposition that the growing Hispanic population will take away jobs from those who are already here. A majority of all four cohorts agree that it is either extremely or very likely that jobs will be lost, though boomers (57.0 percent) and members of the Silent Generation (59.3 percent) are slightly less concerned than Xers (65.2 percent) and members of the G.I. age group (66.4 percent). Taken as a whole, these generational differences do not achieve statistical significance. Still, it is interesting that boomers are a full 8.2 points more tolerant than Xers on the jobs question. It may be the case that thirtysomething and fortysomething boomers (like the Silent Generation) are relatively secure in their jobs and careers and, especially in contrast to younger adults, feel less threatened by the economic threat that an expanding non-Anglo presence might seem to pose in the marketplace. On the other hand, perceptions of economic threat are probably not motivating the retirement-age G.I. Generation, which also expresses a higher level of concern about the loss of jobs. But whatever is causing people to feel the way they do, the distribution of responses raises further doubts about the youthful-tolerance argument.

As for whether growing numbers of Hispanics might lead to higher taxes, at least 60 percent in each cohort—and close to 70 percent among the G.I. and Silent generations—fear they will. Although this item produces the familiar binomial divide that we have encountered on previous occasions (i.e., the older two cohorts more disturbed by the prospect of a tax hike than are boomers and Xers), cross-cohort differences are not statistically significant. Finally, we move to the symbolic question of whether Hispanics will "improve our culture with new ideas and customs." Only a few respondents (16 percent or less in all age groups) anticipate such a result, and the small age-related differences that exist are not significant. Yet Generation X does stand out, by margins of between 2.5 (compared to boomers) and 8.5 (compared to the G.I. Generation) points as the cohort most inclined to believe that Hispanics are *not* a positive cultural force. Considered in tandem with the results for symbolic racism presented in Figure 6.1, the pattern here suggests that, with regard to racial and ethnic stereotyping, the relationship between youth and tolerance posited by Stouffer and others is far from perfect.

The Work Ethic, Intelligence, and Violence

The 1992 ANES included several new items that permit us to delve more deeply into the public's propensity for racial stereotyping. Respondents were asked to place various ethnic groups (whites, blacks, Hispanics, Asian Americans) on seven-point scales according to whether they believed group members to be (1) hard-working or lazy, (2) intelligent or unintelligent, and (3) peaceful or violent (see Appendix for wordings). Scales have been recoded to have a zero midpoint for neutrality (midway between the adjective pair, or an original score of four), positive values for "tolerant" responses (saying that most members of the group are hardworking, intelligent, or peaceful), and negative values for "intolerant" responses; each scale thus ranges between –3 and + 3. Mean scores, broken down by birth cohort, are shown in Figures 6.2 through 6.4.[25]

We begin with Figure 6.2, which presents assessments by non-Hispanic whites (controlling for education) of the work ethic associated with our four target groups. First, the data reveal that birth cohort is a significant predictor of beliefs about the work ethic of whites and blacks, but not of Hispanics and Asian Americans. Second, one is struck by the large gap between the mean scores for whites and Asians versus those for Hispanics and blacks. All four generations apparently feel that the former work harder than the latter. Indeed, the entire subsample of non-Hispanic whites gives blacks an overall negative rating, meaning that blacks tend to be viewed as more lazy than hardworking.

In contrast to the symbolic racial stereotyping scale portrayed in Figure

Figure 6.2
Beliefs about the Work Ethic of Four Ethnic Groups by Cohort, 1992.

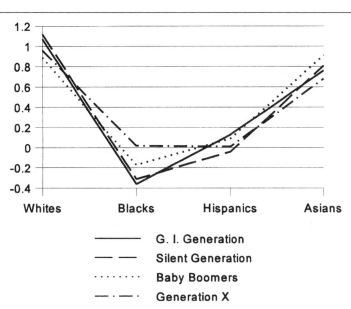

Figures are based on index scores for each age group; see text for explanation and Appendix for question wordings.
Source: American National Election Study, 1992.

6.1, we find a steady progression toward more positive attitudes toward blacks as one moves from old to young, that is, the two younger cohorts are, on balance, more likely than members of the Silent and G.I. generations to believe that blacks are hardworking. Conversely, boomers and Xers are less "tolerant" of whites than are their older counterparts (placing them closer to the lazy end of the continuum), though all four cohorts still tend to view whites as being more hardworking than blacks.[26] In sum, the youthful-tolerance argument gains some modest support here, at least in terms of people's attitudes toward blacks.

The same is true for Figure 6.3, which deals with beliefs about the intelligence of ethnic groups. As before, there are no significant differences among the cohorts in their perceptions of Hispanics and Asian Americans. But while citizens of all ages perceive whites as having more intelligence than blacks, the discrepancy in mean scores is greater for the G.I. and Silent generations than for boomers and Xers (who are statistically indistinguish-

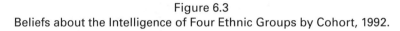

Figure 6.3
Beliefs about the Intelligence of Four Ethnic Groups by Cohort, 1992.

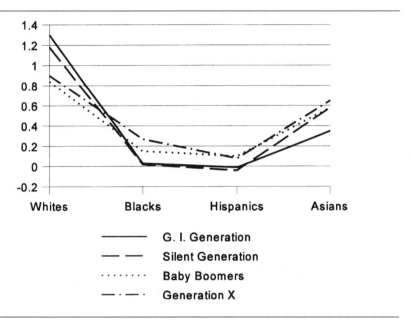

Figures are based on index scores for each age group; see text for explanation and Appendix for question wordings.
Source: American National Election Study, 1992.

able from one another). In other words, younger people tend to see blacks as being more intelligent—and whites as being less so—than their elders do.

Lastly, Figure 6.4 contains some of the most interesting findings that we have seen so far. Unlike the patterns observed for both work ethic and intelligence, birth cohort is a significant predictor of beliefs about the peaceful versus violent proclivities of *all four* ethnic groups: whites, blacks, Hispanics, and Asian Americans. The real surprise, however, lies in the nature of these relationships. Remember that our dependent variable is coded so that decreasing scores reflect the view that members of a group are more violent than peaceful. In the aggregate, there again is a tendency for young and old alike to evaluate whites more favorably (as being less violent) than ethnic minorities, but for boomers and Xers to give whites lower marks (as being more violent) than do older cohorts. What is surprising is the fact that gen-Xers stand out as the most *intolerant* cohort for everyone else as well. That is, Xers are significantly more likely than those born prior to 1964 to suggest

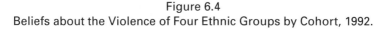

Figure 6.4
Beliefs about the Violence of Four Ethnic Groups by Cohort, 1992.

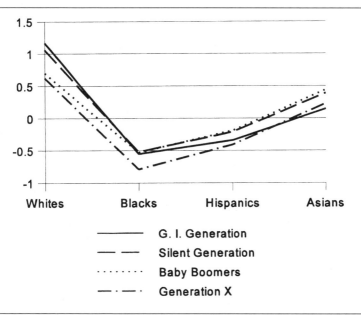

Figures are based on index scores for each age group; see text for explanation and Appendix for question wordings.
Source: American National Election Study, 1992.

that blacks, Hispanics, and Asian Americans are violent rather than peaceful. These results provide further evidence that tolerance is not an inevitable product of youth (see Wilson 1996).

Conclusion

This chapter began with an overview of the literature on age and political tolerance. Nearly all of those who studied popular support for democratic norms during the 1950s, 1960s, and 1970s concluded from their data that, for whatever reason (aging versus life experiences), youth and higher levels of tolerance go hand in hand. An alternative hypothesis is that the perceived rise in tolerance between the 1950s and 1970s was due partly to increased educational opportunities in American society—but also to the coming of age of baby boomers, whose life experiences had indeed predisposed them to be more tolerant (or liberal) in terms of their willingness to "put up with" the beliefs and activities of unpopular out-groups. However, the apparent link between youth and tolerance is not automatic. Unless there is something about the aging process itself that causes people to become less tolerant as they get older, or about the specific life experiences of recent generations that has pushed them in the direction of greater tolerance, there is no reason to expect today's youth to be any more tolerant than their elders.[27]

My approach to studying political tolerance is admittedly different from that used by many other scholars, especially Stouffer (1955) and Sullivan et al. (1982), both of whom were primarily concerned with public tolerance for the civil liberties of either predefined or respondent-selected societal groups. The work presented here follows more closely in the tradition of Sniderman et al. (1989), Prothro and Grigg (1960), and McClosky (1964) in that citizen support for democratic norms is seen as a broader gauge of political and social tolerance in the classically liberal sense. Nevertheless, this discussion has been framed in the context of research done on both general attitudes *and* orientations toward specific out-groups and ethnic minorities. After all, knowing how Americans view certain groups and types of behavior in the 1990s should tell us a lot about our nation's commitment to some of the core values of liberal democracy.

Based on results from the 1992 ANES, we cannot either accept or reject the youthful-tolerance hypothesis without qualification. It seems that there is *some* link between youth and tolerance, most clearly in the areas of support for equality in the abstract, acceptance of behaviors that run counter to conventional social norms, and beliefs about the work ethic and intelligence of African Americans. Yet the review of cohort attitudes toward minority groups yielded a number of inconsistencies, ultimately leaving us with something of a puzzle. How can it be that Generation X is one of the two cohorts (boomers are the other) most supportive of the general idea of equality and most tolerant of newer lifestyles—yet is virtually indistinguishable from its parents' and grandparents' generations on our measure of symbolic racism? And how can it be that Xers (again, with boomers) are more supportive of homosexual rights than their older counterparts, as well as more likely to see blacks as hardworking and intelligent—yet at the same time they acquiesce the least to the notion that Hispanics make a positive contribution to U.S. culture, and they are more inclined than any other cohort to believe that blacks are innately violent?

The answer to these questions probably lies in the fact that gen-Xers have come of political age in a fundamentally different era than did their predecessors. People born between 1943 and 1963 lived as young adults through one of the most tumultuous periods of American history; indeed, many baby boomers helped to change the course of that history through their own direct participation in the political process. Citizens born after 1963 are now living with the backlash against boomer activism, as well as its fiscal and social consequences. It is perhaps telling that Generation X does not even have an illustrative name of its own, but rather is defined in terms of opposition to previous generations. Although the term "baby busters" has been bandied about in the popular press, it is probably no accident that most of those using the term are themselves boomers.

At least two interpretations of the findings reported in this chapter are possible. First, the original hypothesis may be correct, that is, the social and political attitudes of baby boomers are truly anomalous and gen-Xers, with their failure to exhibit the consistently higher tolerance levels normally associated with youth, merely represent a return to more normal patterns. Second, perhaps Generation X is the anomaly: an atavistic, even slightly reactionary group of Americans who have thus far been unable to cope with the mostly positive changes occurring in a nation now run for the most part both politically and financially by boomers. Whatever the truth turns out to be, one fact is beyond dispute: Where attitudes of social and political tolerance are concerned, Generation X is definitely *not* a clone of the baby boomers, nor is it their heir.

Notes

1. Doubts about the existence of such a link are suggested by the support provided by younger German voters for Adolf Hitler's Nazi Party in the 1930s (Childers 1983) and, closer to home, by the opposition to civil rights reform (Lipset 1990) and support for segregationist presidential candidate George Wallace (Converse et al. 1969) among young people in the United States during the 1950s and 1960s.

2. In fact, these were among a number of anticipated social and economic changes (also including greater residential mobility and widespread exposure to images projected by the mass media) that Stouffer (1955, 236) felt would lead to increased tolerance.

3. This reflected a dramatic expansion of educational opportunities (including the G.I. Bill) that made younger Americans much more likely than their parents or grandparents to have finished high school and attended college.

4. This phenomenon reflects the presence of period effects, which "work their will on each generation, reflecting the important events and trends of the time. . . . True period effects have a roughly common impact on all or most segments of society" (Jennings and Niemi 1981, 122; also see Riley 1973).

5. Groups were selected from a list that included targets of both the right (Communists, Socialists, Black Panthers, Symbionese Liberation Army, atheists, pro-abortionists) and the left (fascists, Ku Klux Klan, John Birch Society, anti-abortionists). Presented with this list, respondents were asked to identify which they "liked" the least or "just generally, which group is the most unpleasant?" See Sullivan et al. (1982, 81).

6. In fairness, Sullivan et al. (1982, 31) acknowledged that Stouffer himself was more aware of the limitations of his methodology than were some of those who employed the same or similar questions in their own research.

7. For a sampling of these, see McClosky (1964); Lawrence (1976); Gibson and Bin-

gham (1982); Mueller (1988); Gibson (1992); Chong (1993, 1994); Wilson (1994); Davis (1995).

8. Sniderman and his colleagues also argued that the aggregate increase in tolerance since the 1950s was probably greater than Sullivan et al. are willing to admit (but also see Barnum and Sullivan 1990).

9. These data were made available by the Inter-University Consortium for Political and Social Research. Neither the Consortium nor the original collectors of the data bear any responsibility for the analyses and interpretations presented here.

10. Except for using 1964 rather than 1961 as the starting point for Generation X, this age breakdown follows Strauss and Howe (1991).

11. Further information on these weighting procedures can be obtained upon request from the author.

12. Only Xers eligible to vote in 1992 (born 1964 to 1974) are included in this sample.

13. A further consideration is that, facing the draft and possible military service in Vietnam, many male boomers who might not otherwise have done so chose to pursue graduate work in order to maintain their educational deferment. See U.S. Department of Commerce (1993).

14. See the Appendix for question wordings. The response range for each item was from + 2 (strongest support for the goal of equality) to –2 (least support), with individuals who neither agreed nor disagreed being coded as zero. Cronbach's alpha for the index was .72.

15. Here and throughout the chapter, statistical differences between the four generations are established by Tukey's "Honestly Significant Differences" test. This test indicates whether cohort means on a particular index or single item are sufficiently different from one another to be distinguishable from random fluctuations. See Agresti (1990).

16. Education is, as expected, related to the equality index, with college graduates (especially among boomers) exhibiting the highest levels of support.

17. See the Appendix for question wordings. The response range for each item was again from + 2 to –2 (+ 8 to –8 for the overall index), with zero (neither agree nor disagree) as the true neutral point. Cronbach's alpha for the index was .68.

18. Unlike support for the norm of equality, education is largely unrelated to tolerance for newer lifestyles when birth cohort is controlled.

19. See the Appendix for question wordings. The format in this instance was similar to that described above, with response options ranging from strong support for the policy to strong opposition (and zero as the neutral point). Cronbach's alpha for the index was .75.

20. One's level of formal schooling is a significant predictor in its own right of tolerance for homosexual rights, especially among boomers and Xers.

21. For more on the debate concerning symbolic racism and related attitudes, see Bobo (1983); Bobo and Kluegel (1993); Glaser (1994); Sidanius et al. (1996); Sniderman and Tetlock (1986); Sniderman et al. (1991); Tedin (1994).

22. As one would expect, educational level is related to all of these racial attitudes, i.e., better-educated respondents tend to be more tolerant (or "liberal").

23. See the Appendix for question wordings. As described earlier, individual items were scored from –2 to + 2, with zero as the neutral point. Cronbach's alpha was .76.

24. See the Appendix for question wordings. Although response categories have been combined ("extremely likely" with "very likely," "somewhat likely" with "not at all likely") for presentational purposes, measures of association and statistical significance tests are based on the full range of responses.

25. Because I have not discussed tolerance for Asian Americans (nor is there much prior research dealing with this; but see Wilson 1996; Link and Oldendick 1996), attitudes toward the group are included in this stage of the analysis primarily for comparative purposes.

26. Differences between boomers and gen-Xers are not statistically significant on these items.

27. To the extent that youth *is* associated with greater tolerance, we are left with the question of whether this is due to the effects of life-cycle (remember Winston Churchill) or generational forces—or, conceivably, a combination of the two. Although I have not conducted any formal tests (which would require data that allowed us to observe attitudinal changes occurring within particular cohorts over time), the relative intolerance of young people on at least some of our measures suggests that the "aging conservative" life-cycle argument is seriously flawed.

7

Hazards Lie Ahead: Economic Prospects for Generation X

Steven E. Schier

Some political voices can be heard proclaiming that young Americans today are hurtling toward an economic calamity. For example, there is Third Millennium (1993, 1), a group of some several hundred gen-Xers centered in New York which says, "Like Wile E. Coyote waiting for a twenty-ton Acme anvil to fall on his head, our generation labors in the expanding shadow of monstrous national debt." Ultimately, Xers are seen as facing "the prospect of economic meltdown. At best, the costs of servicing the mushrooming national debt will drain more and more of our national resources. This means a future of economically devastating taxation and minimal government services" (Third Millennium 1993, 3).

What factors would propel the debt to levels so high that the economic welfare of young people might be seriously threatened? Richard Lamm, former Colorado governor and a candidate for the 1996 Reform Party presidential nomination eventually claimed by Ross Perot, believes that we should be especially concerned about the costs associated with funding the retirement of Xers' generational predecessors. According to Lamm, "The gray wave of baby boomers that are heading toward retirement is going to be one of the great challenges in American history. . . . This is going to be a social revolution equal to the civil rights movement in its magnitude" (*St. Paul Pioneer Press* 1996b, A4).

Can the situation really be so bad? How could our national debt, even when it is inflated by higher spending for boomers' retirement, produce such dire consequences for gen-Xers? The following analysis will examine the evidence behind the argument. Although the language cited above is clearly overwrought, there are enough supporting facts to make Xers' future economic prospects worrisome. Reality, in other words, is not altogether consistent with the relative long-term optimism of Xers described earlier in this book (see Chapters 1 and 4). As matters stand currently, serious federal spending problems lie squarely in the path of Generation X. The longer these problems are allowed to fester, the more accurate the dire rhetoric is likely to become.

Since 1969, the federal government has routinely spent more than it takes in, resulting in annual budget deficits for almost the past thirty years. The *national debt* equals the total of all deficits incurred since the nation's beginning. From 1980 to 1996, the debt more than quintupled, growing from $908.5 billion to just over $5 trillion.[1] Future trends, illustrated later in the chapter, indicate continued deficit spending through the year 2006.

What difference have the deficits made thus far? For one thing, they have pushed up the amount of spending devoted merely to paying interest on the national debt. In 1980, the government paid $52.7 billion to finance its borrowing; by 1996, interest payments totaled $240 billion. The difference, $187.3 billion (1.2 percent of all federal spending in 1996), is money that might be used for worthwhile social programs, for cutting taxes, or for reducing the deficit itself. Instead, it goes as interest payments straight to the holders of government securities. We can reclaim this money for other purposes only by reducing the deficit back to its level in 1980, which does not seem likely to occur. Absent some sort of dramatic action, however, the amounts lost for interest payments will grow even larger as the debt continues to rise.

What do these big numbers mean? Some comparisons can provide a fuller perspective on the trends. Economists calculate deficits and national debt in terms of their proportion of the U.S. gross domestic product (GDP), which measures the total worth of a country's production of goods and services in a given year. In 1980, the GDP totaled $2.7 trillion and the budget deficit amounted to $73.8 billion—over 2 percent of GDP. By 1996, the GDP had reached $7.5 trillion with a deficit of $117 billion—1.5 percent of GDP. This looks like progress, except that the deficit peaked in the interim and promises to go up again from now through 2006.

Constant deficits produced another disturbing development: Not only the deficit but also the size of the national debt has been rising as a share of GDP. The proportion more than doubled over fifteen years, from 34.1 percent in 1980 to 70.6 percent in 1995. In fact, our national debt grew much faster than did the overall economy during this same period—a peacetime increase that is unprecedented in our history. Mobilization for World War II drove the ratio as high as 113.8 percent of GDP in 1946, but postwar prosperity reduced it to 26.3 percent by 1979. After that came the new debt explosion. And what did the money buy? Rather than victory in a world war,[2] it bought a private and governmental "consumption binge" (Gramlich 1991, 173–5). Americans enjoyed an artificially high standard of living thanks to public borrowing, a sort of public-sector credit card frenzy. And in the end, they left future generations with the bill in the form of interest payments on a swollen public debt.

What Gen-Xers Will Owe Government

If it is true that, in macroeconomic terms, the recent past has not been especially kind to Generation X (or to any other group of Americans), the more critical question, and one that will occupy our attention for the remainder of this chapter, is what the economic future holds for younger citizens. Our answer begins with a look at federal tax rates for gen-Xers. In 1994, the Clinton administration published an analysis based on "generational accounting" that revealed the probable lifetime tax burdens that would be borne by various generations of Americans. Consistent with the projections of private economists, this analysis provides a benchmark for Generation X's economic welfare.

The results are presented in Table 7.1. Numbers in the table's right-hand column indicate the percentage of lifetime income that people born in different eras have paid or will pay to the federal government (keeping in mind that these totals do not include state and local taxes, which often add another 10 percent to the lifetime rate). Consider the case of a family in which both parents were born in 1920, then had a daughter in 1950; the daughter, in turn, married a man her own age and they had an Xer son in 1970.[3] Whereas the parents will end up paying 29 percent of their lifetime earnings in taxes, their daughter and son-in-law face a tax burden of just over 33 percent—and the Xer grandson will fare worse yet, with a rate of 36.5 percent. Unless changes are made, the situation promises to deteriorate even more dramatically in the years to come, with children of today's gen-Xers (the "future generations" at the bottom of Table 7.1) facing an obviously intolerable tax rate of 82 percent. One reason lifetime rates change in this way over time is that older Americans paid less in during their working years, while benefiting greatly from rising government retirement benefits in recent decades. In effect, current taxpayers pay more now so that current seniors receive more lifetime benefits than they paid in taxes.

Since younger generations pay more, they will not receive nearly as favorable a ratio of benefits to taxes as do older citizens. The cash facts are outlined in Table 7.2. On average, seventy-year-old males in 1992 figured to receive $98,600 more than they paid in; the average net gain for a female of the same age was $124,600.[4] More recent generations do not, however, fare as well. A forty-year-old male baby boomer in 1992 stood to pay $170,900 more in taxes than he will receive in federal benefits, while a forty-year-old female boomer will have to pay $69,100 more in taxes than she receives in benefits. Xers actually fare a little better here, but not much. A male born in 1977 is looking at a lifetime tax loss of $157,200, and a comparable female a loss of $82,500.[5]

The general trend is clear, and it is not good news for either boomers or Xers. In fact, the news is a bit more disturbing than the data presented thus

Table 7.1
Estimated Lifetime Net Federal Tax Rates by Year of Birth

Year of Birth	Lifetime Tax Percentage
1900	23.6
1910	27.2
1920	29.0
1930	30.6
1940	31.9
1950	33.2
1960	35.0
1970	36.5
1980	36.9
1990	36.5
1992	36.3
All future generations	82.0

Source: Office of Management and Budget (1994, 24).

far suggest because the calculations I am using derive from optimistic—and not always realistic—assumptions. One such assumption is that the rate of annual increases in federal health care spending will equal the overall rate of inflation in the economy. As it happens, health care spending, with few exceptions, has exceeded the inflation rate for the past three decades, and according to projections it will continue along the same path. The probable course of spending trends for the 1990s is simply not sustainable. As the administration analysis admits, for example, "A pure extrapolation of recent trends . . . would imply that health care costs would eventually bankrupt the government" (Office of Management and Budget 1994, 24).

Two factors can help us to understand why current spending trends are unsustainable. First, payments on net interest will steadily increase as a percentage of all spending if deficits persist—and the best official estimates are that they will. An even more important factor, however, is that spending on entitlements is set to explode over the next thirty years. *Entitlements*, which amounted to 54 percent of federal government spending in 1994 (Pear 1994,

Table 7.2
Estimated Lifetime Net Tax Payments by Age

Age in 1992	Net Tax Payment (in thousands)*	
	Males	Females
0	78.4	44.1
5	99.3	54.8
10	124.8	67.3
15	157.2	82.5
20	187.7	96.9
25	203.0	101.5
30	201.6	96.9
35	192.4	87.8
40	170.9	69.1
45	132.5	39.7
50	81.0	2.4
55	19.5	-40.2
60	-43.9	-86.3
65	-94.1	-122.5
70	-98.6	-124.6
75	-92.9	-117.9
80	-79.4	-100.5
85	-69.4	-79.3
90	-11.6	-11.1

*Figures are calculated by subtracting tax payments from benefits received. A minus sign indicates that payments are expected to exceed receipts by the amount indicated.
Source: Office of Management and Budget (1994, 26).

A6), are legally mandated, automatic payments to individual citizens. They operate on automatic pilot: When an entitlement becomes law, everyone who qualifies gets the payment unless Congress amends or repeals the program. And restrictions on payments or eligibility are difficult to enact because such programs (e.g., federal health care, including Medicare and

Medicaid; see below) remain popular with most voters. Given their enormous impact on the budget, a closer look at entitlements is in order.

A Tour of the Land of Entitlements

The nation's largest entitlement program is Social Security (OASDI), which provides millions of monthly benefit checks adding up to approximately 22 percent of all federal spending. The acronym OASDI (Old-Age, Survivors and Disability Insurance) indicates the program's beneficiaries. Most recipients are retirees who paid into the fund during their working lives and later began to receive a monthly pension based on their contribution. A payroll tax of 12.4 percent, half paid by the worker and half by the employer, finances the program. An annual COLA, or cost-of-living adjustment, helps to keep benefits in pace with inflation. On top of inflation indexing, benefits for new retirees are raised in line with the growth of real wages (inflation-adjusted wages) in the working sector. This means that each year's new group of retirees starts out at a higher benefit level than the previous year's—a policy that has insured a steady rise in the standard of living among the aged over the past three decades (Morris 1996, 92), but one that has also contributed to Social Security costs' more than doubling over a period of just fourteen years (from $155 billion in 1982 to $348 billion in 1996).[6]

A second major program benefiting retirees is Medicare, a medical insurance plan administered by the federal government. It has two parts. Part A provides hospital insurance, including inpatient stays and related care, and it is automatic for all eligible seniors. Its funding comes from the Medicare portion of the Social Security payroll tax, a 2.9 percent levy divided equally between employers and employees.[7] Part B is an optional insurance program, covering physician and other outpatient costs, available to those who are enrolled in Part A. Although participants pay a monthly premium ($46.10 in 1995) that is deducted from Social Security checks, the general tax revenues of the federal government pay most of the costs of Part B. Despite the benefits included in Parts A and B, Medicare covers less than half the of the health outlays for senior citizens; the remainder is covered (if at all) by private insurance, personal funds, or a third entitlement program that we will be discussing momentarily, Medicaid. Very rapid medical cost inflation has caused the Medicare budget to explode since the early 1980s, from $46.5 billion in 1982 to $197 billion in 1996. Medicare now constitutes 12.5 percent of all federal spending.

Medicaid is yet another health-related entitlement program with a swelling budget. Designed to provide insurance for the medically indigent (those unable to pay for their own care), it is a complex program that is funded and administered—including determination of eligibility—in part by both the state and federal governments. Seventy percent of Medicaid outlays go to fund the elderly poor, though once health care costs deplete the personal assets of other older Americans, the program kicks in to pay for long-term nursing-home care. The federal government's share of Medicaid costs soared from $18 billion in 1982 to $90 billion in 1996 and now comprises 6 percent of all federal spending.

Social Security, Medicare, and Medicaid make up the "big three" of entitlement programs (adding up to 40.5 percent of all federal spending), but they hardly exhaust the list. Many other entitlements (totaling more than 10 percent of federal expenditures) exist as well—for example, civil service and military retirement systems, veterans' benefits, subsidized federal mortgages, and unemployment compensation. And in addition to all of this guaranteed spending, millions of Americans are helped by various tax loopholes, or *tax expenditures*, that lower their taxes below what standard rates would normally require. Howe and Longman (1992, 91) have described such expenditures as "the moral and fiscal equivalent of the government's simply mailing a check. To pay for them, other people's taxes have to be raised, other benefits have to be cut, or the deficit has to be increased." The federal tax deductions for home mortgage payments and employer-paid medical expenses alone bestow about $200 billion in benefits annually.

Who gains the most from entitlements and tax expenditures? Among the biggest winners are the middle class. In 1994, for example, the government in Washington spent $177 billion on entitlements for the poor—but $612 billion on everyone else (Hage et al. 1995, 34). Tax expenditures for health care and home mortgages, in particular, help the middle class (and the rich), since poor people seldom have employer-paid health insurance and do not usually own homes. Adding together tax expenditures and automatic payments to individuals produces a surprising result: In 1991, "One-half (at least $400 billion) of all entitlements went to households with incomes over $30,000. One-quarter (at least $200 billion) went to households with incomes over $50,000" (Howe and Longman 1992, 93). As of 1992, a majority of all households included at least one person receiving an entitlement check, and roughly 30 percent of the overall population enjoyed the benefits of a tax expenditure, such as the home mortgage interest deduction (Congressional Budget Office 1994, xi).

This munificence has its price, and it is one that will weigh heavily on the shoulders of younger Americans over the next several decades. In 1994, President Clinton appointed a bipartisan commission to examine the future of entitlements and taxes. The group issued its report in December 1994 and the news was not good. By a vote of twenty-nine to one, Democrats and Republicans on the commission concluded that (1) by the year 2012, given the continuation of current trends, projected annual spending for entitlements and for interest on the national debt would consume all tax revenues collected by the federal government; (2) by 2030, projected spending for Medicare, Medicaid, Social Security, and federal employee retirement programs alone would have the same effect; and (3) total spending at that point would top 37 percent of GDP, a huge increase from today's level of about 22 percent (Bipartisan Commission on Entitlement and Tax Reform 1994).[8]

Exactly how big a catastrophe are we looking at here? The problems associated with entitlement spending and the burden it will one day place on Xers are finally starting to come into focus, but the longer we wait to address these problems, the more intractable they are likely to become. We do need to recognize, however, that the general pattern is made up of several parts. Some programs face imminent bankruptcy, while others have difficulties that are serious but not yet on the verge of disaster. Let us take a few moments to consider where things stand in a number of different areas.

Medicare: A Clear and Present Crisis

Plainly put, Medicare is in crisis. Both Social Security and Medicare are administered from trust funds, which theoretically accumulate payroll tax revenue that is subsequently distributed in benefits. In practice, it is estimated that Medicare Part A's trust fund (hospitalization insurance) will go bankrupt by the year 2001 (Board of Trustees 1996), after which the fund's projected shortfalls will become ridiculously large (amounting to 4 percent of GDP in 2050) and persist for at least seventy-five years. The spending cuts needed to bring the fund into long-term balance are ten times larger than those proposed in 1995 by President Clinton and five times larger than those proposed by congressional Republicans (Howe and Jackson 1995b). Cuts of this magnitude almost certainly will not be made because most people don't want to kill grandma, but the only other alternative is an increase in taxes to pay for expanded care. Understand, by the way, that these taxes would be *on top of* the higher tax rates for gen-Xers presented in Table 7.1, because those projected rates do not assume a health care crisis like the one that now plagues Medicare Part A.

Medicare Part B (for doctor's fees and supplemental medical services) also faces major funding problems. Spending was $69 billion in 1995 after growing at a 14.8 percent annual clip for the previous twenty-five years. As of 1995, enrollees paid just under 30 percent of total costs through their monthly premiums—while $43.5 billion of the program budget came from general tax revenues. With costs projected to increase rapidly, the proportion that will have to be drawn from general revenues is likely to rise as well.

What has brought us to this point? Demographic factors are part of the story. As life spans steadily lengthen, older Americans use more medical services per capita. Making matters worse, when the large boomer generation retires, the number of Medicare users will skyrocket and costs will escalate even further. Medical technology also plays a role. With medicine more complex and more effective than ever before, it is also more expensive; health care costs for society in general, and for Medicare in particular, increase accordingly. More sick people who would otherwise die are kept alive and receive medical care. In the coming decades, we can expect all of these trends—longer life expectancy, retirees making up a greater proportion of the population, and improved medical technology—to continue, and each will have the effect of pushing up the cost of Medicare. In fact, they already have produced a financial situation that cannot be maintained. An individual who retired in 1990, for example, could look forward to receiving over four dollars in health benefits for every dollar he or she paid into the system (Nasar 1995, 1).

Finally, Medicare also suffers from some fairly serious inefficiencies. A recent study reported that the program pays two-thirds more for certain health treatments than those same treatments cost in Canada (Welch et al. 1993). Although medical inflation has declined in the 1990s, Medicare spending underwent double-digit annual increases. Part of the reason is that no major structural reform of the program has occurred since its creation in 1965, while the organization of private-sector medicine has changed dramatically.[9] Medicare recipients still have an almost unlimited choice of doctors and hospitals, and the government pays for treatments. This gives patients no incentive to economize on care and leaves the government with the bill. More aggressively managed care, common in Canada and in the U.S. private sector, could save Medicare billions of dollars each year.

Medicaid, which has similar inefficiencies and is subject to the same inexorable trends as Medicare, further contributes to the emerging crisis in federal health care funding. Estimates from the nonpartisan Congressional Budget Office (1996a, 46) show federal spending on Medicaid rising from $96 billion in 1996 to $243 billion in 2006, an increase of 253 percent in just ten years. These numbers could become even more daunting if Congress decides to further loosen the requirements for Medicaid eligibility.

Social Security: A Growing Problem

While the growing cost of health care is a clear and present danger to Xers' pocketbooks, the trends in Social Security have yet to reach the crisis stage. Nevertheless, life spans continue to lengthen, and it will not be long before the initial wave of the baby-boom generation begins to retire. The result, inevitably, will be increased spending. It also is important to keep in mind that Xers constitute a much smaller group than boomers. The Social Security Administration estimates that the number of people aged sixty-five (the current retirement age for full benefits) or over will more than double by the year 2030, but the number of working-age people will rise only 25 percent (Congressional Budget Office 1996a, 68)—a development that portends bankruptcy for Social Security trust funds at precisely the time many of today's younger Americans will be nearing fifty and starting to think about retirement themselves.

This will occur even though Social Security is now in the process of accumulating a surplus that should reach $2.3 trillion by 2010 (Board of Trustees 1995, 181). The surplus results from a reform enacted by Congress mandating that, from 1983 to 2013, more money be taken in than is spent in order to build reserves that will be needed when boomers hit retirement age. There is just one problem: The government is not saving the surplus. Instead, it is using the surplus to pay for current operating expenses (see note 6). What the trust funds actually contain, then, is a large supply of Treasury securities, or IOUs. The policy is one that allows the government to spend the surplus as it is collected and thereby shift the bill for boomers' retirement to gen-Xers during the latter's prime earning years. According to Charles Morris (1996, 132), the consequences are that "[w]hen the trust funds begin calling in the government IOUs at an annual average clip of $150 billion-plus fifteen to twenty years from now, the government will have to scramble to raise the cash from that generation of workers and taxpayers. That is not what most people would understand as a 'surplus.' " The longer the system continues to operate as it does, the more money Xers will have to pay later on. Reform of Social Security is clearly in Xers' personal self-interest.

In fairness, Social Security has in one important sense been a grand success: It dramatically improved the lot of senior citizens. The median net worth of those over age sixty-five, for example, is now double that of all other Americans (Shapiro 1995, 4). But let us also recognize that Social Security, with nearly two-fifths of its benefits going to households whose incomes are above the national median (Peterson 1996, 72), helps the affluent elderly as well as the less affluent. Future projections indicate that this cannot continue indefinitely. As with Medicare, the question becomes how much money retirees—especially those who do not need it—are entitled to take from the pockets of working gen-Xers.

Unfunded Liabilities: Other Problems

Beyond Social Security and Medicare lie other financial burdens for members of Generation X. The federal government has legislated numerous additional entitlements to groups of citizens without specifying how they will be paid for. Such *unfunded liabilities*, which are simply legal requirements to provide specified benefits without secure funding, presumably will be covered by future taxes. As we have seen, however, tax revenues will likely prove inadequate to make good the government's promises. Once again, Americans face the prospect of having to make painful adjustments in the coming decades.

Medicare and Social Security are the two largest unfunded liabilities, but others exist. One of these, the civil service retirement system, pays benefits to former civilian employees of the federal government. The present system guarantees more than $1,158 *trillion* in benefits (about 40 percent to current retirees and the rest, calculated on the basis of today's dollars, to those still working when they retire; Longman 1996, 158)—an amount that would require roughly $4,600 from each and every citizen. Unfortunately, no cash reserves exist to defray the costs of this obligation (Office of Personnel Management 1993, 158).

Although federal employees often receive salaries lower than what they would earn in comparable jobs outside of government, their pension system helps to make up the difference. First, the monthly benefits of federal retirees are, on average, more than double those of the average private-sector pension. And second, the median age at which civil servants begin taking a pension is fifty-eight—as opposed to sixty-two in the private sector; Howe and Jackson 1995a. ii). Finally, federal retirees also receive generous health care coverage that is heavily subsidized by taxpayers (Congressional Budget Office 1993).

Military pensions constitute another large unfunded liability that future generations will have to confront. Uniformed military personnel can retire after serving just twenty years on active duty, with pensions ranging from 50 to 75 percent of their final base pay (fully indexed for inflation). In contrast, the typical private-sector pension contains no indexation for inflation and equals 25 to 30 percent of final pay. A military officer who retired in 1996, at age forty-two with twenty years of experience, could expect to receive $1.1 million in pension checks before turning fifty-five, plus another $1 million by age seventy-five. Benefits at the level currently authorized by Congress amount to about $3,000 for every citizen, adding to a grand total of $713.4 billion (U.S. Department of Defense 1994, 13). Moreover, military retirees can count on receiving Social Security benefits at age sixty-two and Medicare at age sixty-five (Goldrich 1993, 1).

There also are substantial guarantees of medical care for the men and women with military service. According to the Department of Veterans Affairs (VA), the present value of promises made to former servicepeople is more than $189 billion (U.S. Department of the Treasury 1993). These benefits include disability checks, which are distributed liberally to claimants. The General Accounting Office, a research arm of Congress, estimates that over 390,000 veterans receive VA compensation payments, totaling $1.2 billion a year, for diseases and physical injuries neither caused nor made worse by military service (Longman 1996, 132). The Department of Veterans Affairs also administers an extensive system of 171 hospitals and 131 nursing homes for veterans. It provides care for illnesses and injuries regardless of whether they are service connected. Not surprisingly, the cost of health care spending for veterans has more than doubled since 1980 (Stewart and Crouse 1993, 1).

Political discourse in the 1990s has rarely addressed the promises that gen-Xers will ultimately be expected to keep with their tax dollars. Defenders of Social Security often point to its existing surplus (no matter that the surplus is made of Treasury bonds rather than cash), and the price tag for other entitlement programs tends to get short shrift as well. The imminent Medicare crisis, however, is close to becoming the first of several big "news events" that will heighten the public visibility of unfunded liabilities, with Social Security and civil service and military pension programs facing similar problems early in the twenty-first century. Recall from our earlier discussion the extent to which lifetime tax rates are projected to increase for gen-Xers (and for future generations). The calculations in Table 7.1 assume the existence of a large cash surplus for Social Security (not IOUs) over the coming decades, along with a sharp decline in health care inflation. Neither condition seems at all likely to be met. To the contrary, unfunded liabilities could lead to an increase in lifetime taxes for Xers above the already high levels shown in the table. These long-term concerns require that we look at federal deficits in a new light.

The Deficit and Debt Revisited

The "good" news concerning recent efforts to reduce the deficit turns out not to be quite as good as it first appeared. Table 7.3 presents two types of deficit calculations. Figures in column 2, based on standard Washington accounting procedures, are the Congressional Budget Office's best estimates of budget deficits from 1996 through 2006. The Congressional Budget Office (1996a, xxv) described the general path here as "not particularly alarming" since deficits are projected to stay within about 3 percent of GDP (column 3)—a level many economists find acceptable. But the fourth column lists annual Social Security surpluses, totaling $1.08 trillion, that should pile up over the same eleven-year period. The problem is that these funds will be borrowed to cover annual expenditures. Thus, in reality, the federal government will be spending more than it collects each year in an amount equal to both the conventional deficit *and* the Social Security surplus. Using 1996 as an example, we see that the government was expected to spend $180 billion more than it took in (column 5), but then borrow $64 billion from Social Security, leaving a conventional deficit of $116 billion (1.9 percent of GDP versus the 2.7 percent indicated in column 6). Gen-Xers should be aware that it is their future tax revenues that will be used to pay off the $1.08

Table 7.3
Conventional and Actual Deficit Calculations, 1996–2006

Year	Conventional Deficit (In billions)	Deficit as Percent of GDP	Social Security Surplus (in billions)	Actual Deficit (In billions)	Deficit Percent of GDP
1996	116	1.5	64	180	2.5
1997	171	2.2	72	243	3.1
1998	194	2.4	76	270	3.3
1999	219	2.5	84	303	3.5
2000	244	2.7	92	336	3.7
2001	259	2.7	97	356	3.7
2002	285	2.9	104	389	4.0
2003	311	3.0	110	421	4.1
2004	342	3.1	117	459	4.2
2005	376	3.3	127	503	4.4
2006	403	3.3	137	540	4.4

Source: Congressional Budget Office (1996a: 31, 54). The 1996 deficit totals are from the Congressional Budget Office (1996b, 12).

trillion in Social Security surpluses that have been used to finance current governmental programs and activities.

The predicament facing gen-Xers is relatively straightforward. First, they will be forced to endure higher lifetime tax rates even if health care inflation plummets and government stops using the Social Security surplus to cover current spending. Second, because of the proliferation of unfunded liabilities, entitlements are projected to consume the entire federal budget by the year 2030. Under the circumstances, there would seem to be only two available courses of action: Either (1) the government gets serious about budget balance now or (2) Xers can count on paying taxes in the coming decades which are even higher than those already anticipated.

Leading economists of both political parties have therefore urged that the government begin running budget surpluses—not deficits—as soon as possible. Republican Alan Greenspan (1994), chairman of the Federal Reserve Board, and Democrat Robert Reischauer (1994), former head of the Congressional Budget Office, are among those who have spoken out in this regard. Surpluses would provide a stronger foundation for dealing with the oncoming crisis in Medicare, and they would bolster Social Security by building up reserves for the day when baby boomers begin to leave the workforce. It is especially imperative that government start saving, because boomers and Xers themselves have not. Overall, our record in total personal and national savings has been miserable during the deficit era; the United States ranks last among the ten largest industrial economies in the world in both areas (Peterson 1993, chart 3.5). Federal deficits combined with low personal savings assure that future problems will be just that much worse.

Economist Lawrence Kotlikoff, creator of "generational accounting," explains the boomers' plight.

> The current low rate of U.S. saving is particularly surprising coming, as it does, at a time when the sizable baby boom generation (those born between 1947 and 1964) should be starting to put some money aside for retirement. The propensity of Americans to retire from their main job at earlier and earlier ages (retirement at age fifty-five is now common), coupled with our increasing life expectancies, spells a long period of retirement for baby boomers. If baby boomers are saving less and are likely to retire early, how will they support themselves in old age (Kotlikoff 1992, 2–3)?

An answer to this question comes from Lawrence Thompson, economist and former Social Security deputy commissioner. "Don't be fooled," he said, speaking of the trust funds he helped to administer. "When the smoke clears, you're either going to have people putting in more while working longer, or accepting lower monthly benefits when they retire" (*St. Paul Pioneer Press* 1996a, A20).

Some analysts take a contrary view, suggesting that continued economic growth will lead to higher living standards for both boomers and Xers and make the trends described earlier less threatening than they appear (Kinsley 1994, A15). Although higher growth would indeed produce more money with which to confront our problems, the deficit numbers in Table 7.3 already assume a 2.1 percent growth rate in real (inflation-adjusted) GDP—a moderate level of economic expansion. Also, an important point to recall is that even if these expectations are exceeded, Xers will not necessarily reap the rewards because of the higher lifetime tax burden they may be asked to bear.

Dealing honestly with the difficulties posed by unfunded liabilities will not be a walk in the park politically. Recent opinion polls reveal that public support for budget cutting is often inversely proportional to the size of the programs to be cut. For example, large majorities want to reduce the amount of aid that the United States sends to foreign countries (less than 2 percent of total spending)—but fewer than one in four endorse reductions in Medicare or Social Security (Peterson 1996, 70). As of today, the average American understands little about current spending patterns or their likely future trends (Penny and Schier 1996, 66–9). That will change, however, as the bad news mounts. The key question is whether it will change in time to make a difference. If reform begins immediately, the dire rhetoric about Generation X's future may prove ill founded. It is therefore critical for gen-Xers to understand better their personal stake in quick and effective action.

The Stakes for Xers

Recent official estimates on the future of Medicare and Social Security can be summarized in personal terms. According to its Board of Trustees (1996), the Medicare Part A (hospitalization insurance) trust fund will go broke in the year 2001, when Xers born in 1975 turn twenty-six. The Board of Trustees (1995) for Social Security reports that those trust funds will run annual operating deficits beginning in 2013, when the same Xers turn thirty-eight. Unless the trust funds have actual surplus money, the government will have to borrow funds from other sources in order to cover its annual deficits. In that sense, Social Security also will be broke, and taxpayers will then be forced to make good on the IOUs that have been accumulating in the trust funds. The president's Bipartisan Commission on Entitlement and Tax Reform (1994) estimated that entitlements and debt interest alone would consume all federal revenue by 2012, when our Xers turn thirty-seven. People in this age bracket will thus have to endure payroll taxes equaling an astronomical 38.4 percent of income in order to receive the Social Security and Medicare benefits that have been promised them beginning at age sixty-five (Longman 1996, 12).

Such discouraging tax news might cause some Xers to panic, but it shouldn't, because the nightmare is unlikely to come true. Before Xers reach retirement, benefits will probably be lower, and taxes, as a result, not as high as anticipated. Still, even if this happens, it is a virtual certainty that Xers (and their children) will have higher lifetime tax rates than even those projected in Table 7.1. In short, younger Americans need to prepare themselves for higher taxes—and fewer benefits—than exist today.

What steps can be taken to improve the lot of gen-Xers? A balanced budget would help. The Congressional Budget Office (1996a, xxiv) calculates that "permanently balancing the budget could raise real incomes in the United States from 10 percent to 15 percent by 2025 and by larger percentages in years thereafter." Lower deficits would lead to lower interest rates, thereby spurring economic activity and raising living standards. Federal Reserve Board chairman Alan Greenspan (1994) estimates that permanent budget balance would reduce interest rates by up to 2 percentage points. And what difference would that make to a gen-Xer?

Take the case of a student who has just graduated from a four-year private college with student loan obligations of $71,000, repayable over ten years (at $876 per month) at 8.25 percent interest. If interest rates drop 2 points, the student's monthly payment declines by $74, for a yearly savings of $888, or $8,885 over the term of the loan. Imagine another student who has graduated from a four-year public university with a typical ten-year loan obligation totaling $34,248. A 2-point drop in interest rates lowers the monthly payment from $420 to $385 and ultimately saves the student $4,263 over the life of the loan. Permanently lower interest rates would make it possible for more Xers to buy cars and homes and to put their children through college.[10]

Balancing the budget, however, requires a complete rethinking of the entitlement state that has been created over the past several decades. How can the growth of Social Security, Medicare, Medicaid, veterans' benefits, civil service and military pensions, and other smaller entitlements be restrained? What tax expenditures can be curtailed? Answering both questions requires a reappraisal of who is really deserving, and in what degree. Yet budget balance remains only a minimal goal. Budget surpluses would be even better because they could avert the need for large tax increases when baby boomers retire. Decisions must be made now with the future in mind. The real conflict is not between today's retirees and taxpayers, but between boomer retirees and the Xer taxpayers of tomorrow.[11]

Conclusion

The dreadful predictions by Third Millennium and Richard Lamm noted at the beginning of this chapter are far from certain to come true. Nevertheless, the longer our political system puts off dealing with the huge costs of federal entitlement, the more accurate the predictions are likely to become. Bennett and Craig (Chapter 1; also see Chapter 4) found that, at least in the early 1990s, gen-Xers were not particularly gloomy, compared to older cohorts, about their economic prospects. Such optimism hardly seems justified when one examines the best evidence available; in fact, that evidence points strongly in the opposite direction. America's national debt is at a level often found at the end of a major war, yet the vast cost of millions of boomer retirees lies only a few years away. It is time for young people to understand what the future holds for them. Budget balance and entitlement reform, if accomplished soon, can provide a sound basis for Xer optimism. But Xers themselves must take responsibility for forcing their political leaders to take the appropriate action, and to do so quickly. According to the Congressional Budget Office (1996a, xxv), "Eliminating deficits projected for the next ten years will provide noticeable economic benefits during that time period and will ameliorate the longer-term budget problem. But the real payoff will come from taking steps to prevent the impending demographic pressures from pushing up the deficit dramatically in the next century. Because the deficits and debt that would result if there are no changes are not sustainable, such changes are inevitable. But the changes will be less painful, and the benefits greater, if the problem is dealt with sooner rather than later."

Notes

1. The historical numbers are from the Council of Economic Advisers (1995), while the 1996 figures are from the Congressional Budget Office (CBO) (1996a). Note that the total national debt reported here is larger than the "debt held by the public" totals employed by the CBO and used in this chapter's tables. A bit more than $1 trillion in additional debt is owed by the government to itself, mostly to various trust funds. As we shall see, the Social Security trust fund is a large potential problem for gen-Xers.

2. There are those, of course, who contend that heightened defense spending during the Reagan years (a major contributor to current deficits) did help to end the cold war by forcing the Soviet Union to allocate money it did not have and could not afford in a futile effort to maintain its own defense capabilities. See, for example, Winik (1996).

3. The daughter here has been allowed to become a mother relatively early in life so that her son (the Xer) would more comfortably fit within one of the birth-cohort frameworks utilized by other contributors to this book. Nevertheless, as should be apparent, my own usage of the term *Generation X* is considerably broader; it includes, as a matter of convenience, young people generally, including those who have not yet entered the electorate—and who future research might find belong to a different political generation altogether (see the discussions in Chapters 1 and 4).

4. The net payment in Table 7.2 "is the difference between the present value of taxes that a member of each generation will pay, on average, over his or her remaining life and the present value of the transfers he or she will receive." See Office of Management and Budget (1994, 26).

5. In all of these calculations, women do better than men because they tend to live longer and therefore collect a larger amount in retirement benefits later in life.

6. Higher costs are not the only problem plaguing Social Security. In fact, the program has for some time been accumulating an annual surplus (more on this later in the chapter) that could be counted as "assets"—the value of which were then subtracted before calculating a deficit figure for the federal government as a whole. The accounting procedure employed here is questionable because the surplus money is only *lent* to the government to pay for current deficit spending; in return, the funds receive what amounts to an IOU in the form of Treasury bonds. Since the bonds must eventually be paid from future tax revenue, what at first appears to be a surplus is actually an unfunded liability that gen-X taxpayers will have to make good at some later point in time. Since 1983, the Congressional Budget Office has been required to report annual deficits both before and after subtracting the money borrowed from Social Security—an approach that, if nothing else, allows for more accurate assessment of the deficit's size in terms of its burden on future taxpayers.

7. In 1994, Congress increased taxes on well-off retirees to help pay for the growing costs of Part A.

8. These projections were based on economic assumptions about the 1990s that proved to be slightly pessimistic. Specifically, the commission assumed that the federal deficit would average 2.5 percent of GDP from 1995 to 1999; it now appears likely to average about 2.3 percent. Such a small change would, however, alter the final numbers very little (see Congressional Budget Office 1996a).

9. An example is the increased emphasis on managed care, in which health providers have restructured medical care in an effort to reduce costs. See Zelman (1996).

10. The examples discussed in this paragraph are taken from Business Roundtable (1996).

11. Most, though not all, economists believe that large perpetual budget deficits are a problem for America's economic future. Some (e.g., Eisner 1994; Heilbroner and Bernstein 1989) actually argue that persistent deficits help the economy.

8

Losing Canada? Generation X
and the Constitutional Crisis

Michael D. Martinez

Canada represents a crucial case for the study of Generation X. As we shall see, contemporary Canadian society is rife with political ambiguities that should be a natural nurturing ground for the sort of resignation and withdrawal often attributed to gen-Xers in the United States (see Chapter 2). Our North American neighbors share a high level of economic development, and their 1989 Free Trade Agreement and the 1993 North American Free Trade Agreement with Mexico have only served to strengthen an economic interdependence that has existed to some extent since the middle of the nineteenth century.

However, despite these strong economic links and the penetration of American entertainment into Canadian media markets, clear differences in the cultures of the two countries remain (Lipset 1990; Merelman 1991). Canadians are more communally oriented, more likely to respect the importance of maintaining order, and more egalitarian in their approach to social issues. Ethnic tensions are felt in both countries, but ethnic politics in Canada are complicated by the politics of language and the very real threat of Quebec's separation. Any similarities between Canadian and American Xers would therefore be testimony to the power of social and economic forces to effect generational change across political and cultural boundaries. On the other hand, significant differences between Americans and Canadians of this generation would suggest the importance of a nation's political culture in shaping change. This chapter will review recent political changes in Canada and examine their impact on the attitudes of different age groups in that country.

Canadians who came of political age in the 1980s and 1990s entered a political culture in suspended transition. Since its Confederation in 1867, Canada has been home to both an English-speaking (anglophone) majority and a French-speaking (francophone) minority. In recent years, the French-speaking population in Canada has become increasingly concentrated geographically in the province of Quebec. While the proportion of francophones in Canada has declined from 29 percent in 1951 to 24 percent in 1991, due to differences in birth rates and migration, the francophone share of Quebec's population increased slightly over the same period (from 82.5 to 83.2 percent). By 1991, fully 86 percent of Canada's francophones lived in Quebec (Gibbins 1994, 97–108).

These changes in population patterns have corresponded to a shift in identity among many Quebec francophones from "Canadiens" to "Québécois," as well as a rise in pro-independence movements and political parties (Saywell 1977). Parti Québécois governments have called referenda on sovereignty twice, and both times Quebec voters declined the invitation to secede (59 percent to 41 percent in 1980; 50.6 percent to 49.4 percent in 1995). But the later vote was so close that the government of Quebec has promised another referendum soon, and Canadians continue to wait and debate their country's future. The very existence of Canada as a bilingual nation has been continually debated during the entire lifetime of gen-Xers, who have witnessed their political elders' disagreements about both Canada's history and its future.

While the Quebec question has forced a reconsideration of what kind of national identity could bind the country together, Canadians have also been faced with the ever-present question of what makes their country distinct from the United States. The new political uncertainty is compounded by the continued and expanded American influences on Canadian culture (LeDuc and Murray 1983), including the perceived Americanization of entertainment (Fletcher and Taras 1995, 298–301), the Canadian economy (Williams 1995), and the judicial system (Jhappan 1995; Knopf and Morton 1992). To be sure, American influence has loomed large throughout Canada's history, but tightened economic interdependence and technological innovations (including cable, satellite, and the Internet) have rapidly increased American penetration into Canadian markets. Thus, the question of national identity has at least two dimensions: First, what commonalities tie together as "Canadians" anglophones, francophones, natives, and others from across the vast territorial expanse? And, second, what distinguishes Canada from the United States?

Recent political developments highlight the national unity debate. For example, the 1993 national election saw the rise of two federal political parties (the Bloc Québécois in Quebec and Reform in Western Canada), each of which reinforced existing regional divisions,[1] and the decline of two traditional parties (Progressive Conservatives and the New Democratic Party) that had tried to bridge these cleavages. Only the Liberals, under Prime Minister Jean Chrétien, were able to elect candidates from each of Canada's regions to the House of Commons in 1993. The Bloc Québécois, committed to representing Quebec's interests in Ottawa while working for the province's separation, captured 54 of Quebec's 75 seats and became the official Opposition in the House. Reform, largely reflecting Western populism and a hard line on accommodations to Quebec, emerged as the third largest party in the House. The Progressive Conservatives, who had formed the previous government and for many years tried to promote unity through brokerage politics, were reduced from a majority government to two seats in the House. The New Democratic Party, which preached national unity through a social democratic ideology, also suffered big losses in the 1993 election (see Nevitte et al. 1995).

In short, recent changes in the Canadian political landscape underscore the regional cleavages that have accumulated over the last thirty years. From quite different perspectives, Quebec nationalists and Western regionalists have grown frustrated at the center's attempts to fiddle compromises while Canada burns, and the prospects for a successful resolution of the constitutional crisis only seem to be getting worse as the arena for resolution has shifted from elite consociationalism to public referenda (Gibbins 1995). While the potential for disintegration in the form of Quebec's separation continually hovers over the country, its realization has thus far been frustrated by the ambivalence of Quebec voters and by internal divisions among its political elite. Canadians, Canadiens, Québécois, and Quebeckers[2] have not decided on a divorce just yet, but their marriage has been in trouble for nearly two decades. At the same time, there is a growing realization that public-sector deficits have been consuming ever-greater shares of the nation's economic output—thereby casting some doubt as to whether Canada (with or without Quebec) can continue to provide the combination of growth and compassion necessary to maintain what is, according to the United Nations Human Development Index, one of the world's most enviable living standards.

Nevertheless, although gen-Xers in Canada are indeed pessimistic about the country's future, the following analysis will show that pessimism is rooted more in perceptions of Canada's political challenges than in any lack of confidence about its economic opportunities. While their neighbors to the south may be anxious about their place in a rapidly changing economy, Canadian Xers are actually more confident about Canada's economic prospects than about its political future. Ironically, such concerns are coupled with attitudes that are at least somewhat more accommodating to a potential resolution of the national crisis. Whether those attitudes will endure long enough for this generation to gain political power is an open question.

Defining Cohorts

In this chapter, cohorts are defined by political history. Canadians born before 1943 entered adulthood (roughly, age eighteen)[3] during a time in which questions of national identity were more concerned with removing the legacy of the British Empire from national symbols than with Quebec's place within Canada. Although the British government abdicated any authority to interfere with Canadian legislation in the 1930s, the flag featuring the Union Jack and the official national anthem, "God Save the Queen," served as reminders of the colonial past until they were replaced in the 1960s by the maple leaf flag and "O Canada."[4]

There is, of course, little doubt that Canada's linguistic cleavages were important in shaping these debates, but through the 1950s the French-speaking majority in Quebec were more likely to think of themselves as Canadiens than as Québécois. The Catholic Church's control of educational and social policy, combined with economic dominance by anglophone Canadian and U.S. entrepreneurs, left most Quebec francophones with just enough skills and resources to provide the labor for anglophone capital. Nevertheless, francophones achieved significant political representation in the Canadian government as traditions of alternating power and allocation of powers developed in a number of institutions (McRoberts 1995). Alienation was also developing among Canadians in the Maritime and Western provinces, where citizens felt dominated by the financial and political center of the country (defined as various permutations of Ontario, Quebec, and the federal government).

Early baby boomers, identified here as the cohort born from 1943 to 1957, came of age during a truly revolutionary era. In the mid–1960s, Canada changed its national symbols, including the national anthem and flag, to further distance the country from its colonial roots. But it also began to hear new demands from francophones that they not be treated as strangers in their own country and that francophone Québécois become *maîtres chez nous* (masters in our own house). A 1963 report of the Royal Commission on Bilingualism and Biculturalism noted a strong association between speaking French and *lower* incomes in Quebec, a finding which captured the economic stratification that existed among English-speaking entrepreneurs and managers, bilingual foremen, and francophone laborers (Dion 1992, 97).

This report reflected some of the frustrations expressed by Quebec francophones in the Quiet Revolution that had spread across the province. French-speaking intellectuals rose in opposition to the Church's dominance over education, labor demanded more public services from the provincial government, and a budding entrepreneurial class demanded greater access to capital. Some intellectuals, including Pierre Trudeau, advocated a liberal conception of language as an important right of all *individuals*, requiring protection by a strong national policy of bilingualism. Others, including René Lévesque, sought to strengthen the hand of the Quebec provincial government in protecting and promoting francophone *society* within the province itself.

Quebec voters either ignored or failed to recognize the tension between these approaches, providing strong support for the federal Liberal Party under Trudeau throughout the 1960s and 1970s, as well as growing support for French nationalist parties (such as the new Parti Québécois) in provincial elections (Dion 1992). The federal government passed the Official Languages Act in 1969, thereby securing the right of any Canadian to receive services from the federal government in either English or French. Language and cultural issues had transformed politics in Quebec and throughout Canada.

Late boomers, born from 1958 to 1971, entered political adulthood as Canada began seriously to question its own survival. The Parti Québécois came to power in the 1976 Quebec elections and pledged a referendum on separation from the rest of Canada. Sovereignists argued that French culture and language could not be protected under the Canadian federal system in which francophones represented a permanent (and diminishing) minority population. Federalists, led by Prime Minister Trudeau, pledged a renewed federalism under a new constitutional arrangement. When the question was finally posed to the Quebec electorate in 1980, 60 percent of voters (including an overwhelming majority of anglophones and a simple majority of francophones) voted against a somewhat ambiguous proposal for "sovereignty-association."[5] However, Prime Minister Trudeau's attempt to remove the last vestiges of British colonialism through patriation of the Canadian constitution in 1982 exacerbated rather than resolved the crisis.[6]

The constitutional package was approved without the assent of Quebec's separatist premier, René Lévesque, prompting Quebec sovereignists and others to accuse Trudeau of betraying the promises he had made during the 1980 referendum campaign (Gibbins 1994, 338–9). A 1987 agreement by Brian Mulroney, the first Progressive-Conservative prime minister from Quebec, and the ten provincial premiers (including a Liberal premier of Quebec) meeting at Meech Lake appeared to resolve the crisis, but opposition later intensified, and the pact expired in 1990 without the required ratification by provincial legislatures in Manitoba and Newfoundland (Dion 1992, 111–7). As late boomers entered adulthood, they saw Pierre Trudeau, a Liberal prime minister from Quebec, fail to satisfy the government of his home province, and Brian Mulroney, a Progressive-Conservative prime minister from Quebec, fail to obtain the needed support from the rest of Canada. These unsuccessful constitutional negotiations left the nation exhausted and the unity crisis unsettled.

Generation X, composed of those born since 1972, has come of political age under this cloud of doubt about the nation's future. In 1992, they saw another package of constitutional amendments attempting to resolve the crisis fail under the weight of the politics of inclusion. The public debate on constitutional revision had sparked others to clamor for their own share of the political pie. Specifically, Westerners demanded a greater share of power in the central government, and aboriginals insisted on a greater share of self-government. An accord reached at Charlottetown between Prime Minister Mulroney and the ten provincial premiers created a formula that was designed to address all of these demands, as well as those introduced by the Liberal Quebec government.[7]

While the ministers who negotiated the agreement had hoped to create a "logroll" of public support by agreeing to each sector's principal demand, the 1992 national referendum campaign that followed became more of an "inverted logroll" in which each sector objected to the provisions meant to satisfy other groups (Johnston 1993). Québécois opposed provisions that would have increased the institutional power base of Westerners, while many anglophones disapproved of the effort to placate Quebec demands for its recognition as a distinct society and a guaranteed share of seats in the House of Commons (Gibbins 1994, 349–52). The crisis thus remained unresolved. In the subsequent federal election, two new regional parties (Bloc Québécois and Reform) emerged as opposition to the new Liberal government under Chrétien, and two old national parties (Progressive Conservatives and New Democrats) were reduced to electoral rubble (Nevitte et al. 1995). The Parti Québécois was returned to power in Quebec in 1994, giving the province another referendum on sovereignty in October 1995. Again, federalists staved off a majority vote for separation, but by the barest of margins (50.4 percent to 49.6 percent).

We shall see that the evolving and unresolved political uncertainty has left a generation of new Canadians uncertain about their country's future yet, ironically, possessing attitudes that seem more conducive than those of their elders to a resolution of the national crisis. The new economic uncertainty plaguing many advanced postindustrial societies has not created an apathetic or angry cohort of young Canadians. Instead, political uncertainties prominent in recent years have left this group pessimistic and divided about what it means to be a Canadian.

Affect for Canada, 1974

The unresolved debate about Canada's constitution and its future has taken a toll on the overall level of popular support for the country. One measure of support is the "feeling thermometer," in which survey respondents are asked to indicate how warmly they feel about something or someone. Scores range between zero (indicating a "very cool" or negative evaluation) and 100 (indicating a "very warm" or positive assessment). Feeling thermometers are commonly used in the United States (see Appendix) and Canada to measure overall affective evaluations of political leaders

(Markus and Converse 1979; Brody 1991; Johnston et al. 1992), parties (Wattenberg 1994; Craig 1985), and social groups (Conover and Feldman 1981).

Canadian scholars have often employed feeling thermometers to assess overall affect for Canada as a whole and for its various provinces. Looking at surveys conducted between 1974 and 1980, Harold Clarke and his colleagues found that Canada evoked warm feelings among its citizens and, as expected, that the country was ranked higher on the feeling thermometer than either its government or its politicians. However, there were some notable variations across both region and time. Affect for Canada was highest in Ontario, somewhat lower in the west and in Atlantic Canada, and lowest in Quebec (Clarke et al. 1979, 70). Further, the average feeling-thermometer score fell slightly in the five years between the 1974 and 1979 federal elections (from 84 degrees to 80) before rebounding to 83 in the following year (Clarke et al. 1984, 41–2). Perhaps more importantly, the Clarke group discovered that older people tended to rate Canada higher than younger people did. Among Westerners in 1974, for example, the average rating for the oldest cohort (those born before 1915) was 91 degrees, while Westerners born between 1945 and 1955 gave Canada a mean score of 82. There were similar patterns in Quebec and Atlantic Canada, although differences among age groups in Ontario were much less pronounced (Clarke et al. 1979, 76).

Why are older Canadians' feelings for their country warmer than those of younger cohorts? There are two kinds of explanations for age differences: life-cycle and generational (also see Chapter 1). A life-cycle explanation would suggest that as a person gets older, his or her feelings for Canada are enhanced by a myriad of changes in lifestyle and an accumulation of life experiences. As one ages, for example, one might pay more attention to the news media and its relative emphasis on Canada (as opposed to the heavy attention given to U.S.-produced entertainment), thereby causing a greater appreciation for Canada and identification with other Canadians. In addition, as one becomes older and participates more frequently in community activities and elections, a stronger interest in the country's political system might develop. Warmer feelings for Canada as one's home also could be subtly reinforced on every return from a shopping trip to Buffalo, a sporting event in Detroit, or a winter respite in Florida or Arizona.

On the other hand, a generational interpretation suggests that the historical context existing during one's formative years shapes feelings that endure over most of a person's lifetime. Under this model, older Canadians have warmer feelings for Canada than gen-Xers do because the two groups were raised in different time periods. Many who became politically conscious before the social upheaval in Quebec in the 1960s may have viewed Canada as a harmonious, relatively prosperous, orderly, tolerant nation. For those coming of age later, the very idea of Canada was becoming contentious; for some, it represented a distant or even "foreign" authority. Of course, the age differences in feelings for Canada might be the result of a combination of life-cycle and generational effects.

A survey is simply a snapshot of public opinion at one point in time. The data from the 1974 survey alone cannot be used to determine whether those differences are more consistent with life-cycle or generational effects. The cohorts in that survey diverged not only in their affect for Canada, but also in terms of (1) the formative periods during which their attitudes began to develop (generation) and (2) the accumulation of life experiences (life cycle). Fortunately, surveys from 1992 and 1993 also included the feeling-thermometer measures tapping affect for Canada, so we have some leverage to disentangle these effects. If mean scores increased between 1974 and 1992 for each birth cohort, it would be reasonable to infer the presence of life-cycle effects. If they remained roughly the same *within* each birth cohort, but younger cohorts were less supportive of Canada than their elders, generational effects would be indicated.

A Brief Look at Data

The data used here are taken from opinion surveys conducted by Richard Johnston, André Blais, Henry Brady, Elisabeth Gidengil, and Neil Nevitte.[8] Their extraordinarily rich design yielded a combination of weekly samples of interviews conducted throughout both the 1992 Charlottetown referendum and the 1993 federal election campaigns, plus straight cross-sectional (postelection) telephone interviews and a mail follow-up. There were 4,876 respondents in all, 4,251 of whom participated in more than one wave of the survey; 887 respondents participated in all five waves. Interviewers generally began the conversation in French for people living in Quebec and in English for people living elsewhere, but then switched to the other language if that was the individual's preference. The mail questionnaire was available in both French and English. For our purposes, language of the interview should suffice as a measure of language preference.[9] Respondents were assigned to a cohort based on the year of birth that they reported in each wave of the survey.[10]

Affect for Canada, 1992

When the mean 1992 thermometer scores for Canada are broken down by birth cohort and language (see row 1 of Table 8.1), we find patterns that, on balance, resemble those reported by Clarke from the 1970s surveys. Mean affect for the country as a whole is still high in the early 1990s, but

Table 8.1
Feeling Thermometer Scores by Language and Cohort, 1992*

	Anglophones				Francophones			
	Preboomers	Early Boomers	Late Boomers	Gen-X	Preboomers	Early Boomers	Late Boomers	Gen-X
Feeling thermometer: Canada (mean score)	89.1	85.8	83.3	80.2	70.2	61.3	61.8	56.5
Feeling thermometer: Quebec (mean score)	58.9	58.9	55.4	55.8	76.8	78.5	78.0	80.8
Correlation between Canada and Quebec thermometers	.41†	.36†	.42†	.49†	.51†	.24†	.20†	.00
Sample N =	453	585	540	140	111	189	188	39

*Feeling thermometer scores range from 0 (very cold) to 100 (very warm), as described in the text. Correlations are Pearson's r (see note 15); coefficients marked by a cross (†) are statistically significant at the .01 level or better.
Source: Canadian National Election Study 1993, incorporating the 1992 Referendum Study on the Charlottetown Accord.

lower than in the 1974–1980 period. Not surprisingly, anglophones exhibit consistently higher (more positive) affect across cohorts than do francophones, but there is also variation between age groups. Among anglophones, the average feeling thermometer for Canada drops from 89.1 degrees for respondents over age 50 to 80.2 for gen-Xers. Among francophones, the drop is from 70.2 for the eldest cohort to 56.5 for the youngest. Once again, younger cohorts who came of age during this prolonged period of debate appear to have developed much less positive attitudes about the country.

Are older Canadians more supportive of Canada because of life-cycle effects or because of generational effects? We can solve the puzzle by tracking the various birth cohorts in these two sets of surveys. The early boomers, born between 1943 and 1957, were aged seventeen to thirty-one in 1974 and gave Canada relatively low thermometer ratings in surveys conducted at that time. By 1992, this same group was aged from thirty-five to forty-nine. If early boomers are "warming up" to Canada as they age (a life-cycle pattern), their 1992 thermometer ratings should be higher than their 1974 scores. If, on the other hand, generational differences account for the relationship between age and affect, we would not expect any substantial change in early boomers' feelings for the country over this eighteen-year period.

The results (not shown) are clearly consistent with a generational-effects model for both anglophones and francophones. Anglophone early boomers gave Canada an 85.5 average rating in 1974[11] and a nearly identical 85.8 score in 1992. Those born between 1925 and 1942 showed no change at all (a mean score of 89.1 in both surveys), while support levels among the 1915–1924 birth cohort remained static (89.7 and 88.4, respectively) as well. In sum, the life-cycle model's prediction of a sizable *increase* in affect is not observed for any anglophone age group. Also worth noting is the fact that Xers' 1992 scores (80.2) were somewhat lower than those of early boomers in 1974 (85.5)—a finding which suggests that generational factors may be serving to undermine support for Canada among younger anglophones.

Among francophones, the story is slightly different but even less in line with a standard life-cycle interpretation. Early boomers gave Canada an average score of 68.1 in 1974 and a significantly *lower* score of 61.3 in 1992. Far from growing more supportive of Canada as they aged, this cohort seemed to distance itself psychologically from Canada during the period under examination. A similar pattern is evident among those born between 1915 and 1942, although their drop in support was not quite as large as that for early boomers. Finally, the gap between Xers in 1992 (56.5) and early boomers in 1974 (68.1) denotes the presence of generational effects even more potent than those affecting young anglophones.[12] In addition to dampening national support among older French-speaking Canadians, the debate over Quebec sovereignty and relations with Ottawa thus appears to have taken a rather dramatic toll on the young. Canada simply does not inspire a great deal of affection among most young francophones in the 1990s—and if the generational model continues to hold, there is little hope for an increase in psychological attachment in the foreseeable future.[13]

It is helpful that the 1992 survey included thermometer questions measuring respondents' feelings not only for Canada as a whole but also for Quebec specifically. The results presented in Table 8.1 (row 2) dispel the notion that boomers and gen-Xers are more skeptical than their elders about *everything*, since the mean score on the Quebec item is essentially flat across both francophone and anglophone birth cohorts. In other words, the prolonged crisis has diminished younger cohorts' affect for their country much more than their affect for the dissident province.[14] Further, among young francophones (but not anglophones), feelings about Quebec and about Canada were quite distinct from each other in 1992 (see row 3 in Table 8.1). For all Canadians born prior to 1943, there was a moderately strong correlation[15] between affect for Canada and for its predominantly francophone province. Most of these individuals felt warmly toward both, and those who felt most warmly toward one also tended to express the most favorable sentiments about the other. Later anglophone cohorts exhibited a similar pattern. Later francophone cohorts, however, showed much weaker relationships between their feelings for Quebec and for Canada. For francophone Xers, knowing their affect toward Quebec tells us nothing about their affect toward Canada. The two polities are completely separate in the hearts of young francophones.

A number of explanations for these findings are possible, but I will offer one here based on the premise that affect toward polities is largely shaped early in a person's life (e.g., see Easton and Dennis 1969). For most francophones and anglophones who reached maturity before the onset of the current crisis over the status of Quebec, Canada is seen as the traditional mosaic in which the beauty of the whole stems from the brilliance of its many distinct components; the very idea of Canada is a positive reflection of the mutual enhancement of each culture by the other. But succeeding cohorts came of age during times when the beauty of the mosaic was being questioned. Younger francophones feel as positively toward Quebec as do their elders, and yet they fail to see Quebec's reflection in the whole of Canada. Younger anglophones also feel as positively about Quebec as do *their* elders (if less so than francophones), but their overall view of Canada is dampened by a perception that the tiles of the mosaic clash more than they complement one another.

There are several other hints that the crisis has taken its toll on the nation's collective bicultural identity. Not surprisingly, efforts to recognize Quebec as a distinct society either within or apart from Canada have resonated more with francophones than with anglophones, and that is reflected in the differing levels of agreement with the statement "We should make no distinctions, we are all Canadians," shown in Table 8.2. Equally important is the fact that younger anglophones *and* younger francophones were more inclined to reject this statement than were their elders—so much so that support for the idea that "we are all Canadians" was no higher among younger anglophones than among older francophones. For anglophones, such attitudes may be a recognition of (or resignation to) Quebec's distinctiveness or a perception of the inequalities of power in the rest of Canada. Whatever its roots, it is felt more by younger birth cohorts. There is also a greater tendency for young people of both language groups to believe that Quebec is either "somewhat" or "very" likely to separate from Canada. Cohort differences in 1992 were not drastic, but they were consistent across language groups. About a quarter of anglophone Xers (and late boomers) expected that Quebec eventually would separate, compared with only 18 percent of English-speaking Canadians over age 50. A majority of francophone Xers (54.3 percent, compared with 50.6 percent of early boomers and less than half of preboomers and late boomers) anticipated the same result. Younger generations thus appeared to be more pessimistic about the prospects for Canadian unity (or more optimistic about the prospects for Quebec's separation), in spite of the fact that they were usually more likely to believe that "an agreement *could* be reached that would satisfy most people" (emphasis added; see question 3 in Table 8.2).

The moral here is that the crisis of unity in Canada has had a telling impact on the national identity of the next generation. Canadian Xers are at the tail end of a generational trend line that is increasingly skeptical about the very idea of Canada. Decades of unresolved conflict have left this cohort, including both anglophones and francophones, (1) with diminished affect for the country as a whole; (2) less likely than their elders to agree that the concept of "Canadian" overcomes other distinctions; and (3) more pessimistic about Canada's ability to remain intact with its predominantly francophone province.[16] With contending factions unable to reach a consensus on any of the alternative national visions that have been offered, the new generation possesses growing doubts about the country as it now exists.

It's Not the Economy, Stupid

In the United States, the social and political attitudes of Generation X are often attributed to a frustration with its economic lot in the 1990s and beyond (Strauss and Howe 1991; Meacham 1995). Faced with an uncertain future in postindustrial societies, some Xers have criticized the boomer generation for creating an expectation of extrinsically and intrinsically rewarding work in a steadily expanding economy. A significant part of Xers'

Table 8.2
Attitudes toward Quebec Separation by Language and Cohort, 1992*

	Anglophones				Francophones			
	Preboomers	Early Boomers	Late Boomers	Gen-X	Preboomers	Early Boomers	Late Boomers	Gen-X
1. "We should make no distinctions, we are all Canadians."								
Agree	97.3%	91.0%	91.7%	82.6%	84.5%	71.0%	75.3%	57.9%
Disagree	2.7	9.0	8.3	17.4	15.5	29.0	24.7	42.1
2. How likely is it "that Quebec will separate from Canada?"								
Very/somewhat likely	18.0%	22.6%	25.7%	24.3%	47.5%	50.6%	46.9%	54.3%
Very/somewhat unlikely	82.1	77.4	74.3	75.7	52.4	49.5	53.1	45.7
3. How likely is it "that an agreement could be reached that would be acceptable to most Canadians?"								
Very/somewhat likely	37.6%	41.6%	41.7%	52.5%	52.9%	42.5%	42.6%	51.3%
Very/somewhat unlikely	62.3	58.4	58.4	47.5	47.2	57.4	57.4	48.8
Sample N (pre-election) =	453	585	540	140	111	189	188	39
Sample N (postelection) =	448	579	535	131	110	189	187	39

*Table entries are column percentages adding to 100% (respondents with missing values on a particular item are not included in the calculations). Question 1 is from the pre-election wave of the 1992 survey, while questions 2 and 3 are from the postelection wave.

Source: Canadian National Election Study 1993, incorporating the 1992 Referendum Study on the Charlottetown Accord.

(alleged) anger and pessimism supposedly stems from their recognition that they are doomed to enter stagnating economies overburdened by many years of extravagant spending. In fact, this is not at all an accurate picture of the youngest cohorts in Canada. Their pessimism about the country's future is essentially unrelated to their mildly *optimistic* assessments of their own economic future.

Respondents in the 1993 pre-election wave of the survey were asked if they were better or worse off now than one year ago, whether the federal government's policies had made them better or worse off, and whether they expected to be better or worse off one year later. In general, anglophones were more positive than francophones, with younger members of each language group being more positive than their elders in terms of both retrospective and prospective economic outlooks. Specifically, Table 8.3 shows that the older cohorts, not the younger ones, felt worse off as a result of economic changes over the previous year. Younger people (especially young francophones) also were least likely to attribute any perceived decline in their own economic status to federal economic policies. Finally, looking ahead, younger cohorts were in general more likely to believe that they would be better off "a year from now" than were older cohorts.

While the levels of economic optimism are not exceedingly high for a country ranked first in the world in overall human development, it is not the younger cohorts who are especially gloomy about their status. Moreover, these patterns suggest that dismay over the economy is not the source of the younger cohorts' relatively cool evaluation of the country and pessimism about its political future.

Politics of Reconciliation

Given the long history of struggle to define Quebec's place either within or alongside Canada, and the resulting pessimism about Canada's future that is present among the younger cohorts, some observers might conclude that the best solution is really no solution. In this section, we will see evidence of what appears to be a national *ambivalence* regarding the viability of a bicultural nation—an ambivalence that is strongest among the young. Younger anglophones, in particular, express a greater willingness to accommodate the French language and other Quebec concerns than do their elders. The problem is that, on specific proposals, these individuals are not always so understanding of Quebec's approach to a resolution of the crisis.

One of the question experiments in this survey involved an effort to measure differences in the degree of support for the French language versus support for Quebec itself. Half of all respondents in the 1993 pre-election wave of the study were asked, "How much do you think should be done to

Table 8.3

Economic Evaluations by Language and Cohort, 1993*

	Anglophones				Francophones			
	Preboomers	Early Boomers	Late Boomers	Gen-X	Preboomers	Early Boomers	Late Boomers	Gen-X
1. "Would you say that you are better off or worse off financially than you were a year ago?"								
Better off	12.0%	21.3%	33.7%	52.3%	6.5%	12.1%	24.4%	39.6%
Same (volunteered)	33.9	21.4	22.4	11.0	46.7	27.4	30.7	29.7
Worse off	54.1	57.3	44.0	36.7	46.8	60.5	44.9	30.6
2. "Have the policies of the federal government made you better off, worse off, or haven't they made much of a difference either way?"								
Better off	5.1%	3.2%	4.7%	2.8%	3.5%	3.7%	2.4%	4.2%
Not much difference	47.9	41.4	58.6	76.4	66.9	49.1	60.2	83.1
Worse off	47.0	55.4	36.7	20.8	29.6	47.2	37.4	12.6
3. "Do you think that a year from now you will be better off financially, worse off, or just about the same as now?"								
Better off	14.4%	24.3%	37.5%	33.7%	15.2%	18.4%	24.8%	29.7%
Same	60.7	51.7	49.0	58.9	66.7	60.9	64.9	65.4
Worse off	24.9	24.0	13.5	7.4	18.1	20.7	10.3	4.9
Sample N =	798	991	914	144	232	329	300	50

*Table entries are column percentages adding to 100% (respondents with missing values on a particular item are not included in the calculations).

Source: Canadian National Election Study 1993, incorporating the 1992 Referendum Study on the Charlottetown Accord.

promote [the French language in Canada]?"; the other half were asked, "How much do you think should be done for Quebec?" Table 8.4 shows the *percentage difference index* for each language group and birth cohort. For example, in row 1 of the table, the 77.6 score listed for the eldest francophone cohort represents the difference in the proportion of that group who said that more should be done to promote the French language (81.2 percent) and the proportion who believed that less should be done (3.6 percent). Not surprisingly, francophones at all stages of the life cycle were much more supportive of both the French language and Quebec interests overall (especially the latter)[17] than were anglophones; that is, a profound language gap can be seen in every age group. Looking only at anglophones, however, there is a fairly sizable cohort effect as we move from old to young. Indeed, for English-speaking Xers, the proportion who favor doing more to promote the French language is actually greater (by 10.7 points) than the proportion wanting to do less, and almost as many want to do more for Quebec (22.3 percent) as want to do less (28.9 percent).

The next two sets of entries in Table 8.4 involve specific issues associated with the 1992 Charlottetown referendum campaign. The proposals to guarantee Quebec's representation in the House of Commons against an erosion of its relative population size (question 3), and to explicitly recognize the province as a "distinct society" within Canada (question 4), were made in an attempt to obtain Quebec's backing for the agreement—but instead helped to undermine popular support outside of Quebec. If younger anglophones, including Xers, are more willing (as they say they are) to promote Quebec's interests, then we should expect to see corresponding age differences on these concrete proposals. At best, the evidence is ambiguous. First, less than 20 percent of anglophones (with very little variation across cohorts) agreed that Quebec should be formally allocated one-quarter of all seats in the House. Second, although there was greater anglophone support for the Quebec government's most basic demand that the province be recognized as a distinct society, only Xers came close to hitting the 50 percent mark (49.3 percent agree)—and even this is less than we might have expected given younger anglophones' higher level of professed support for Quebec in the abstract. When principle gives way to action, English-speaking Xers do not differ much from older anglophones in terms of their willingness to accommodate Quebec's specific interests.

Other aspects of the Charlottetown Accord addressed the demands of Western provinces. For example, Canada currently has a system of "asymmetrical bicameralism" (Lijphart 1984): On paper, the Senate is nearly a coequal House of Parliament; by convention, however, that appointed and malapportioned body usually defers to the will of the elected representatives in the House of Commons.[18] Some in the West and the Maritimes argue that reform is the key to providing them with an effective voice in the federal

Table 8.4

Support for Quebec, the French Language, and Constitutional Proposals, 1992 and 1993*

	Anglophones				Francophones			
	Preboomers	Early Boomers	Late Boomers	Gen-X	Preboomers	Early Boomers	Late Boomers	Gen-X
1. "How much do you think should be done to promote [the French language in Canada]?"								
Percentage Difference Index†	-35.5	-27.4	-19.7	10.7	77.6	71.5	70.9	75.0
2. "How much do you think should be done for Quebec?"								
Percentage Difference Index†	-42.0	-39.8	-29.3	-6.6	82.7	83.3	74.2	86.4
3. "Do you agree or disagree with ... giving Quebec a guarantee of one-quarter of the seats in the House of Commons?"								
Agree	17.2%	17.7%	15.7%	13.7%	65.9%	72.8%	68.7%	57.1%
Disagree	82.8	82.3	84.3	86.3	34.1	27.2	31.3	42.9
4. "Do you agree or disagree with ... recognizing Quebec as a distinct society?"								
Agree	42.8%	45.3%	41.9%	49.3%	82.8%	87.6%	86.3%	73.7%
Disagree	57.2	54.7	58.1	50.7	17.2	12.4	13.7	26.3
Sample N (1992) =	448	579	535	131	110	189	187	39
Sample N (1993) =	798	991	914	144	232	329	300	50

*Questions 1 and 2 are from the pre-election wave of the 1993 survey; questions 3 and 4 are from the postreferendum wave of the 1992 survey. Table entries for the latter are column percentages adding to 100% (respondents with missing data on an item are excluded from the calculations).

†Percentage difference index is calculated by subtracting the percent saying that (either somewhat or much) "less" should be done from the percent saying that (either somewhat or much) "more" should be done. Each of these questions was asked of a randomly selected half of the full sample. *Source:* Canadian National Election Study 1993, incorporating the 1992 Referendum Study on the Charlottetown Accord.

government, and they have called for a "Triple E" Senate that would confer on the Senate the legitimacy it needs to be an effective legislative body.[19] Senate reform was included as the price of Western acquiescence, though it turned out to be the lightning rod leading to Quebec's rejection of the Charlottetown Accord. In an equal Senate, the natural home of one of Canada's two founding cultures would be reduced to a status comparable to Prince Edward Island and possibly overwhelmed by the nine other provinces collectively.

If young anglophones were truly more sensitive to Quebec's interests, we would expect to find less agreement among them for two questions related to Senate reform. Once again, the data (not shown) indicate that this is not the case. Most anglophones approved of making the Senate a more effective body, with Xers (and late boomers) actually being more inclined than their elders to say that the Accord would have given the upper chamber either "too little" or "the right amount" of power. Close to 60 percent of all anglophones (with little variation across age groups)[20] also supported the proposal to allocate Senate representation on an equal basis. Coming on top of what we already have learned, these patterns suggest that younger cohorts' relative willingness to "do more for Quebec" may be somewhat superficial.[21]

Nevertheless, there are some issues relevant to the national debate on which younger anglophones do seem to be closer to francophone public opinion than are their elders. In the survey's mail-back wave, respondents were asked whether they agreed or disagreed with the statement "Federal government services should be provided in only one language, French in Quebec and English in the rest of the country." A policy of "bifurcated unilingualism" has been advocated by the Reform Party in an attempt to reconcile its Western base with Quebec's desire to control language issues within its own borders. In some ways, this reflects the experience of Canadians who matured before the Quiet Revolution of the 1950s and 1960s, and in fact the idea (results not shown) resonates fairly well (51.4 percent agree) with preboomer anglophones. Yet those who have come of age since bilingualism became the official policy of the federal government are considerably less enthusiastic. Only about a quarter of anglophone Xers supported such an approach, not much more than the 20 percent observed for all francophones (among whom cohort differences are negligible).

On another level, younger generations are slightly more supportive of maintaining public involvement in efforts to resolve the crisis—which may serve to complicate the process. Gibbins (1995) argued that as the constitutional debate in Canada unfolded, the arena for resolution shifted as well. Prior to the 1982 patriation of the constitution, it was customary for the British Parliament to accede to a collective request by federal and provincial political executives for amendments to the British North America Act. But in 1982, responsibility for ratifying constitutional amendments was shifted to the national and provincial legislatures; then, in later years, emergent populist sentiment in both Quebec and the Western provinces led to the submission of the 1992 Charlottetown Accord to advisory referenda.

As difficult as it may be to achieve consensus among Canada's first ministers on major issues, legislative and popular ratification have thus far proved insurmountable. Both the Meech Lake and Charlottetown agreements were endorsed by the federal prime minister and provincial premiers, which would have been sufficient under pre-1982 conventions. But Meech Lake was not ratified by the legislatures in Manitoba and Newfoundland, and Charlottetown fell in a nationwide referendum. Although the public has grown understandably skeptical of politicians' ability to reach a just settlement to the crisis, popular involvement in the process obviously presents problems of its own. And this does not seem likely to change anytime soon: Whereas francophones and anglophones of all ages are solidly in favor of constitutional ratification by referendum (as opposed to ratification by elected officials), it is younger cohorts—again including late boomers as well as Xers—who exhibit the highest levels of support for the populist approach.[22]

Conclusion

Generation Xers in Canada have reached adulthood amid a sea of challenges to their national identity. Even as Canadians celebrated their country's premier ranking on the United Nations Human Development Index, they were faced with the prospect of a "divorce" structured largely along ethnic lines. It should come as no surprise that after decades of fomenting nationalism, young Québécois francophones have weak affective ties with Canada. What is mildly surprising is that the debate has also taken its toll on the support levels of anglophone Xers. As a group, the latter still express stronger support for Canada than does any francophone cohort, but the incessant questioning of the concept of Canada in public constitutional debates appears to have left the youngest anglophones with a somewhat tenuous love for their country. Moreover, the evidence suggests that these Canadians are unlikely to "grow out of" this affective skepticism if the political contours of the debate do not change.

The crisis, as we have seen, is not an economic one, or at least the economy is not at its forefront. National and regional economies in Canada are closely tied to—and quite dependent upon—the U.S. economy (Williams 1995), which might lead one to expect that American Xers' economic concerns, such as they are (see Chapter 1), would be echoed or even exaggerated among their Canadian counterparts. Yet there is little evidence that younger

Canadians are any more dissatisfied with, critical of, or pessimistic about the economy than older citizens are. Perhaps greater educational opportunities have opened up economic opportunities for more people, or maybe the political crisis has simply left younger Canadians with such low expectations that they are easier to satisfy economically. Either way, it is clear that economic satisfaction has not translated into an optimism about the country's political future. Whereas the pessimism of gen-Xers in the United States is often said to stem from the gap between expectations and realities in the workplace (Strauss and Howe 1991), in Canada this gap has more explicitly political origins. Despite a new emphasis on the existence of one political community with two official languages representing multiple cultures, mutual respect and accommodation have been difficult to realize.

For those who favor Canada's remaining a single nation, in one form or another, generational politics presents some cruel paradoxes. At an abstract level, anglophone Xers seem to be more conciliatory toward Quebec than their elders are. But francophone Xers have already psychologically distanced themselves from Canada, and younger anglophones themselves are ambivalent about the resolution of the crisis. In principle, they are more supportive of efforts to promote both the French language and Quebec generally, but that support does not always extend to specific proposals that might satisfy an actual government in Quebec. In time, such ambivalence could resolve itself; unfortunately, time can only prolong the crisis that produced the ambivalence in the first place.

Notes

1. There are very weak ties between the federal and provincial parties in many areas of Canada. In recent history, some parties have successfully competed in federal elections but not in provincial elections (e.g., Reform), while others have been competitive in provincial elections but not at the federal level (e.g., Social Credit in British Columbia from 1952 to 1991). There are often separate organizations for federal and provincial parties that share the same name, and "split" partisanships also are common among citizens in various parts of the country (Clarke and Stewart 1987; Martinez 1990).

2. Until the Quiet Revolution (discussed later), most francophones referred to themselves as Canadiens, and francophones outside Quebec still do. Most francophones inside Quebec now think of themselves as Québécois, while some anglophones and allophones (citizens whose native language is neither English nor French) consider themselves Quebeckers.

3. It should be noted, however, that this has been the age of the franchise in Canadian federal elections only since 1969.

4. Among other things, the Statute of Westminster in 1931 acknowledged that the colonial authority to "disallow" Canadian legislation had become obsolete, and it recognized a distinction between the Canadian and British Crowns. Although Elizabeth II nominally reigns as the Queen of *Canada*, since 1951 the monarch has appointed (upon the recommen-

dation of the Canadian prime minister) a Canadian as governor-general to exercise her formal responsibilities. "God Save the Queen" remains the Royal Anthem.

5. In the hope of ameliorating fears of economic isolation, the PQ government asked Quebeckers for the authority to negotiate for "sovereignty-association," which was widely interpreted as meaning *political* sovereignty combined with an *economic* association with the rest of Canada.

6. An Act of the British Parliament, the British North America Act of 1867, was the constitution of Canada until 1982. While the British government had routinely approved requests of the Canadian national and provincial governments for amendments to the Act, Trudeau sought and eventually received the British Parliament's endorsement of constitutional amendments that removed its role in any future amendments. This final Act of the British Parliament was known as the patriation of the Canadian constitution.

7. Some of the specific agreements reached at Charlottetown will be discussed later in this chapter.

8. These data were made available by the Inter-University Consortium for Political and Social Research (ICPSR Study number 6571). Neither the Consortium nor the original collectors of the data bear any responsibility for the analyses and interpretations presented here.

9. Of the 4,251 respondents who participated more than once, only ten were coded as having switched languages between waves of the study. These data reflect the geographic cleavage in language noted earlier: 92 percent of Quebec respondents were interviewed in French, while 99 percent of non-Quebec respondents were interviewed in English.

10. Due to the unreliability of respondent reports and/or coding errors in the data, fifty-one respondents who participated more than once were coded into different birth cohorts. This should have a negligible impact on the findings presented here.

11. The data from the 1974 Canadian National Election Study were made available by the Inter-University Consortium for Political and Social Research (ICPSR Study number 7379). For comparability with Clarke et al. (1979), the preboomer cohorts in 1974 and 1992 were divided into either two (francophone) or three (anglophone) separate age categories.

12. The results reported here very likely reflect a combination of generational and *period* effects, the latter referring to a general lowering of affect for Canada across *all* (francophone) cohorts at the same time. For a more complete discussion of life-cycle, generational, and period effects, see Jennings and Niemi (1981, Chapter 5).

13. In passing, we might speculate that the drop in support for Canada among francophone pre- and early boomers has been stimulated to some degree by changes in the nation's language patterns. Although one can find francophone communities scattered throughout Canada (including Acadians in New Brunswick as well as smaller populations in Ontario, Manitoba, Saskatchewan, and other provinces), most of Canada's French speakers live in Quebec. In the nearly two decades between these two surveys, Quebec became more French speaking itself through (1) greater assimilation of allophones (see note 2), combined with (2) an exodus of anglophones—the net result being that it is now home to a larger proportion of all French speakers than ever before (Gibbins 1994, 96–108). Thus, the decline in francophone support for Canada has occurred at a time when the francophone population is becoming sparser *outside* of Quebec and more heavily concentrated *within* Quebec.

14. Interestingly, among anglophones living outside of Quebec, younger cohorts express lower affect both for Canada and for one's own province.

15. Correlation coefficients, in this case Pearson's r, range between 0.0 (no relationship) and plus or minus 1.0 (a perfect relationship). A coefficient of plus or minus 1.0 means that knowing a respondent's relative score on the first variable allows one to predict, with perfect accuracy, his or her relative score on the second variable. A score of 0.0 means that there is no tendency at all for high (or low) scores on one variable to occur among individuals who score high (or low) on the other. Except for francophone Xers, for whom there is no relation-

ship, the correlations listed in row 3 of Table 8.1 indicate that those who feel warmly toward Canada also *tend* to score higher on the Quebec thermometer (and vice versa).

16. Part of the problem may be that Canadian Xers (and others) see themselves as the victims of constitutional architects who created political expectations that are unrealizable.

17. This modest difference suggests that francophones are at least somewhat more likely to see the national conflict in terms of Quebec versus the rest of Canada, rather than as a conflict between the two official languages. In contrast, anglophones are more sympathetic (or less antagonistic) to the language than to the province.

18. Many Westerners see three related problems with the present Senate. First, it is malapportioned. In theory, the Senate provides approximately equal representation to four regions (the Maritimes, Quebec, Ontario, and the West), with the result that the population per senator varies among the provinces from 32,000 in Prince Edward Island to 527,000 in British Columbia (Gibbins 1993, 166). Second, although senators "represent" the provinces, they are appointed by the federal government to serve until age seventy. This can lead to a situation like that of Alberta, where in 1993 the Reform Party won twenty-two of twenty-six seats in the House of Commons, where Progressive Conservatives controlled the provincial government, and yet the incumbent Liberal prime minister had the authority to fill any vacancies from Alberta in the Senate. Third, the Senate is largely ineffective. Because the chamber is seen as undemocratic, senators usually defer to the will of the elected government and the House of Commons. There are occasions, however, when the Senate has blocked or delayed important legislation, as in the case of the implementation of the 1988 Free Trade Agreement with the United States.

19. A "Triple E" Senate would emulate the constitutional structure of its U.S. counterpart. Proponents contend that if each province had an equal number of *elected* senators, then the Senate would have greater legitimacy as a democratic institution to be an effective counterweight to the House of Commons. Others note, however, that this reform would come at the expense of the principle of "responsible government" (Gibbins 1993). Ontario and Quebec have the most to lose under the "Triple E" proposal, since their shares of seats in the Senate would be reduced at the same time as the Senate is granted more power.

20. A small number of respondents, mostly pre- and early boomers, responded to each of these questions by saying that the Senate should be abolished altogether.

21. Such contradictions may stem from any of several related processes. First, prior research on public opinion has found that people often express support for abstract concepts such as democracy but then, for whatever reasons, fail to apply those same principles to concrete situations (Prothro and Grigg 1960). Second, Craig and Halfacre report in Chapter 4 that gen-Xers in the United States are more likely than other cohorts to hold multiple, or ambivalent, attitudes on issues involving the role of big government and the redistribution of resources (see Zaller and Feldman 1992; Wildavsky 1990). Although the multiwave Canadian data do not permit a direct test of this phenomenon, the aggregate pattern suggests that many citizens—especially younger ones, and anglophones Xers most of all—do possess a similar ambivalence on matters relating to the constitutional crisis (for example, being generally sympathetic to Quebec interests but also believing in the importance of individual rights that could be threatened by constitutional recognition of Quebec as a distinct society). Finally, gen-Xers and other young (mainly anglophone) Canadians may be making a sharper distinction between support for community, regime, and authorities (Easton and Dennis 1969; Kornberg and Stewart 1983) than their elders do. That is, there may be a disjuncture between some anglophones' (diffuse) support for the Quebec community and their (specific) support for the proposals offered by a single Quebec regime or a particular set of Quebec authorities.

22. Respondents in 1992 were asked the following: "Who should have the final say in changing the constitution? The people in a referendum, or our elected representatives at the federal and provincial levels?" Between 70 and 80 percent of all boomers and Xers chose the former.

Appendix

Wording of Survey Questions

The following questions have been drawn from the 1992, 1993, and 1994 American National Election Study (ANES) surveys.

Partisan and Ideological Self-Identification

1. Generally speaking, do you usually think of yourself as a Republican, a Democrat, an Independent, or what? (If Republican or Democrat) Would you call yourself a strong . . . or a not very strong . . . ? (If Independent) Do you think of yourself as closer to the Republican Party or to the Democratic Party? NOTE: Partisan strength (as opposed to direction) is measured by "folding over" responses to this question: strong Republicans are combined with strong Democrats, not very strong Republicans with not very strong Democrats, Independents leaning Republican with Independents leaning Democrat, and Independents who do not lean one way or the other are left as a separate category.

2. We hear a lot of talk these days about liberals and conservatives. Here is a seven-point scale on which the political views that people might hold are arranged from extremely liberal (1) to extremely conservative (7). Where would you place yourself on this scale, or haven't you thought much about this? NOTE: Respondents also are asked to place various political figures, e.g., candidates for president, and for House and Senate, on this same scale.

Performance Evaluations and Partisan Choice

1. Do you approve or disapprove of the way George Bush is handling his job as president? Do you approve/disapprove strongly or not strongly?

2. In general, do you approve or disapprove of the way the U.S. Congress has been handling its job? Do you approve/disapprove strongly or not strongly?

3. Do you think there are any important differences in what the Republicans and Democrats stand for? (yes or no)

4. Which political party do you think would be most likely to get the government to do a better job in dealing with [whatever has been previously named as the single most important problem the country faces]—the Republicans, the Democrats, or wouldn't there be much difference between them?

5. Which party do you think would do a better job of (a) handling the nation's economy, (b) handling foreign affairs, (c) solving the problem of poverty, (d) making health care more affordable—the Democrats, the Republicans, or wouldn't there be much difference between them?

6. Which presidential candidate do you think would do a better job at (a) handling the nation's economy, (b) handling foreign affairs, (c) solving the problem of poverty, (d) handling the problem of pollution and protecting the environment, (e) making health care more affordable, (f) reducing the budget deficit—George Bush, Bill Clinton, or wouldn't there be any difference between them?

7. Do you think it is better when one party controls both the presidency and Congress, better when control is split between the Democrats and Republicans, or doesn't it matter?

Economic Assessments and Materialism/Postmaterialism

1. We are interested in how people are getting along financially these days. Would you say that you (and your family living here) are better off or worse off financially than you were a year ago? Is that much better/worse off or somewhat better/worse off?

2. Now looking ahead, do you think that a year from now you (and your family living here) will be better off financially, or worse off, or just about the same as now? Is that much better/worse off or somewhat better/worse off?

3. Do you think that twenty years from now, the standard of living for the people who are just children now will be better, about the same, or worse than it is today?

4. For a nation, it is not always possible to obtain everything one might wish. [In this booklet], several different goals are listed. If you had to choose among them, which one seems most desirable to you—maintaining order in the nation, giving the people more say in important political decisions, fighting rising prices, protecting freedom of speech? Which one would be your second choice?

Issue and Policy Views

1. There has been some discussion about abortion during recent years. Which one of the opinions on this page best agrees with your view? (a) By law, abortion should never be permitted. (b) The law should permit abortion only in case of rape, incest, or when the woman's life is in danger. (c) The law should permit abortion for reasons other than rape, incest, or danger to the woman's life, but only after the need for the abortion has been clearly established. (d) By law, a woman should always be able to obtain an abortion

as a matter of personal choice. NOTE: Respondents also are asked to place the views of major candidates for president on this same scale.

2. Would you favor or oppose a law in your state that would allow the use of government funds to help pay for the costs of abortion for women who cannot afford them? Do you favor/oppose government funding for abortions strongly or not strongly?

3. Recently there has been a lot of talk about women's rights. Some people feel that women should have an equal role with men in running business, industry, and government. Others feel that women's place is in the home. Where would you place yourself on this [seven-point] scale, or haven't you thought much about this?

4. Do you favor or oppose laws to protect homosexuals against job discrimination? Do you favor/oppose such laws strongly or not strongly?

5. Do you think homosexuals should be allowed to serve in the United States Armed Forces, or don't you think so? Do you feel strongly or not strongly that homosexuals should/should not be allowed to serve in the United States Armed Forces?

6. Do you think gay or lesbian couples, in other words, homosexual couples, should be legally permitted to adopt children? Do you feel strongly or not strongly that homosexual couples should be legally permitted to adopt children?

7. Some people think the government should provide fewer services, even in areas such as health and education, in order to reduce spending. [Others] feel it is important for the government to provide many more services even if it means an increase in spending. Where would you place yourself on this [seven-point] scale, or haven't you thought much about this?

8. Some people feel the government in Washington should see to it that every person has a job and a good standard of living. Others think the government should just let each person get ahead on their own. Where would you place yourself on this [seven-point] scale, or haven't you thought much about this?

9. Would you personally be willing to pay more in taxes so that the government could spend more on the services you favor, or would you rather keep your taxes the same even if this meant the government couldn't increase its spending as you would like?

10. There is much concern about the rapid rise in medical and hospital costs. Some people feel there should be a government insurance plan which would cover all medical and hospital expenses for everyone. Others feel that all medical expenses should be paid by individuals, and through private insurance plans like Blue Cross or other company-paid plans. Where would you place yourself on this [seven-point] scale, or haven't you thought much about this?

11. Do you think government should provide child care assistance to

low- and middle-income working parents, or isn't it the government's responsibility?

12. Some people say the U.S. should maintain its position as the world's strongest military power even if it means continuing high defense spending. Would you say that you agree strongly, agree somewhat, neither agree nor disagree, disagree somewhat, or disagree strongly?

13. In the future, how willing should the United States be to use military force to solve international problems—extremely willing, very willing, somewhat willing, not very willing, or never willing?

14. Some people believe that we should spend much less money for defense. Others feel that defense spending should be greatly increased. Where would you place yourself on this [seven-point] scale, or haven't you thought much about this?

15. Some people feel that the government in Washington should make every effort to improve the social and economic position of blacks. Others feel that the government should not make any special effort to help blacks because they should help themselves. Where would you place yourself on this [seven-point] scale, or haven't you thought much about this?

16. Some people say that because of past discrimination, blacks should be given preference in hiring and promotion. Others say that such preference in hiring and promotion of blacks is wrong because it gives blacks advantages they haven't earned. What about your opinion—are you for or against preferential hiring and promotion of blacks? Do you favor/oppose preference in hiring and promotion strongly or not strongly?

17. Some people say that because of past discrimination, it is sometimes necessary for colleges and universities to reserve openings for black students. Others oppose quotas because they say quotas give blacks advantages they haven't earned. What about your opinion—are you for or against quotas to admit black students? Do you favor/oppose quotas strongly or not strongly?

18. Some people say that the civil-rights people have been trying to push too fast. Others feel they haven't pushed fast enough. How about you? Do you think that civil-rights leaders are trying to push too fast, are going too slowly, or are they moving at about the right speed?

19. Do you favor the death penalty for persons convicted of murder? Do you favor/oppose the death penalty for persons convicted of murder strongly or not strongly?

20. Which of the following views comes closest to your opinion on the issue of school prayer? (a) By law, prayers should not be allowed in public schools. (b) The law should allow public schools to schedule time when children can pray silently if they want to. (c) The law should allow public schools to schedule time when children, as a group, can say a general prayer

not tied to a particular religious faith. (d) By law, public schools should schedule a time when all children would say a chosen Christian prayer.

21. Should federal spending on . . . be increased, decreased, or kept about the same? (a) welfare programs; (b) programs that assist blacks; (c) child care; (d) poor people.

Group Attitudes and Attachments

1. Ratings of persons and groups on the "feeling thermometer" (with scores of 0–49 degrees reflecting a *less* favorable evaluation, 51–100 degrees a *more* favorable evaluation, and exactly 50 degrees indicating that the respondent feels neither "warm" nor "cold" toward the indicated person/group): (a) gay men and lesbians (homosexuals); (b) the Republican Party; (c) the Democratic Party; (d) the federal government in Washington.

Feelings about the Role of Government

1. Some people are afraid the government in Washington is getting too powerful for the good of the country and the individual person. Others feel that the government in Washington is not getting too strong. . . . What is your feeling, do you think the government is getting too powerful or do you think the government is not getting too strong? (If not getting too strong) Do you think the government should become more powerful or should it stay the way it is?

2. I am going to ask you to choose which of two statements I read comes closer to your own opinion. You might agree to some extent with both, but we want to know which one is closer to your views. (a) One, the less government the better; or two, there are more things that government should be doing. (b) One, we need a strong government to handle today's complex economic problems; or two, the free market can handle these problems without government being involved. (c) One, the main reason government has become bigger over the years is because it has gotten involved in things that people should do for themselves; or two, government has become bigger because the problems we face have become bigger.

Support for Equality

1. Our society should do whatever is necessary to make sure that everyone has an equal opportunity to succeed. (strongly agree to strongly disagree)

2. We have gone too far in pushing equal rights in this country. (strongly agree to strongly disagree)

3. This country would be better off if we worried less about how equal people are. (strongly agree to strongly disagree)

4. It is not really that big a problem if some people have more of a chance in life than others. (strongly agree to strongly disagree)

5. If people were treated more equally in this country, we would have many fewer problems. (strongly agree to strongly disagree)

6. One of the big problems in this country is that we don't give everyone an equal chance. (strongly agree to strongly disagree)

Support for Traditional Values and Lifestyles

1. The world is always changing and we should adjust our view of moral behavior to those changes. (strongly agree to strongly disagree)

2. We should be more tolerant of people who choose to live according to their own moral standards, even if they are very different from our own. (strongly agree to strongly disagree)

3. This country would have many fewer problems if there were more emphasis on traditional family ties. (strongly agree to strongly disagree)

4. The newer lifestyles are contributing to the breakdown of our society. (strongly agree to strongly disagree)

Racial/Ethnic Attitudes

1. Irish, Italians, Jewish and many other minorities overcame prejudice and worked their way up. Blacks should do the same without any special favors. (strongly agree to strongly disagree)

2. Over the past few years, blacks have gotten less than they deserve. (strongly agree to strongly disagree)

3. It's really a matter of some people not trying hard enough; if blacks would only try harder, they could be just as well off as whites. (strongly agree to strongly disagree)

4. Generations of slavery and discrimination have created conditions that make it difficult for blacks to work their way out of the lower class. (strongly agree to strongly disagree)

5. How likely is it that the growing number of Hispanics [in the United States] will improve our culture with new ideas and customs—extremely likely, very likely, somewhat likely, or not at all likely?

6. [How likely is it that the growing number of Hispanics in the United States will] cause higher taxes due to more demands for public services—extremely likely, very likely, somewhat likely, or not at all likely?

7. [How likely is it that the growing number of Hispanics in the United States will] take away jobs from people already here—extremely likely, very likely, somewhat likely, or not at all likely?

8. Ratings of different groups in society (whites, blacks, Hispanics, Asian Americans) on three seven-point scales: (a) hardworking vs. lazy; (b) intelligent vs. unintelligent; and (c) violent vs. peaceful. Respondents are instructed to give a score of 1 or 7 if they believe that "almost all of the people" in a group share a particular characteristic, 4 if they believe that "most people in the group are not closer to one end or the other," or any number in between that best reflects their views.

Political Trust

1. How much of the time do you think you can trust the government in Washington to do what is right—just about always, most of the time, or only some of the time?
2. Do you think that people in the government waste a lot of the money we pay in taxes, waste some of it, or don't waste very much of it?
3. Would you say the government is pretty much run by a few big interests looking out for themselves or that it is run for the benefit of all the people?
4. Do you think that quite a few of the people running the government are crooked, not very many are, or do you think hardly any of them are crooked at all?

Political Effectiveness and Government Responsiveness

1. I don't think public officials care much what people like me think. (strongly agree to strongly disagree)
2. People like me don't have any say about what the government does. (strongly agree to strongly disagree)
3. Sometimes politics and government seem so complicated that a person like me can't really understand what's going on. (strongly agree to strongly disagree)
4. Over the years, how much attention do you feel the government pays to what the people think when it decides what to do—a good deal, some, or not much?
5. And how much do you feel that having elections makes the government pay attention to what the people think—a good deal, some, or not much?

Patriotism

1. When you see the American flag flying, does it make you feel extremely good, very good, somewhat good, or not very good?

2. How strong is your love for your country—extremely strong, very strong, somewhat strong, or not very strong?

Political Involvement

1. We would like to find out about some of the things people do to help a party or a candidate win an election. During the campaign, did you (a) talk to any people and try to show them why they should vote for or against one of the parties or candidates? (b) wear a campaign button, put a campaign sticker on your car, or place a sign in your window or in front of your house? (c) go to any political meetings, rallies, speeches, dinners, or things like that in support of a particular candidate? (d) do any [other] work for one of the parties or candidates? (e) give money to an individual candidate running for public office? (yes or no)

2. In talking to people about elections, we often find that a lot of people were not able to vote because they weren't registered, they were sick, or they just didn't have time. How about you—did you vote in the elections this November? (yes or no)

3. Some people don't pay much attention to political campaigns. How about you? Would you say that you have been very much interested, somewhat interested, or not much interested in the political campaigns so far this year?

4. Some people seem to follow what's going on in government and public affairs most of the time, whether there's an election going on or not. Others aren't that interested. Would you say you follow what's going on in government and public affairs most of the time, some of the time, only now and then, or hardly at all?

References

Abramson, Paul R. 1975. *Generational Change in American Politics*. Lexington, MA: D. C. Heath.

———. 1983. *Political Attitudes in America: Formation and Change*. San Francisco: W. H. Freeman.

Abramson, Paul R., and Ronald Inglehart. 1994. "Education, Security, and Postmaterialism: A Comment on Duch and Taylor's 'Postmaterialism and the Economic Condition.'" *American Journal of Political Science*. 38 (August): 797–814.

Agresti, Alan. 1990. *Statistical Methods for the Social Sciences*, 3rd ed. San Francisco: Dellen Publishing.

Aldrich, John H. 1995. *Why Parties? The Origin and Transformation of Political Parties in America*. Chicago: University of Chicago Press.

Aldrich, John H., and Richard G. Niemi. 1995. "The Sixth American Party System: Electoral Change, 1952–1992." In *Broken Contract? Changing Relationships Between Americans and Their Government*, ed. Stephen C. Craig. Boulder, CO: Westview.

Almond, Gabriel A., and Sidney Verba. 1963. *The Civic Culture: Political Attitudes and Democracy in Five Nations*. Princeton: Princeton University Press.

Alwin, Duane F., Ronald L. Cohen, and Theodore M. Newcomb. 1991. *Political Attitudes Over the Life Span: The Bennington Women After Fifty Years*. Madison: University of Wisconsin Press.

American Enterprise. 1994. "Public Opinion and Demographic Report." January/February: 81–104.

Andersen, Kristi. 1978. "Book Review." *American Political Science Review*. 72 (June): 663–4.

Atkeson, Lonna R., James A. McCann, Ronald B. Rapoport, and Walter J. Stone. 1996. "Citizens for Perot: Assessing Patterns of Alienation and Activism." In *Broken Contract? Changing Relationships Between Americans and Their Government*, ed. Stephen C. Craig. Boulder, CO: Westview.

Auer, Bernhard M. 1967. "A Letter from the Publisher." *Time*. January 6: 11.

Barber, Benjamin. 1984. *Strong Democracy: Participatory Politics for a New Age*. Berkeley: University of California Press.

Barna, George. 1994. *The Baby Busters: The Disillusioned Generation*. Chicago: Northfield.

Barnum, David G., and John L. Sullivan. 1990. "The Elusive Foundations of Political Freedom in Britain and the United States." *Journal of Politics*. 52 (August): 719–39.

Bash, Alan. 1993. "Generation X: Redefining the American Dream." *USA Today*. September 23: D6.

Beck, Paul Allen. 1974. "A Socialization Theory of Partisan Realignment." In *The Politics of Future Citizens*, by Richard G. Niemi and Associates. San Francisco: Jossey-Bass.

———. 1984. "The Dealignment Era in America." In *Electoral Change in Advanced Industrial Democracies: Realignment or Dealignment?*, ed. Russell J. Dalton, Scott C. Flanagan, and Paul Allen Beck. Princeton: Princeton University Press.

Beck, Paul Allen, and M. Kent Jennings. 1991. "Family Traditions, Political Periods, and the Development of Partisan Orientations." *Journal of Politics*. 53 (August): 742–63.

Bellah, Robert N., Richard Madsen, William M. Sullivan, Ann Swidler, and Steven M. Tipton. 1985. *Habits of the Heart*. Berkeley and Los Angeles: University of California Press.

Bengtson, Vern L., Michael J. Furlong, and Robert S. Laufer. 1974. "Time, Aging, and the Continuity of Social Structure: Themes and Issues in Generational Analysis." *Journal of Social Issues*. 30 (no. 2): 1–30.

Bennett, Linda L. M., and Stephen Earl Bennett. 1990. *Living with Leviathan: Americans Coming to Terms with Big Government*. Lawrence: University Press of Kansas.

———. 1996. "Looking at Leviathan: Dimensions of Opinion about Big Government." In *Broken Contract: Changing Relationships Between Americans and Their Government*, ed. Stephen C. Craig. Boulder, CO: Westview.

Bennett, Stephen Earl. 1986. *Apathy in America, 1960–1984*. Ardsley-on-Hudson, NY: Transnational Publishers.

———. 1995. "Americans' Knowledge of Ideology, 1980–1992." *American Politics Quarterly*. 23 (July): 259–78.

———. 1996. "Resolving Different Views of Americans' Knowledge about Public Affairs." Unpublished manuscript. University of Cincinnati.

Bennett, Stephen Earl, John R. Baker, Richard S. Flickinger, Staci R. Rhine, and Linda L. M. Bennett. 1996. "Citizens' Knowledge of Foreign Affairs." *Harvard International Journal of Press/Politics*. 1 (March): 10–21.

Bennett, Stephen Earl, and Linda L. M. Bennett. 1989. "Interest in American Presidential Election Campaigns." *Polity*. 22 (September): 341–54.

Bennett, Stephen Earl, and Eric Rademacher. 1994. "The Politics of 'Generation X': America's Post-Boomer Birth Cohort Comes of Age." Paper presented at the Annual Meetings of the American Political Science Association, New York.

Bennett, W. Lance. 1996. *News: The Politics of Illusion*, 3rd ed. New York: Longman.

Berelson, Bernard R., Paul F. Lazarsfeld, and William N. McPhee. 1954. *Voting: A Study of Opinion Formation in a Presidential Campaign*. Chicago: University of Chicago Press.

Billingsley, Keith R., and Clyde Tucker. 1987. "Generations, Status and Party Identification: A Theory of Operant Conditioning." *Political Behavior*. 9 (no. 4): 305–22.

Bipartisan Commission on Entitlement and Tax Reform. 1994. *Entitlement Reform Discussion: Document*. Washington: Bipartisan Commission on Entitlement and Tax Reform.

Black, Chris. 1990. "America's Young Have Tuned Out on Politics." *Boston Sunday Globe*. May 13: A17, A20.

Black, Gordon S., and Benjamin D. Black. 1994. *The Politics of American Discontent*. New York: Wiley.

Blum, John Morton. 1991. *Years of Discord: American Politics and Society, 1961–1974*. New York: Norton.

Board of Trustees, Federal Hospital Insurance Trust Fund. 1996. *Annual Report*. Washington: Government Printing Office.

Board of Trustees, Federal Old-Age and Survivors Insurance and Disability Insurance Trust Funds. 1995. *Annual Report*. Washington: Government Printing Office.

Bobo, Lawrence. 1983. "Whites' Opposition to Busing: Symbolic Racism or Realistic Group Conflict?" *Journal of Personality and Social Psychology*. 45 (December): 1196–210.

Bobo, Lawrence, and James R. Kluegel. 1993. "Opposition to Race-Targeting: Self-Interest, Stratification Ideology, or Racial Attitudes?" *American Sociological Review*. 58 (August): 443–64.

Booth, William. 1994. "Polls: Young Tuned-Out Voters Feel 'Party Stuff Is Getting in the Way.' " *Washington Post*. November 6: A29.

Braungart, Richard G., and Margaret M. Braungart. 1984. "Political Generations." *Micropolitics*. 3 (no. 4): 349–415.

———. 1987. "Generational Politics." In *Annual Review of Political Science*, vol. 2, ed. Samuel Long. Norwood, NJ: Ablex Publishing.

———. 1991. "The Effects of the 1960s Political Generation on Former Left- and Right-Wing Youth Activist Leaders." *Social Problems*. 38 (August): 297–315.

Brody, Richard A. 1991. "Stability and Change in Party Identification: Presidential to Off-Years." In *Reasoning and Choice: Explorations in Political Psychology*, ed. Paul Sniderman, Richard A. Brody, and Philip E. Tetlock. New York: Cambridge University Press.

Bruce, John M., John A. Clark, and John H. Kessel. 1991. "Advocacy Politics in Presidential Parties." *American Political Science Review*. 85 (December): 1089–1105.

Burnham, Walter Dean. 1970. *Critical Elections and the Mainsprings of American Politics*. New York: Norton.

Business Roundtable. 1996. *Effect of Interest Rate Reductions on Consumer Debt*. Washington: Business Roundtable.

Butler, David, and Donald Stokes. 1976. *Political Change in Britain*, 2nd college ed. New York: St. Martin's.

Campbell, Angus, Philip E. Converse, Warren E. Miller, and Donald E. Stokes. 1960. *The American Voter*. New York: Wiley.

Cassel, Carol A. 1993. "A Test of Converse's Theory of Party Support." *Journal of Politics*. 55 (August): 664–81.

Chanley, Virginia. 1994. "Commitment to Political Tolerance: Situational and Activity-Based Differences." *Political Behavior*. 16 (September): 343–63.

Childers, Thomas. 1983. *The Nazi Voter: The Social Foundations of Fascism in Germany, 1919–1933*. Chapel Hill: University of North Carolina Press.

Chong, Dennis. 1993. "How People Think, Reason, and Feel about Rights and Liberties." *American Journal of Political Science*. 37 (August): 867–99.

———. 1994. "Tolerance and Social Adjustment to New Norms and Practices." *Political Behavior*. 16 (March): 21–53.

Citrin, Jack. 1974. "Comment: The Political Relevance of Trust in Government." *American Political Science Review*. 68 (September): 973–88.

Clarke, Harold D., Jane Jenson, Lawrence LeDuc, and Jon H. Pammett. 1979. *Political Choice in Canada*. Toronto: McGraw-Hill Ryerson.

————. 1984. *Absent Mandate: The Politics of Discontent in Canada.* Toronto: Gage Educational Publishing Company.

Clarke, Harold D., and Marianne C. Stewart. 1987. "Partisan Inconsistency and Partisan Change in Federal States: The Case of Canada." *American Journal of Political Science.* 31 (May): 383–407.

Clubb, Jerome M., William H. Flanigan, and Nancy H. Zingale. 1980. *Partisan Realignment: Voters, Parties, and Government in American History.* Beverly Hills, CA: Sage.

Congressional Budget Office. 1993. *Reducing the Deficit: Spending and Revenue Options.* Washington: Government Printing Office.

————. 1994. *Reducing Entitlement Spending.* Washington: Government Printing Office.

————. 1996a. *The Economic and Budget Outlook: Fiscal Years 1997–2006.* Washington: Government Printing Office.

————. 1996b. *An Economic and Budget Outlook Update.* Washington: Government Printing Office.

Conover, Pamela Johnston, and Stanley Feldman. 1981. "The Origins and Meaning of Liberal/Conservative Self Identifications." *American Journal of Political Science.* 25 (November): 617–45.

Converse, Philip E. 1964. "The Nature of Belief Systems in Mass Publics." In *Ideology and Discontent*, ed. David E. Apter. New York: Free Press.

————. 1969. "Of Time and Partisan Stability." *Comparative Political Studies.* 2 (July): 139–71.

————. 1975. "Public Opinion and Voting Behavior." In *Handbook of Political Science*, vol. 4, ed. Fred I. Greenstein and Nelson W. Polsby. Reading, MA: Addison-Wesley.

————. 1976. *The Dynamics of Party Support: Cohort-Analyzing Party Identification.* Beverly Hills, CA: Sage.

————. 1990. "Popular Representation and the Distribution of Information." In *Information and Democratic Processes*, ed. John A. Ferejohn and James H. Kuklinski. Urbana: University of Illinois Press.

Converse, Philip E., Warren E. Miller, Jerrold D. Rusk, and Arthur C. Wolfe. 1969. "Continuity and Change in American Politics: Parties and Issues in the 1968 Election." *American Political Science Review.* 63 (December): 1083–1105.

Converse, Philip E., with Richard G. Niemi. 1971. "Non-voting Among Young Adults in the United States." In *Political Parties and Political Behavior*, 2nd ed., ed. William J. Crotty, Donald S. Freeman, and Douglas S. Gatlin. Boston: Allyn and Bacon.

Council of Economic Advisers. 1995. *Economic Report of the President.* Washington: Government Printing Office.

Coupland, Douglas. 1991. *Generation X: Tales for an Accelerated Culture.* New York: St. Martin's.

Craig, Stephen C. 1985. "The Decline of Partisanship in the United States: A Reexamination of the Neutrality Hypothesis." *Political Behavior.* 7 (no. 1): 57–78.

————. 1993. *The Malevolent Leaders: Popular Discontent in America.* Boulder, CO: Westview.

————. 1996a. "Change and the American Electorate." In *Broken Contract? Changing Relationships Between Americans and Their Government*, ed. Stephen C. Craig. Boulder, CO: Westview.

————. 1996b. "The Angry Voter: Politics and Popular Discontent in the 1990s." In *Broken Contract? Changing Relationships Between Americans and Their Government*, ed. Stephen C. Craig. Boulder, CO: Westview.

Craig, Stephen C., and Thomas L. Hurley. 1984. "Political Rhetoric and the Structure of Political Opinion: Some Experimental Findings." *Western Political Quarterly.* 37 (December): 632–40.

Craig, Stephen C., Richard G. Niemi, and Glenn E. Silver. 1990. "Political Efficacy and Trust: A Report on the NES Pilot Study Items." *Political Behavior.* 12 (September): 289–314.

Crispell, Diane. 1993. "Where Generations Divide: A Guide." *American Demographics.* May: 9–10.

Cutler, Blayne. 1989. "Up the Down Staircase." *American Demographics.* April: 32–41.

Cutler, Stephen J., and Robert L. Kaufman. 1975. "Cohort Changes in Political Attitudes: Tolerance of ideological Nonconformity." *Public Opinion Quarterly.* 39 (Spring): 69–81.

Dalhouse, Marie, and James S. Frideres. 1996. "Intergenerational Congruency: The Role of the Family in Political Attitudes of Youth." *Journal of Family Issues.* 17 (March): 227–48.

Davies, A. F. 1973. "The Child's Discovery of Nationality." In *Socialization to Politics: A Reader*, ed. Jack Dennis. New York: Wiley.

Davis, Darren W. 1995. "Exploring Black Political Intolerance." *Political Behavior.* 17 (March): 1–22.

Davis, James A. 1975. "Communism, Conformity, Cohorts, and Categories: American Tolerance in 1954 and 1972–73." *American Journal of Sociology.* 81 (November): 491–513.

Dawson, Richard E., and Kenneth Prewitt. 1969. *Political Socialization.* Boston: Little, Brown.

Delli Carpini, Michael X. 1986. *Stability and Change in American Politics: The Coming of Age of the Generation of the 1960s.* New York: New York University Press.

————. 1989. "Age and History: Generations and Sociopolitical Change." In *Political Learning in Adulthood: A Sourcebook of Theory and Research*, ed. Roberta S. Sigel. Chicago: University of Chicago Press.

Delli Carpini, Michael X., and Scott Keeter. 1996. *What Americans Know about Politics and Why It Matters.* New Haven: Yale University Press.

Dennis, Jack. 1966. "Support for the Party System by the Mass Public." *American Political Science Review.* 60 (September): 600–15.

————. 1970. "Support for the Institution of Elections by the Mass Public." *American Political Science Review.* 64 (September): 819–35.

————. 1975. "Trends in Public Support for the American Party System." *British Journal of Political Science.* 5 (April): 187–230.

————. 1980. "Changing Public Support for the American Party System." In *Paths to Political Reform*, ed. William J. Crotty. Lexington, MA: D. C. Heath.

———. 1986. "Public Support for the Party System, 1964–1984." Paper presented at the Annual Meeting of the American Political Science Association, Washington, DC.

———. 1988. "Political Independence in America, Part I: On Being an Independent Partisan Supporter." *British Journal of Political Science*. 18 (January): 77–109.

———. 1994. "The Perot Constituency." Report to the Board of Overseers of the American National Election Studies, March 10.

Dewar, Helen, and Thomas B. Edsall. 1996. "Some Good News for Clinton." *Washington Post*. May 12: A12.

Diggins, John Patrick. 1988. *The Proud Decades: America in War and Peace, 1941–1960*. New York: Norton.

Dion, Stéphane. 1992. "Explaining Quebec Nationalism." In *The Collapse of Canada?*, ed. R. Kent Weaver. Washington: Brookings Institution.

Dowdy, Zachary R. 1993. "New Generation of Activists Makes Mark for City's Young." *Boston Globe*. October 11: A1.

Duch, Raymond M., and Michaell A. Taylor. 1993. "Postmaterialism and the Economic Condition." *American Journal of Political Science*. 37 (August): 747–79.

———. 1994. "A Reply to Abramson and Inglehart's 'Education, Security, and Postmaterialism.' " *American Journal of Political Science*. 38 (August): 815–24.

Dunn, William. 1993. *The Baby Bust: A Generation Comes of Age*. Ithaca, NY: American Demographics Books.

Easterlin, Richard A., and Eileen M. Crimmins. 1991. "Private Materialism, Personal Self-Fulfillment, Family Life, and Public Interest: The Nature, Effects, and Causes of Recent Changes in the Values of American Youth. *Public Opinion Quarterly*. 55 (Winter): 499–533.

Easton, David. 1965. *A Systems Analysis of Political Life*. New York: Wiley.

———. 1975. "A Re-Assessment of the Concept of Political Support." *British Journal of Political Science*. 5 (October): 435–57.

Easton, David, and Jack Dennis. 1969. *Children in the Political System: Origins of Political Legitimacy*. New York: McGraw-Hill.

Eilperin, Juliet. 1996a. "Members Push Effort to Rock Net Vote." *Roll Call*. April 22: 12.

———. 1996b. "Partisanship Debate Rocks High-Profile National Effort to Register Youth Voters." *Roll Call*. June 6: 13, 20.

Eisner, Robert. 1994. *The Misunderstood Economy: What Counts and How to Count It*. Boston: Harvard Business School Press.

Elazar, Daniel J. 1976. *The Generational Rhythm of American Politics*. Philadelphia: Center for the Study of Federalism, Temple University.

Eldersveld, Samuel J. 1964. *Political Parties: A Behavioral Analysis*. Chicago: Rand McNally.

Erikson, Erik H. 1963. *Childhood and Society*, rev. and enlarged ed. New York: Norton.

———. 1968. *Identity, Youth and Crisis*. New York: Norton.

Fallows, James. 1996. *Breaking the News: How the Media Undermine American Democracy*. New York: Pantheon Books.

Feldman, Stanley, and John Zaller. 1992. "The Political Culture of Ambivalence: Ideological Responses to the Welfare State." *American Journal of Political Science*. 36 (February): 268–307.

Finkel, Steven E. 1985. "Reciprocal Effects of Participation and Political Efficacy: A Panel Analysis." *American Journal of Political Science.* 29 (November): 891–913.

Fiorina, Morris P. 1981. *Retrospective Voting in American National Elections.* New Haven: Yale University Press.

Flacks, Richard. 1971. *Youth and Social Change.* Chicago: Markham.

Fletcher, Frederick J., and Daphne Gottlieb Taras. 1995. "The Mass Media: Private Ownership, Public Responsibilities." In *Canadian Politics in the 1990s*, ed. Michael S. Whittington and Glen Williams. Scarborough, Ontario: Nelson Canada.

Free, Lloyd A., and Hadley Cantril. 1967. *The Political Beliefs of Americans.* New Brunswick, NJ: Rutgers University Press.

Gamson, William A. 1968. *Power and Discontent.* Homewood, IL: Dorsey.

———. 1971. "Political Trust and Its Ramifications." In *Social Psychology and Political Behavior: Problems and Prospects*, ed. Gilbert Abcarian and John W. Soule. Columbus, OH: Charles E. Merrill.

Gibbins, Roger. 1993. "A Tale of Two Senates." In *Canada and the United States: Differences that Count*, ed. David Thomas. Peterborough, Ontario: Broadview.

———. 1994. *Conflict and Unity: An Introduction to Canadian Political Life.* Scarborough, Ontario: Nelson Canada.

———. 1995. "Constitutional Turmoil and Frustration: From Trudeau to Mulroney." In *Canadian Politics in the 1990s*, ed. Michael S. Whittington and Glen Williams. Scarborough, Ontario: Nelson Canada.

Gibson, James L. 1992. "Alternative Measures of Political Tolerance: Must Tolerance Be 'Least-Liked'?" *American Journal of Political Science.* 36 (May): 560–77.

Gibson, James L., and Richard D. Bingham. 1982. "On the Conceptualization and Measurement of Political Tolerance." *American Political Science Review.* 76 (September): 603–20.

Giles, Jeff. 1994. "Generalizations X." *Newsweek.* June 6: 63–72.

Gitlin, Todd. 1980. *The Whole World Is Watching.* Berkeley: University of California Press.

Glaser, James M. 1994. "Back to the Black Belt: Racial Environment and White Racial Attitudes in the South." *Journal of Politics.* 56 (February): 21–41.

Glenn, Norval D. 1977. *Cohort Analysis.* Beverly Hills, CA: Sage.

Goldrich, Robert L. 1993. "Military Retirement and Separation Benefits: Major Legislative Issues." *Congressional Research Service Issues Brief*, September 8.

Graber, Doris A. 1994. "Why Voters Fail Information Tests: Can the Hurdles Be Overcome?" *Political Communication.* 11 (October): 331–46.

———. 1996. "Wrong Questions, Wrong Answers: Measuring Political Knowledge." Paper presented at the Annual Meetings of the Midwest Political Science Association, Chicago.

Gramlich, Edward M. 1991. "U.S. Budget Deficits: Views, Burdens, and New Developments." In *Debt and the Twin Deficits Debate*, ed. James W. Rock. Mountain View, CA: Mayfield.

Greenberg, Stanley B. 1995. *Middle Class Dreams: The Politics and Power of the New American Majority.* New York: Times Books.

Greenspan, Alan. 1994. Testimony before the Bipartisan Commission on Entitlement and Tax Reform, Washington, DC, July 15.

Greenstein, Fred I. 1960. "The Benevolent Leader: Children's Images of Political Authority." *American Political Science Review*. 54 (December): 934–43.

———. 1969. *Children and Politics*, rev. ed. New Haven: Yale University Press.

Gross, David, and Sophronia Scott. 1990. "Proceeding with Caution." *Time*. July 16: 56–62.

Hage, David, David Fischer, and Robert Black. 1995. "America's Other Welfare State." *U.S. News and World Report*. April 10: 34–37.

Heilbroner, Robert L., and Peter L. Bernstein. 1989. *The Debt and the Deficit: False Alarms/Real Possibilities*. New York: Norton.

Hess, Robert D., and Judith V. Torney. 1967. *The Development of Political Attitudes in Children*. Chicago: Aldine.

Hibbing, John R., and Elizabeth Theiss-Morse. 1995. *Congress as Public Enemy: Public Attitudes Toward American Political Institutions*. New York: Cambridge University Press.

Hochschild, Jennifer L. 1981. *What's Fair? American Beliefs about Distributive Justice*. Cambridge, MA: Harvard University Press.

Howe, Neil, and Richard Jackson. 1995a. *The Facts about Federal Pensions*. Washington: Concord Coalition.

———. 1995b. *What We Need to "Save" Medicare*. Washington: Concord Coalition.

Howe, Neil, and Phillip Longman. 1992. "The Next New Deal." *Atlantic Monthly*. April: 88–99.

Howe, Neil, and William Strauss. 1992. "The New Generation Gap." *Atlantic Monthly*. December: 67–89.

———. 1993a. *13th Gen: Abort, Retry, Ignore, Fail?* New York: Vintage.

———. 1993b. "At Issue: Will the Generation Entering the Workforce Today Have a Lower Standard of Living Over Their Lifetime Than Their Parents Enjoyed? YES." *CQ Researcher*. July 23: 641.

Hyman, Herbert H. 1959. *Political Socialization*. Glencoe, IL: Free Press.

Inglehart, Ronald. 1971. "The Silent Revolution in Europe: Intergenerational Change in Post-Industrial Societies." *American Political Science Review*. 65 (December): 991–1017.

———. 1977. *The Silent Revolution: Changing Values and Political Styles among Western Publics*. Princeton: Princeton University Press.

———. 1990. *Culture Shift in Advanced Industrial Society*. Princeton: Princeton University Press.

Inglehart, Ronald, and Paul R. Abramson. 1994. "Economic Security and Value Change." *American Political Science Review*. 88 (June): 336–54.

Isreal, Betsy. 1993. "Lost in the Name Game." *New York Times*. February 14, section 9: 1.

Jackman, Robert W. 1972. "Political Elites, Mass Publics, and Support for Democratic Principles." *Journal of Politics*. 34 (August): 753–73.

Jackman, Robert W., and Ross A. Miller. 1996. "A Renaissance of Political Culture?" *American Journal of Political Science*. 40 (August): 632–59.

Janowitz, Morris. 1983. *The Reconstruction of Patriotism: Education for Civic Consciousness*. Chicago: University of Chicago Press.

Jennings, M. Kent. 1987. "Residues of a Movement: The Aging of the American Protest Generation." *American Political Science Review*. 81 (July): 367–82.

———. 1996. "Political Knowledge over Time and across Generations." *Public Opinion Quarterly.* 60 (Summer): 228–52.

Jennings, M. Kent, and Gregory B. Markus. 1984. "Partisan Orientations over the Long Haul: Results from the Three-Wave Political Socialization Panel Study." *American Political Science Review.* 78 (December): 1000–18.

Jennings, M. Kent, and Richard G. Niemi. 1974. *The Political Character of Adolescence: The Influence of Families and Schools.* Princeton: Princeton University Press.

———. 1981. *Generations and Politics: A Panel Study of Young Adults and Their Parents.* Princeton: Princeton University Press.

Jhappan, Radha. 1995. "The Charter and the Courts." In *Canadian Politics in the 1990s*, ed. Michael S. Whittington and Glen Williams. Scarborough, Ontario: Nelson Canada.

Johnston, Richard. 1993. "An Inverted Logroll: The Charlottetown Accord and the Referendum." *PS: Political Science and Politics.* 26 (March): 43–48.

Johnston, Richard, André Blais, Henry Brady, and Jean Crête. 1992. *Letting the People Decide: Dynamics of a Canadian Election.* Stanford: Stanford University Press.

Jones, Landon Y. 1980. *Great Expectations: America and the Baby Boom Generation.* New York: Ballantine Books.

Jones, Robert, and Michael Demarest. 1967. "Man of the Year." *Time.* January 6: 18–23.

Jutkowitz, Alexander, and Jeffrey Pollock. 1996. "Solving for X: Which Way Will Young Voters Go?" *Campaigns and Elections.* May: 44–45.

Kasschau, Patricia L., H. Edward Ransford, and Vern L. Bengtson. 1974. "Generational Consciousness and Youth Movement Participation: Contrasts between Blue Collar and White Collar Youth." *Journal of Social Issues.* 30 (no. 3): 69–94.

Keniston, Kenneth. 1968. *Young Radicals: Notes on Committed Youth.* New York: Harcourt, Brace and World.

———. 1971. *Youth and Dissent: The Rise of a New Opposition.* New York: Harcourt Brace Jovanovich.

Kerbel, Matthew Robert. 1995. *Remote and Controlled: Media Politics in a Cynical Age.* Boulder, CO: Westview.

Key, V. O., Jr. 1955. "A Theory of Critical Elections." *Journal of Politics.* 17: 3–18.

———. 1959. "Secular Realignment and the Party System." *Journal of Politics.* 21 (May): 198–210.

Kim, Jae-On, and Charles W. Mueller. 1978a. *Introduction to Factor Analysis: What It Is and How to Do It.* Beverly Hills, CA: Sage.

———. 1978b. *Factor Analysis: Statistical Methods and Practical Issues.* Beverly Hills, CA: Sage.

Kinder, Donald R., and David O. Sears. 1981. "Prejudice and Politics: Symbolic Racism versus Racial Threats to the Good Life." *Journal of Personality and Social Psychology.* 40 (March): 414–31.

———. 1985. "Public Opinion and Political Action." In *Handbook of Social Psychology*, 3rd ed., ed. Gardner Lindzey and Elliot Aronson. New York: Random House.

Kinsley, Michael. 1994. "Post-Boomer Bellyaching." *Washington Post.* March 4: A15.

Klein, Joe. 1995. "Stalking the Radical Middle." *Newsweek.* September 25: 32–36.

Knopf, Rainer, and F. L. Morton. 1992. *Charter Politics.* Scarborough, Ontario: Nelson Canada.

Kornberg, Allan, and Harold D. Clarke. 1992. *Citizens and Community: Political Support in a Representative Democracy*. Cambridge: Cambridge University Press.

Kornberg, Allan, and Marianne C. Stewart. 1983. "National Identification and Political Support." In *Political Support in Canada: The Crisis Years*, ed. Allan Kornberg and Harold D. Clarke. Durham, NC: Duke University Press.

Kornhauser, William. 1959. *The Politics of Mass Society*. Glencoe, IL: Free Press.

Kotlikoff, Lawrence J. 1992. *Generational Accounting: Knowing Who Pays, and When, for What We Spend*. New York: Free Press.

Ladd, Everett Carll. 1981. "The Brittle Mandate: Electoral Dealignment and the 1980 Presidential Election." *Political Science Quarterly*. 96 (Spring): 1–25.

———. 1993. "The Twentysomethings: 'Generational Myths' Revisited." *Public Perspective*. January/February: 14–18.

Ladd, Everett Carll, with Charles D. Hadley. 1975. *Transformations of the American Party System*. New York: Norton.

Lawrence, David G. 1976. "Procedural Norms and Tolerance: A Reassessment." *American Political Science Review*. 70 (March): 80–100.

LeDuc, Lawrence, and Alex Murray. 1983. "A Resurgence of Canadian Nationalism: Attitudes and Policy in the 1980s." In *Political Support in Canada: The Crisis Years*, ed. Allan Kornberg and Harold D. Clarke. Durham, NC: Duke University Press.

Leland, John, and John McCormick. 1996. "The Children of Gridlock." *Newsweek*. July 1: 33.

Light, Paul C. 1988. *Baby Boomers*. New York: Norton.

Lijphart, Arend. 1984. *Democracies: Patterns of Majoritarian and Consensus Government in Twenty-One Countries*. New Haven: Yale University Press.

Link. Michael W., and Robert W. Oldendick. 1996. "Social Construction and White Attitudes toward Equal Opportunity and Multiculturalism." *Journal of Politics*. 58 (February): 149–68.

Lipset, Seymour Martin. 1990. *Continental Divide: The Values and Institutions of the United States and Canada*. New York: Routledge.

Lipsky, David, and Alexander Abrams. 1994. *Late Bloomers: Coming of Age in Today's America—The Right Place at the Wrong Time*. New York: Times Books.

Littwin, Susan. 1986. *The Postponed Generation: Why America's Grown-Up Kids Are Growing Up Later*. New York: William Morrow.

Longman, Phillip. 1996. *The Return to Thrift: How the Collapse of the Middle Class Welfare State Will Reawaken Values in America*. New York: Free Press.

Luttbeg, Norman R., and Michael M. Gant. 1995. *American Electoral Behavior, 1952–1992*, 2nd ed. Itasca, IL: Peacock.

MacManus, Susan A., with Patricia A. Turner. 1996. *Young v. Old: Generational Combat in the 21st Century*. Boulder, CO: Westview.

Maddox, William S., and Stuart A. Lilie. 1984. *Beyond Liberal and Conservative: Reassessing the Political Spectrum*. Washington: Cato Institute.

Malkin, Michelle. 1994. "Changing Times: Generation X's Fiscal Reality Bites." *Dayton Daily News*. February 28: A7.

Mannheim, Karl. 1952. "The Problem of Generations." In *Essays on the Sociology of Knowledge*, by Karl Mannheim. London: Routledge & Kegan Paul Ltd.

————. 1974. "What Is a Social Generation?" In *The Youth Revolution: The Conflict of Generations in Modern History*, ed. Anthony Esler. Lexington, MA: D. C. Heath.

Markus, Gregory B. 1979. "The Political Environment and the Dynamics of Public Attitudes: A Panel Study." *American Journal of Political Science.* 23 (May): 338–59.

Markus, Gregory B., and Philip E. Converse. 1979. "A Dynamic Simultaneous Equation Model of Electoral Choice." *American Political Science Review.* 73 (December): 1055–70.

Martin, David. 1993. "The Whiny Generation." *Newsweek.* November 1: 10.

Martinez, Michael D. 1990. "Partisan Reinforcement in Context and Cognition: Canadian Federal Partisanships, 1974–1979." *American Journal of Political Science.* 34 (August): 822–45.

Maslow, Abraham H. 1954. *Motivation and Personality.* New York: Harper and Row.

McClosky, Herbert. 1964. "Consensus and Ideology in American Politics." *American Political Science Review.* 58 (June): 361–82.

McPhee, William N., and Jack Ferguson. 1962. "Political Immunization." In *Public Opinion and Congressional Elections*, ed. William N. McPhee and William A. Glaser. Glencoe, IL: Free Press.

McRoberts, Kenneth. 1995. "Quebec: Province, Nation, or 'Distinct Society'?" In *Canadian Politics in the 1990s*, ed. Michael S. Whittington and Glen Williams. Scarborough, Ontario: Nelson Canada.

Meacham, Jon. 1995. "The Truth About Twenty-somethings." *Washington Monthly.* January/February: 21–26.

Medvic, Stephen K. 1994. "The Political Attitudes of Generation X: A Preliminary Inquiry." Paper presented at the Annual Meetings of the Midwest Political Science Association, Chicago.

Merelman, Richard. 1991. *Partial Visions: Culture and Politics in Britain, Canada, and the United States.* Madison: University of Wisconsin Press.

Miller, Arthur H. 1974a. "Political Issues and Trust in Government: 1964–1970." *American Political Science Review.* 68 (September): 951–72.

————. 1974b. "Rejoinder to 'Comment' by Jack Citrin: Political Discontent or Ritualism." *American Political Science Review.* 68 (September): 989–1001.

Miller, Arthur H., and Stephen A. Borrelli. 1991. "Confidence in Government during the 1980s." *American Politics Quarterly.* 19 (April): 147–73.

Miller, Arthur H., Patricia Gurin, Gerald Gurin, and Oksana Malanchuk. 1981. "Group Consciousness and Political Participation." *American Journal of Political Science.* 25 (August): 494–511.

Miller, Arthur H., Vicki L. Hesli, and William M. Reisinger. 1995. "Comparing Citizen and Elite Belief Systems in Post-Soviet Russia and Ukraine." *Public Opinion Quarterly.* 59 (Spring): 1–40.

Miller, Arthur H., Warren E. Miller, Alden S. Raine, and Thad A. Brown. 1976. "A Majority Party in Disarray? Policy Polarization in the 1972 Election." *American Political Science Review.* 70 (September): 753–78.

Miller, Warren E. 1991. "Party Identification, Realignment, and Party Voting: Back to the Basics." *American Political Science Review.* 85 (June): 557–68.

Miller, Warren E., and Levitin, Teresa E. 1976. *Leadership and Change: The New Politics and the American Electorate.* Cambridge: Winthrop.

Minton, Torri. 1993. "Young People Who Get a Kick Out of Helping Urban Service Project Kids Dig Right In." *San Francisco Chronicle*. September 30: D7.

Mitchell, Susan. 1993. "How to Talk to Young Adults." *American Demographics*. April: 50–54.

Morin, Richard. 1994. "Maybe If They Televised It On MTV?" *Washington Post*. August 9: D3.

Morris, Charles R. 1996. *The AARP: America's Most Powerful Lobby and the Clash of Generations*. New York: Times Books.

Mueller, John. 1988. "Trends in Political Tolerance." *Public Opinion Quarterly*. 52 (Spring): 1–25.

Nardulli, Peter F. 1995. "The Concept of a Critical Realignment, Electoral Behavior, and Political Change." *American Political Science Review*. 89 (March): 10–22.

Nasar, Sylvia. 1995. "Older Americans Cited in Studies of National Savings Rate Slump." *New York Times*. February 21: A1.

Nelson, Jason. 1994. "Generation X vs. Generation W." *University of Oklahoma Daily*. April 5: 4.

Neuman, W. Russell, Marion R. Just, and Ann N. Cigler. 1992. *Common Knowledge: News and the Construction of Political Meaning*. Chicago: University of Chicago Press.

Nevitte, Neal, Richard Johnston, André Blais, Henry Brady, and Elisabeth Gidengil. 1995. "Electoral Discontinuity in the 1993 Canadian Federal Election." *International Social Science Journal*. 47 (December): 583–99.

New York Times. 1984. "Vietnam Link to College Enrollment Found." September 2: A17.

Nie, Norman H., Sidney Verba, and John R. Petrocik. 1976. *The Changing American Voter*. Cambridge, MA: Harvard University Press.

Nunn, Clyde Z., Harry J. Crockett, Jr., and J. Allen Williams, Jr.. 1978. *Tolerance for Nonconformity*. San Francisco: Jossey-Bass.

Office of Management and Budget. 1994. *Budget of the U.S. Government: Analytical Perspectives, Fiscal Year 1995*. Washington: Government Printing Office.

Office of Personnel Management. 1993. *Civil Service Retirement and Disability Fund: An Annual Report to Comply with the Requirements of Public Law 95–595*. Washington: Government Printing Office.

Ornstein, Norman, Andrew Kohut, and Larry McCarthy. 1988. *The People, the Press, and Politics*. Reading, MA: Addison-Wesley.

Owen, Diana, and Jack Dennis. 1987. "Preadult Development of Political Tolerance." *Political Psychology*. 8 (December): 547–61.

———. 1988. "Gender Differences in the Politicization of American Children." *Women and Politics*. 8 (July): 23–43.

———. 1992. "Sex Differences in Preadult Political Learning." *Women and Politics*. 12 (December): 19–41.

———. 1996. "Anti-partyism in the USA and Support for Ross Perot." *European Journal of Political Research*. 29 (April): 383–400.

Owen, Diana, and Stephen J. Farnsworth. 1995. "Generational Differences in Political Support: The Implications for Political Participation." Paper presented at the Annual Meetings of the American Political Science Association, Chicago.

Page, Benjamin I., and Robert Y. Shapiro. 1992. *The Rational Public: Fifty Years of Trends in Americans' Policy Preferences*. Chicago: University of Chicago Press.

Patterson, Thomas E. 1993. *Out of Order*. New York: Alfred A. Knopf.

Pear, Robert. 1994. "Panel on Deficits Sees Storm Brewing on Costs." *New York Times*. June 14: A6.

Penny, Timothy J., and Steven E. Schier. 1996. *Payment Due: A Nation in Debt, A Generation in Trouble*. Boulder, CO: Westview.

People for the American Way. 1990. *Democracy's Next Generation*. Washington: People for the American Way.

Peterson, Karen S. 1993. "Baby Busters Rise Above Elders' Scorn." *USA Today*. September 23: D1.

Peterson, Peter E. 1993. *Facing Up: How to Rescue the Economy from Crushing Debt and Restore the American Dream*. New York: Simon and Schuster.

———. 1996. "Will America Grow Up Before It Grows Old?" *Atlantic Monthly*. April: 55–86.

Petrocik, John R. 1981. *Party Coalitions: Realignments and the Decline of the New Deal Party System*. Chicago: University of Chicago Press.

Pew Research Center. 1996. "TV News Viewership Declines: Fall-Off Greater for Young Adults and Computer Users." Report issued by the Pew Research Center for the People and the Press, May 13.

Pomper, Gerald M. 1975. *Voters' Choice: Varieties of American Electoral Behavior*. New York: Dodd, Mead.

Popkin, Samuel L. 1994. *The Reasoning Voter: Communication and Persuasion in Presidential Campaigns*, 2nd ed. Chicago: University of Chicago Press.

Prothro, James W., and Charles M. Grigg. 1960. "Fundamental Principles of Democracy: Bases of Agreement and Disagreement." *Journal of Politics*. 22 (May): 276–94.

Public Perspective. 1996. "Young Americans: Where Are They Politically?" June/ July: 50–51.

Putnam, Robert D. 1993a. *Making Democracy Work: Civic Traditions in Modern Italy*. Princeton: Princeton University Press.

———. 1993b. "What Makes Democracy Work." *National Civic Review*. 82 (January): 101–7.

———. 1993c. "The Prosperous Community: Social Capital and Economic Growth." *American Prospect*. Spring: 35–42.

Raine, Alden S. 1977. *Change in the Political Agenda: Social and Cultural Conflict in the American Electorate*. Beverly Hills, CA: Sage.

Ratan, Suneel. 1993. "Why Busters Hate Boomers." *Fortune*. October 4: 56–70.

Reich, Charles. 1970. *The Greening of America*. New York: Random House.

Reischauer, Robert D. 1994. Testimony before the Bipartisan Commission on Entitlement and Tax Reform, Washington, DC, July 15.

Rice, Tom W., and Tracey A. Hilton. 1996. "Partisanship Over Time: A Comparison of United States Panel Data." *Political Research Quarterly*. 49 (March): 191–202.

Riley, Matilda White. 1973. "Aging and Cohort Succession: Interpretations and Misinterpretations." *Public Opinion Quarterly*. 37 (Spring): 35–49.

Robertson, James L. 1970. *What Generation Gap?* Washington: Acropolis Books.

Rosenbaum, Walter A., and James W. Button. 1993. "The Unquiet Future of Intergenerational Politics." *Gerontologist.* 33 (August): 481–90.

Rosenberg, Milton J., Sidney Verba, and Philip E. Converse. 1970. *Vietnam and the Silent Majority.* New York: Harper and Row.

Rosenstone, Steven J., and John Mark Hansen. 1993. *Mobilization, Participation, and Democracy in America.* New York: Macmillan.

Rossiter, Clinton L. 1960. *Parties and Politics in America.* Ithaca, NY: Cornell University Press.

Rothenberg, Stuart. 1996. "Forget Gen X: Seniors Are Prize Age Group for '96." *Roll Call.* April 4: 13.

Russell, Cheryl. 1993. "The Master Trend." *American Demographics.* October: 28–37.

Sabato, Larry J. 1991. *Feeding Frenzy: How Attack Journalism Has Transformed American Politics.* New York: Free Press.

St. Paul Pioneer Press. 1996a. "Everybody's Issue: Fixing Social Security." May 12: A20.

———. 1996b. "Looking for an Opening in the Political Center." July 15: A4.

Samuelson, Robert J. 1993. "At Issue: Will the Generation Entering the Workforce Today Have a Lower Standard of Living Over Their Lifetime Than Their Parents Enjoyed? YES." *CQ Researcher.* July 23: 641.

Saywell, John. 1977. *The Rise of the Parti Québécois 1967–1976.* Toronto: University of Toronto Press.

Schalch, Kathleen. 1996. "Voting in America: Who Votes and Why." National Public Radio, *Morning Edition*, July 3. Transcript #1903–6.

Schuman, Howard, and Cheryl Rieger. 1992. "Historical Analogies: Generational Effects and Attitudes toward War." *American Sociological Review.* 57 (June): 315–26.

Schuman, Howard, and Jacqueline Scott. 1989. "Generations and Collective Memories." *American Sociological Review.* 54 (June): 359–81.

Scott, Jacqueline, and Lilian Zac. 1993. "Collective Memories in Britain and the United States." *Public Opinion Quarterly.* 57 (Fall): 315–31.

Searing, Donald D., Joel J. Schwartz, and Alden E. Lind. 1973. "The Structuring Principle: Political Socialization and Belief Systems." *American Political Science Review.* 67 (June): 415–32.

Sears, David O. 1983. "The Persistence of Early Political Predispositions: The Roles of Attitude Object and Life Stage." In *Review of Personality and Social Psychology*, vol. 4, ed. Ladd Wheeler. Beverly Hills, CA: Sage.

Sears, David O., and Donald R. Kinder. 1985. "Whites' Opposition to Busing: On Conceptualizing and Operationalizing Group Conflict." *Journal of Personality and Social Psychology.* 48 (May): 1141–7.

Shafer, Byron E., ed. 1991. *The End of Realignment? Interpreting American Electoral Eras.* Madison: University of Wisconsin Press.

Shafer, Byron E., and William J. M. Claggett. 1995. *The Two Majorities: The Issue Context of Modern American Politics.* Baltimore: Johns Hopkins University Press.

Shapiro, Robert. 1995. "Rethinking Social Security." *The New Democrat.* September/October: 1–6.

Sidanius, Jim, Felicia Pratto, and Lawrence Bobo. 1996. "Racism, Conservatism, Affirmative Action, and Intellectual Sophistication: A Matter of Principled Conservatism or Group Dominance?" *Journal of Personality and Social Psychology.* 71 (March): 476–90.

Smith-Rowsey, Daniel. 1991. "The Terrible Twenties. *Newsweek.* July 1: 10–11.

Sniderman, Paul M., Thomas Piazza, Philip E. Tetlock, and Ann Kendrick. 1991. "The New Racism." *American Journal of Political Science.* 35 (May): 423–47.

Sniderman, Paul M., and Philip E. Tetlock. 1986. "Symbolic Racism: Problems of Motive Attribution in Political Analysis." *Journal of Social Issues.* 42 (no. 2): 129–50.

Sniderman, Paul M., Philip E. Tetlock, James N. Glaser, Donald Philip Green, and Michael Hout. 1989. "Principled Tolerance and the American Mass Public." *British Journal of Political Science.* 19 (February): 25–45.

Squire, Peverill, Raymond E. Wolfinger, and David P. Glass. 1987. "Residential Mobility and Voter Turnout." *American Political Science Review.* 81 (March): 45–65.

Stewart, Anne C., and William Crouse. 1993. "Major Veterans' Legislation in the 103rd Congress." *Congressional Research Service Report for Congress.* Washington: Government Printing Office.

Stoker, Laura, and M. Kent Jennings. 1995. "Life-Cycle Transitions and Political Participation: The Case of Marriage." *American Political Science Review.* 89 (June): 421–33.

Stone, Walter J., Ronald B. Rapaport, and Alan I. Abramowitz. 1994. "Party Polarization: The Reagan Revolution and Beyond." In *The Parties Respond: Changes in American Parties and Campaigns,* 2nd ed., ed. L. Sandy Maisel. Boulder, CO: Westview.

Stouffer, Samuel A. 1955. *Communism, Conformity, and Civil Liberties.* New York: Doubleday.

Strauss, William, and Neil Howe. 1991. *Generations: The History of America's Future, 1584 to 2089.* New York: William Morrow.

Sullivan, John L., Amy Fried, and Mary G. Dietz. 1992. "Patriotism, Politics, and the Presidential Election of 1988." *American Journal of Political Science.* 36 (February): 200–234.

Sullivan, John L., James Pierson, and George E. Marcus. 1982. *Political Tolerance and American Democracy.* Chicago: University of Chicago Press.

Sundquist, James L. 1983. *Dynamics of the Party System: Alignment and Realignment of Political Parties in the United States,* rev. ed. Washington: Brookings Institution.

Tedin, Kent L. 1994. "Self-Interest, Symbolic Values, and the Financial Equalization of the Public Schools." *Journal of Politics.* 56 (August): 628–49.

Teixeira, Ruy A. 1987. *Why Americans Don't Vote: Turnout Decline in the United States, 1960–1984.* New York: Greenwood Press.

———. 1992. *The Disappearing American Voter.* Washington: Brookings Institution.

Third Millennium. 1993. *Third Millennium Declaration.* New York: Third Millennium.

Thomas, L. Eugene. 1974. "Generational Discontinuity in Beliefs: An Exploration of the Generation Gap." *Journal of Social Issues.* 30 (no. 3): 1–22.

Thompson, Dennis F. 1970. *The Democratic Citizen: Social Science and Democratic Theory in the Twentieth Century.* Cambridge: Cambridge University Press.

Times Mirror. 1990a. "The Age of Indifference." News release issued by the Times Mirror Center for the People and the Press. June 14.

————. 1990b. "The American Media: Who Reads, Who Watches, Who Listens, Who Cares." News release issued by the Times Mirror Center for the People and the Press, July 15.

————. 1991. "The Age of Indifference." Report issued by the Times Mirror Center for the People and the Press, April.

————. 1994. "Public Expects GOP Miracles." Report issued by the Times Mirror Center for the People and the Press, December 8.

Tocqueville, Alexis de. [1835] 1945. *Democracy in America*, vol. 1, ed. Phillips Bradley. New York: Alfred A. Knopf.

Turow, Scott. 1996. "Where Have All the Radicals Gone?" *Newsweek*. September 2: 47.

U.S. Department of Commerce. 1993. "Education in the United States: 1940–1991." Special Demographic Analysis CDS93–1. Washington: Bureau of the Census.

U.S. Department of Defense, Office of the Actuary. 1994. "Valuation of Military Retirement System: September 30, 1994." Washington: Department of Defense.

U.S. Department of the Treasury, Financial Management Service. 1993. *Statement of Liabilities and Other Financial Commitments of the United States Government as of September 30, 1992*. Washington: Government Printing Office.

U.S. News and World Report. 1969. "One Generation Speaks to Another." July 7: 28–31.

Van Deth, Jan W. 1989. "Interest in Politics." In *Continuities in Political Action*, by M. Kent Jennings and Associates. Berlin: Walter de Gruyter.

Van Dongen, Rachel. 1996. "A New Generation of Twentysomething Candidates Takes the Political Challenge." *Roll Call*. July 18: 13, 17.

Van Sant, Rick. 1993. "Generation X: 20–Somethings Fear Boom Years Are Past." *Cincinnati Post*. December 7: A1, A3.

Wattenberg, Martin P. 1994. *The Decline of American Political Parties, 1952–1992*. Cambridge, MA: Harvard University Press.

Welch, W. Pete, Steven J. Katz, and Stephen Zuckerman. 1993. "Physician Fee Levels: Medicare versus Canada. Assessing Cost Containment in the U.S. and Canada." Urban Institute Working Paper No. 6185–02. Washington: Urban Institute.

Wheeler, John. 1984. *Touched with Fire: The Future of the Vietnam Generation*. New York: Avon Books.

Wildavsky, Aaron. 1990. "A World of Difference: The Public Philosophies and Political Behaviors of Rival American Cultures." In *The New American Political System*, ed. Anthony King. Washington: AEI Press.

Williams, Glen. 1995. "Regions within Region: Continentalism Ascendant." In *Canadian Politics in the 1990s*, ed. Michael S. Whittington and Glen Williams. Scarborough, Ontario: Nelson Canada.

Wilson, Thomas C. 1994. "Trends in Tolerance toward Rightist and Leftist Groups, 1976–1988: Effects of Attitude Change and Cohort Succession." *Public Opinion Quarterly*. 58 (Winter): 539–56.

————. 1996. "Cohort and Prejudice: Whites' Attitudes toward Blacks, Hispanics, Jews, and Asians." *Public Opinion Quarterly*. 60 (Summer): 253–74.

Winik, Jay. 1996. *On the Brink: The Reagan Era and the Men and Women Who Won the Cold War*. New York: Simon and Schuster.

Wolfinger, Raymond E., and Steven J. Rosenstone. 1980. *Who Votes?* New Haven: Yale University Press.

Wood, Genevieve. 1996. "Wanted: Spokesperson for Generation X." *Generation NEXT.* May: 24.

Zaller, John R. 1992. *The Nature and Origins of Mass Opinion.* New York: Cambridge University Press.

Zaller, John, and Stanley Feldman. 1992. "A Simple Theory of the Survey Response: Answering Questions versus Revealing Preferences." *American Journal of Political Science.* 36 (August): 579–616.

Zelman, Walter A. 1996. *The Changing Health Care Marketplace: Private Ventures, Public Interests.* San Francisco: Jossey-Bass.

Index

activism: political, *see* political activism; social, 1

adults: behavior pattern shifts by, 7; social roles, 25

advertising, 2–3. *See also* media

advocacy groups, 12

affect, measurement of, 150–51. *See also* patriotism

affirmative action, 116. *See also* race; tolerance

African-Americans, 115–17, 118–21. *See also* race; tolerance

aging, 3, 41–42n20; effect on partisanship, 59, 61n10, 65, 77, 82n4; effect on political effectiveness perception, 97; effect on political participation, 31, 37; effect on tolerance, 109; interaction with experience, 4; reaction to historical events and, 5, 65; susceptibility to change and, 65, 69–70

aging (life-cycle) effects: defining, 7–8, 17; re economics, 14; re issues' effect, 74; re patriotism, 100, 151, 152, 154; re political involvement, 23, 36

alienation, 53, 89, 94; in Canadians, 148

Almond, Gabriel A., 26

Alwin, Duane, 7

ambivalence, 69, 77–80, 81, 166n21; in baby boomers, 67; political, 89–90, 145; re Quebec separation issue, 146, 158, 164; in tolerance levels, 122

American National Election Studies (ANES), 22, 45, 69, 92; re Congress, 96; on economics, 14–15; on educational level, 13; on political parties, 54, 61n7; respondent demographics, 112; survey questions, 167–74; re tolerance, 111, 116, 117; on trust in government, 88, 92

Anderson, Kristi, 70

ANES. *See* American National Election Studies

anomie, 49, 87

apathy. *See* political apathy

Asian-Americans, 118–21

attitudinal inconsistency, 75–77

Auer, Bernhard, 1

baby boomers: ambivalence on policy issues, 67; belief structures, 67, 72; Canadian, 148, 149; characterization of, 1, 9; cohort defined, 4, 111; division of, 24–25; ideals, 67; inconsistency in views, 75–77; individualism and, 68; issues and, 67; libertarian tendencies, 68; on party system, 54–56; political involvement of, 1, 9, 24, 26–27; political opinions, 67, 71; political party attachment, 45–47, 50, 59; as pragmatics, 67; tolerance levels of, 107, 110, 116, 122; values of, 1, 66; view of Xers, 10; volatility of, 67

baby busters. *See* Generation X

belief structures, 67, 72, 81

Bennett, Linda L. M., 24

Bennett, Steven Earl, 16, 17, 24, 26, 142

Bipartisan Commission on Entitlement and Tax Reform, 133–34, 141

birth cohorts, 3, 6, 24; defining, 18, 19n6, 24, 70, 92, 111, 147–48; differences within, 9–10, 12–13, 28; generalizations re, 21; life experiences, 108

Blais, André, 152

Brady, Henry, 152

budget deficit. *See* national debt

Bush, George, 25, 77, 89, 97

Canada: American influence on, 145, 146, 151; British control of, 148, 162–63, 164–65n4, 165n6; Charlottetown Accord, 150, 160, 162, 163; constitutional

Social Security (OASDI), 132, 135–36; future of, 141–42; taxes, 11; trust fund, 134, 136. *See also* entitlements
social structure, effect on event perception, 5–6, 23
societal institutions, 2. *See also* economics; family life; government
Soren, Tabitha, 43
standard of living, 11; of aged, 132; Canadian, 147; expectations re, 15, 19n8, 82n13; increases in, 141; national debt and, 128. *See also* economic security
Stouffer, Samuel (tolerance study), 107, 108, 109, 110, 111, 114, 122
Strauss, William, 10, 11, 67, 68, 87
Sullivan, John L., 110, 111, 114, 122
Sundquist, James L., 69
Supreme Court, 96

taxation, 90, 127; increases, 134; middle class, 133; rates for Xers, 129, 134, 138, 140, 141–42; views re, 80
television. *See* media
terms, meaning of, 4
Theiss-Morse, Elizabeth, 92
Third Millenium, 12, 127, 142
Thompson, Lawrence, 140
Times Mirror/Pew Research Center for the People and the Press, 12, 31
tolerance, 6–7, 107–23; abstract, 110–11, 112–14; re African-Americans, 115–17; defined, 111, 122; education's relationship to, 107, 108, 109, 112, 114, 121; re homosexuals, 115; increase in, 109, 121; re Latinos, 117–18; re lifestyles, 114–15; measurement of, 110; specific, 110–11, 114; specified groups, 108, 110, 111, 114, 122; youth's relationship to, 107, 109, 115, 117, 118, 121–22, 125n27
Trudeau, Pierre, 148, 149

Turow, Scott, 9
Twenty-Sixth Amendment, 5
twentysomethings. *See* Generation X

unemployment, 11, 16, 25
United Nations Human Development Index, 147, 163
United We Stand America, 57

values: of baby boomers, 66; clashes of, 9; democratic, 17, 26; economic conditions' effect on, 15, 16; materialist, 15–16; multiplicity of, 110; political conditions' effect on, 15, 16; work ethic, 118
Verba, Sidney, 26
Vietnam, 6, 24, 89, 110, 111; baby boomers and, 24; differentiated impact of, 5–6; as generation-defining event, 23
violence, tendency toward, 120–21
voting, 29–31, 86; minimum age, 5, 40n2; reports of, 41n12; turnout enhancement efforts, 43; by Xers, 29, 44

war, 24, 66
Watergate, 6, 25, 89
work ethic, 118

Xers. *See* Generation X

youth, 3; affect toward politics, 155; idealism and, 87; identification with, 28; political apathy in, 23, 36–37; reaction to historical events, 5; relation to tolerance, 107, 109, 115, 117, 118, 121–22, 125n27; typical differences from elders, 8; voting rates, 29
Youth Voices (1996) study, 92; re community, 100; re government responsiveness, 99, 100; re institutional evaluation, 96; re politicians, 97; re trust in government, 94

About the Editors

Stephen C. Craig (Ph. D. Northwestern University 1979) is professor of political science at the University of Florida and director of the university's Graduate Program in Political Campaigning. Dr. Craig is author of *The Malevolent Leaders: Popular Discontent in America* (Westview 1993), editor of *Broken Contract? Changing Relationships Between Americans and Their Government* (Westview 1995), and has published numerous articles and book chapters on political trust, partisanship, voting behavior, and the changing character of mass opinion in the United States. He has worked extensively with both academic and political surveys and recently served as a member of the Secretary of State's Blue Ribbon Commission charged with proposing reforms to increase voter turnout in Florida.

Stephen Earl Bennett (Ph. D. University of Illinois at Urbana-Champaign 1972) is professor and head of political science at the University of Cincinnati. Dr. Bennett's research interests are in American political behavior, with concentrations in public opinion and political communication. He has written four books, including *Apathy in America, 1960–1984* (Transnational 1986) and *Living with Leviathan: Americans Coming to Terms with Big Government* (University of Kansas Press 1990, with Linda L. M. Bennett), as well as numerous journal articles, essays, and book chapters. He is currently working on a book to be titled *Americans' Views of Congress: The Vigilant Spirit?* (co-authored with Linda L. M. Bennett).

About the Contributors

Jack Dennis is Hawkins Professor of political science at the University of Wisconsin-Madison. He is co-author of *Children in the Political System* (with David Easton), editor of *Socialization to Politics: A Reader*, and has written extensively on such topics as political socialization, electoral behavior, political participation, political psychology, and political communication. He has served as president of the Midwest Political Science Association, and is currently chair of the Political Psychology section of the American Political Science Association.

Angela C. Halfacre is a Ph. D. student in political science at the University of Florida. Her research interests include American national institutions, environmental and regulatory policy making, and issues relating to race and gender. Her dissertation deals with the impact of minority risk perception on feelings of institutional trust.

Kevin A. Hill is assistant professor of political science at Florida International University. His articles on such topics as political parties, interest groups, congressional elections, and political organization and activity on the Internet have appeared in a variety of professional journals and book chapters.

Michael D. Martinez is associate professor of political science at the University of Florida and director of the Florida Institute for Research on Elections. His articles on political socialization, public opinion, voting behavior, and partisanship in the United States and Canada have appeared in several professional journals, and he is currently working on a book that deals with the consequences of voter turnout.

Diana Owen is assistant professor of government at Georgetown University. She is author of *Media Messages in American Presidential Elections*, co-author of *New Media in American Politics* (with Richard Davis), and has written numerous articles dealing with elections, voting behavior, the mass media, political socialization, and political culture in the United States.

Eric W. Rademacher is a Ph. D. student in political science and a research analyst at the University of Cincinnati's Institute for Policy Research. His research interests include American politics, public opinion, and survey research. His dissertation looks at the impact of Generation X's economic fortunes on its political attitudes and behavior.

Steven E. Schier is professor and chair of political science at Carleton College in Northfield, Minnesota. He has authored numerous articles and books, including *A Decade of Deficits: Congressional Thought and Fiscal Action, Payment Due: A Nation in Debt, A Generation in Trouble* (with former Congressman Timothy Penny), and *The Rules and the Game: Democratic National Convention Delegate Selection in Iowa and Wisconsin*, and is currently working on a book that examines political activists and their effects on national politics.